101 Small Business Ideas for Under $5,000

Corey Sandler
Janice Keefe

WILEY

John Wiley & Sons, Inc.

Published by John Wiley & Sons, Inc., Hoboken, New Jersey.
Published simultaneously in Canada.

For general information on our other products and services please contact our Customer Care Department within the United States at (800) 762-2974, outside the United States at (317) 572-3993 or fax (317) 572-4002.

Wiley also publishes its books in a variety of electronic formats. Some content that appears in print may not be available in electronic books. For more information about Wiley products, visit our web site at *www.Wiley.com.*

Library of Congress Cataloging-in-Publication Data

Sandler, Corey, 1950–
    101 small business ideas for under $5000 / Corey Sandler, Janice Keefe.
        p. cm.
    Includes index.
    ISBN 0-471-69287-5 (pbk.)
    1. New business enterprises. 2. Home-based businesses. 3. Small business. I. Title: Small business ideas for under $5000. II. Title: One hundred one small business ideas for under $5000. III. Title: One hundred and one small business ideas for under $5000. IV. Keefe, Janice. V. Title.

HD62.5.S272 2005
658.1'141—dc22   2004059648
Printed in the United States of America
10 9 8 7 6 5 4 3 2 1

To William Sandler, about to embark on the first of what may be 101 jobs in his career. Here's hoping every one of them is a success.

Contents

Preface ix

Acknowledgments xi

How to Use This Book xiii

Chapter 1 Business Insurance and Risk Management 1

Chapter 2 Legalities and Taxes 11

Chapter 3 Setting Your Price 17

Chapter 4 Financing a Small Business 25

Chapter 5 Home Services (Exterior) 29
  1 Lawn Mowing Service
  2 Snow Removal
  3 Garden Tilling
  4 Window Cleaning
  5 Deck Cleaning
  6 Landscape Designer
  7 Deck Construction
  8 Storage Sheds, Playhouses, Doghouses
  9 Children's Outdoor Playset Installer
  10 Low-Voltage Outdoor Electrical Wiring
  11 Stonemason and Decorative Brick Worker

Chapter 6 Home Services (Interior) 59
  12 Housecleaning
  13 Rug Cleaner
  14 Interior Decorator
  15 Upholstery and Slipcover Maker
  16 Wallpaper Hanger
  17 Specialty Indoor Painting
  18 Furniture Stripping
  19 Furniture Repair

20 Closet Organizer
21 Bookcase and Shelf Builder
22 Indoor Plant Care
23 Custom Silk and Dried Flower Arrangements

Chapter 7 Home Services (Specialty)   **89**
24 Handyperson
25 Errand Runner
26 Vacation Home Caretaker
27 Vacation House Watcher
28 House Painting
29 Chimney Cleaning
30 Pool Service
31 Firewood Delivery
32 On-demand Trash Removal
33 Christmas Tree Service
34 Small Engine Repair

Chapter 8 Parties, Entertainment, and Special Events   **119**
35 Party Planner
36 Children's Event Organizer
37 Party and Special-Event Rentals
38 Catering
39 Visiting Chef
40 Specialty Cake Baker
41 Prepared Custom-Meal Service
42 Freelance Bartender
43 Entertainer
44 Holiday Decoration Service

Chapter 9 Personal Services   **149**
45 Personal Shopper
46 Personalized Gift Basket Maker
47 Travel Planner
48 Historical Tours
49 Personal Fitness Trainer
50 Sports Trainer

Chapter 10 Children, Family, and Pet Services   **165**
51 Babysitting
52 Babysitting Agency

53 Children's Night Out
54 Vacation Child Care
55 Dog Walking and Vacation Pet Visits
56 Pet Sitter and Doggie Day Care
57 Elder Companion
58 Elder Care Consultant
59 Genealogical Research
60 Family Biographer

Chapter 11 Educational Services   **195**
61 Tutoring
62 Language Instructor
63 Music Teacher
64 Computer Instructor
65 SAT or ACT College Test Preparation
66 College Selection Advisor
67 College Application Consultant
68 Instructor at Community School

**Chapter 12 Arts, Crafts, Jewelry, Clothing,
and Musical Instruments**   **217**
69 Alterations
70 Custom Tailoring
71 Custom Knitting, Sweater, and Afghan Design
72 Custom Quiltmaker
73 Jewelry Making
74 Portraiture from Photographs
75 Custom-Built Dollhouses
76 Musical Instrument Tuning and Repair

Chapter 13 Transportation, Delivery, and Auto Services   **237**
77 Car Service
78 Independent Delivery Contractor
79 Auto Detailing

Chapter 14 Computers, Graphics, and Photography   **247**
80 Computer Buying Consultant
81 Computer Repair and Upgrade
82 Web Design and Maintenance
83 Graphic Designer
84 Freelance Photographer

85 Film to Digital Scanning
86 Photo and Document Restorer
87 Videographer

Chapter 15 Office and Professional Services   **271**
88 Temporary Secretary
89 Transcription Services
90 Temporary Worker at Conventions and Business Meetings
91 Bookkeeping
92 Billing Service
93 Resume Design
94 Letter Writing

Chapter 16 Sales   **287**
95 Yard Sale Organizer
96 Consignment Resale
97 Antiques and Collectibles Wholesaler
98 Used Book Reseller
99 Tool and Equipment Rentals
100 Newspaper Delivery Route
101 Online Auctions: EBay and Beyond

Appendix   Government and Private Resources for Small Businesses   309
Index   313

Preface

Every business—from neighborhood to global—begins with an idea.

The next General Motors or Wal-Mart or Microsoft will not spring forth fully developed from the back of an envelope. Big ideas need big funding.

But your next job, or your next source of supplemental income, *can* begin with a small idea and grow from there.

The two keys to success in small business are these:

1. Find something that makes good use of your skills and experience.
2. Market that idea to people and businesses that need your product.

In *101 Small Business Ideas for under $5000,* you'll find a realistic guide to turning your ideas and skills into a business that you can run part-time or full-time or even as an absentee owner.

Some of the other books about starting a small business are little more than a laundry list of job ideas, some practical, some ridiculously fanciful. There *may* be millions to be made in recycling toxic waste, but it's not realistic to consider setting up a processing plant in your backyard pool. You *may* be able to earn a nice income running a dog-walking business, but you *do* need to give serious thought to things like liability, health codes, and personal safety.

Some jobs, such as babysitting or vacation house watch service, are simple to set up and run, and we discuss those and show you how to keep it simple and beneath the radar. Other jobs very quickly become more complex. For these, we discuss the real-world issues an entrepreneur will face:

- Start-up costs
- Legal matters
- Accounting and tax issues
- Liability insurance
- Zoning

We help you draw up a sensible business plan that can be used to direct the start-up; to present to a banker, government agency, or foundation for funding; or to help design a publicity, marketing, and sales program. We give suggestions on how a successful business can be *scaled up* from a one-person start-up to a mini-empire.

Icons help you quickly identify the type of business, required skills, estimated start-up costs, and an indication of legal, zoning, and insurance requirements.

Most of the jobs can be set up for just a few hundred to a few thousand dollars; for the more expensive start-ups, we show ways to ease into full operation one step at a time.

Acknowledgments

A book is a piece of business that begins with an idea, followed by months of hard work. In the case of the book you hold in your hand, the idea originated with editor Michael Hamilton of John Wiley & Sons, in conjunction with trusted agent Gene Brissie.

Though this finished book bears just two names on the cover, dozens of capable and creative people were involved in its conceptualization, design, production, and distribution.

We'd like to thank the capable editors and production staff at John Wiley and North Market Street Graphics, including Linda Witzling, Christine Furry, Lainey Harding, Mary Jo Fostina, and Tracy Pitz.

We also thank you, the reader, for buying this book. We wish you great success in starting your own small business and expanding it as far and wide as you can dream.

Corey Sandler and Janice Keefe

How to Use This Book

Various levels of professional assistance will be required in setting up your small business. We have tried to make it easy for you to zero in on some of the major issues you may confront and who can best help to solve them. Following is an explanation of the visual devices used in this book for quick reference.

When to Seek Professional Advice

① **Legal**

② **Legal**

③ **Legal**

④ **Accounting**

⑤ **Insurance**

⑥ **Insurance**

① Legal

Consult an attorney for assistance in drawing up a contract that spells out the duties you will perform, the type and quality of materials you will use, the compensation you will receive for your work, and the schedule for payment. The contract should also identify any safety and security responsibilities of the client, and limit your liability for accidents, errors, and omissions.

② Legal

If you will be entering a client's property, home, or office while they are there, or if you will be given a key, alarm code, or permission to enter a client's property, home, or place of business, the contract should include specific language limiting your liability for any incident that might be related to your access.

③ **Legal**

Your attorney should also be able to advise about the need for a business license, permits, or any special conditions, including noise ordinances, health codes, limitations on signs, and zoning concerns, including off-street parking for home-based businesses. Certain businesses also have to meet state and federal occupational safety regulations.

④ **Accounting**

Seek advice from an accountant about the form of business, tax reporting requirements, and an acceptable accounting system to keep track of expenses, income, and profits. The accountant should also be able to advise about special requirements for setting up business bank accounts.

⑤ **Insurance**

Discuss with an insurance agent the possible need for a business owner's policy, separate liability insurance, and the need for commercial licensing and insurance for any vehicles that might be used. Depending on your state and the nature of your business, you may need workers' compensation coverage for yourself; if you have any employees, laws generally require such coverage for them. Some commercial clients may require outside contractors to supply evidence of workers' compensation coverage before they will permit you to perform work on their premises.

⑥ **Insurance**

If you will be working with valuable possessions, including collectibles and antiques, make sure your insurance coverage protects you in the event of damage or loss, or that the owners have proper coverage that protects items on and off their property.

There can be a huge difference between the actual value of an item (which takes into account depreciation) and the guaranteed replacement value (which is the cost to buy an equivalent substitute). In the case of antiques and collectibles, an insurance company may insist on an independent appraisal to determine an item's value.

Informational Icons Used

Categories

 Service

 Product

 Trade (skilled trade or craft)

 Creative (artistic or creative skills)

 Virtual company

Challenges

 Seasonal

 Liability (exposes business to liability)

 Hazardous (dangerous to the business operator)

 Children (involves working with children)

 Pets (involves working with pets)

Skills

 Technical

 Computer

Training or certification

Food

Complexity

Tools and equipment (requires specialized tools and equipment)

 Licenses or Permits (requires licenses, permits)

Helper (requires helper)

Web and phone sales

Handicapped or homebound (can be conducted by physically challenged)

Capital Expenditures (not including vehicle or rental space)

$0 to $1,000

$1,001 to $3,000

$3,001 to $5,000

Business Insurance and Risk Management

Once you've let your mind run rampant with dreams of profits, fun, and more profits, take a moment and ask yourself this question: What could possibly go wrong?

Let us suggest a few moments of doom and gloom:

- One of your clients, or perhaps a delivery person, trips and falls over the crack in the driveway you've been meaning to fix for the past three years.

- You somehow manage to lose the only copy of a precious family photograph that was entrusted to you to restore.

- You fail to advise a client of a critical deadline in filing a college application, causing her to be rejected for admission.

- A slip of a chisel cracks and destroys a priceless antique chair you've been asked to refinish.

- When you clean a chimney you overlook a wobbly interior brick that falls into the flue weeks later, resulting in a smoky blaze that destroys the house.

- A product that you sell, even if you did not make it yourself or perform any alterations on it, fails and causes damage to a person or property.

There's a lot more to say than "oops" when you run a business. An accident, error, omission, or a negligent act by you or anyone in your employ could ruin your business and even result in a claim against your personal assets. The severity of the threat could depend on:

- The way your business is set up
- The amount (or lack) of insurance you have
- The care with which the contract with the customer is drawn

That's why we recommend you consult at least two commercial insurance agents for a risk assessment. Listen to the advice you are offered; ask lots of questions. Don't be shy about requesting time: If agents don't offer you good service *before* they've cashed your check, what makes you think they'll be any better once you're a client?

We suggest you meet with more than one agent, at competitive companies. You may find one easier to understand or work with than another, or you might find a better deal.

Don't hide the fact that you are shopping around. The smartest entrepreneurs are those who *buy* goods and services instead of being *sold* goods and services. And the best businesspeople are those who realize that they have to offer real value to their customers in the form of price, service, or both.

Do the same when you seek a civil attorney who can help you protect yourself with limits of liability in your contracts and the form of your business. Ask for an introductory meeting with at least two lawyers. (In most instances, a short preliminary session is offered without charge.) Ask for advice and for an estimate of costs for specific services.

Business Insurance Basics

Everything we do involves some amount of risk. Some risks are relatively minor: You could lose or break an inexpensive item; you could put a minor dent in the bumper of your car by hitting the trash can in your own garage; you could trip and fall in the driveway and skin a knee. In these minor accidents, you have no one to blame but yourself, and you are willing to shrug them off as ordinary events of life.

Now consider the following risks: You could lose or break an expensive musical instrument entrusted to you for repairing; you could have an accident with your car while driving someone to the airport as part of your car service business; the FedEx delivery person could trip and fall in your driveway and break a leg. In each of these incidents, you and your small business—no matter how undersized—are liable to be sued for damages, sometimes for huge amounts of money.

You also face the risk of loss due to theft of your equipment and supplies. Your business could be damaged by fire, flood, loss of heating, and other unforeseen events.

Liability does not stop with obvious things like accidents. If you are operating a business, you face liability for injuries and losses caused by your services and products and for errors and omissions or negligence in advisory and consultative services.

How Small Is Too Small?

When we were kids, we gave no thought to lawsuits, liability, and insurance when we took jobs babysitting for the neighbors, mowing lawns, clearing snow, or selling cookies and bread at ball games.

We would be remiss if we did not warn any reader of this book that we live in a litigious world. We'd like to think that any of the jobs we include in this book can be performed without risk to our readers or their customers, but that's simply not true.

We're not lawyers, and we're not insurance agents. We recommend that *at the very least* anyone planning to start a business find a capable and honest insurance agent and have a meeting to discuss a reasonable level of coverage for a small business. You may find that the job you have in mind—at least in its small, early stages—is protected by personal coverage you already have for your home or vehicle. Or you may find that the agent has serious concerns about your exposure to risk and recommends purchase of a new policy to protect you. It becomes a cost of doing business.

What is the price for a basic insurance policy? There is no simple answer to that question, because insurance companies rate applicants based on the type of business and their experience in paying claims. Rates also differ depending on geographic region, and within regions on whether the work takes place in an urban or a rural setting.

In the broadest terms, we estimate that a basic business owner's policy for an occupation that is not particularly hazardous would cost somewhere between

$250 and $1,000 per year. You may also need to obtain coverage for inventory and for a vehicle used for commercial purposes.

In the worst case, you may find that the insurance costs will be so high that it makes your business plan unrealistic. In that situation, you should look for ways to reduce the risk and the cost, or find a different small business to start.

Who Goes There? Liability for Home-Based Businesses

Let's think about the types of people who might enter your home or place of business (which may be in your home, or elsewhere).

Invitees are those who enter *with your permission* and *for the purposes of your business or otherwise for your benefit.* Included in this group would be those making deliveries, pickups, garbage collections, and providing service or maintenance. You need to make a reasonable effort to be on the lookout for dangerous conditions and post warnings about them.

Licensees are those who enter *with your permission* but *for their own purposes.* For example, licensees include a government inspector, a member of the police or fire department, or a utility worker permitted to gain access because of an easement. In general, your obligation to a licensee is to make them aware of any dangerous conditions: Post a sign warning of slippery floors; install a proper railing on stairs; keep gates to hazardous areas closed.

Trespassers are those who enter *without your permission.* In general, you do not have any legal responsibility to a trespasser, although there are situations, including those called *attractive nuisances,* where you may have some liability even to those who break into your property or otherwise enter without your consent. For example, in most localities you have to take reasonable steps to prevent easy break-in to a swimming pool, to keep a cute but ferocious dog fenced in, or to protect unwanted visitors from getting close to dangerous power tools and other equipment. Consult an attorney and your insurance agent to help assess risks in this area.

Be sure to consult with your insurance agent and attorney about any state or local laws or regulations that would affect your area, and ask about any particular liabilities associated with your type of business. Your homeowner's or business insurance should protect against personal injuries. Your attorney can advise you in setting up a form of business that shields your personal assets from most lawsuits and liability, shifting responsibility to your business.

Assessing Your Risks

Advisors recommend that business owners include a careful assessment of risks faced by an enterprise, no matter how small. Risk management starts with identifying various exposures to risk and then deciding on the best way to deal with each of them.

With each exposure to risk, determine how serious it would be, and whether the loss is one that you could afford to bear or whether you need to find a way to offset that risk in some way.

One of the first things you should do as you draw up your business plan is to make contact with a capable and well-informed commercial insurance agent. Shop around to find an agent who is able to communicate with you and (this is hardest to find) willing to put your interests above all, even above his or her sales commission. Ask friends, family, and business acquaintances for recommendations.

One way to deal with the possibility of risk is to mount an active campaign to *reduce exposure*. For example, you might choose not to accept very valuable items for repair unless the owner relieves you of liability or pays for special insurance coverage. You might choose not to sell particular products because of an increased likelihood of liability: for example, trampolines, diving boards, and weapons.

You might choose to insist on replacing broken parts with new ones instead of making repairs, because new parts have higher reliability. You might choose to accept a babysitting job but refuse to transport children to or from school or other activities.

Some insurance companies will provide free or low-cost consulting services to their clients to help them reduce exposure to loss, something that benefits both the policyholder and the issuer.

Another option is *risk retention* or *self-insurance*. A business might decide it can accept occasional losses as part of the ordinary cost of doing business and build the expense into prices. A garden nursery cannot expect to collect for the loss of a few plants because of an unexpected freeze; the selling price for healthy plants includes an allowance to cover previous or anticipated losses.

This is the sort of decision we might make for our personal automobile: If it is more than a few years old and has declined in value, it might make sense to eliminate collision coverage and reduce the value of the replacement cost. (At the same time, you would not want to skimp on liability coverage to protect you from claims for damage to others or to their property.

The third option is to *transfer the risk*. This can be done by purchasing insurance for your company, or you may be able to find ways to have others assume risks as part of your business relationship with them.

One way you could transfer risk would be to hire an independent trucking company to make pickups and deliveries for your company.

We discuss various types of insurance you can purchase later in this chapter.

Understanding Insurable Risks

What, exactly, are you protecting against when you purchase a business policy? Typical named risks include the following.

Physical Damage

Losses due to fire, storm damage, vandalism, broken pipes, failed heating systems, and other incidents may be insured against. You could lose finished goods, raw materials, tools, and other elements of your business. The loss could also occur to your clients' property that has been deposited with you for repair, maintenance, or processing.

If your business is operated in a room of your home, it may be possible to add a rider or extension to your homeowner's or renter's policy to cover a small business.

Criminal Activity

You could lose property, your own or items belonging to customers, due to theft or robbery. If you will be working with valuable items such as jewelry or works of art, make sure you are fully covered.

Liability

A business or its owner may be required to pay for bodily injury or destruction of property suffered by others. The payment may be required as the result of a court ruling in a legal case, an out-of-court settlement of a lawsuit, or as an element of a contract that makes you or your company responsible for certain types of losses.

Liability insurance usually includes the costs of defending you against a lawsuit for a claim that is covered under the policy.

A company can also be required by law to assume liability for certain occurrences such as injuries that fall under workers' compensation coverage.

Public liability refers to injuries or losses by customers, visitors, and others who are not employees. The liability is incurred as the result of provable negligence or fault. The exposure here would include an injury due to broken pavement, a slippery floor, improper installation or repair of a product provided to a customer, or a new product that is defective.

If you rent a home, office, or place of business, your lease may transfer liability for injury from the owner of the property to the renter; consult an attorney to be sure of your responsibility.

Liability to employees generally falls under *workers' compensation* laws, which vary from state to state. In some states, not all types of businesses are required to have such policies, and in some localities, the owner of a one-person business is exempt from the requirement to have such a policy. Again, consult with a capable insurance agent to find out the laws that apply in your area.

If you will be starting and running a small business that will take you into the offices and workplaces of other companies, you may find that their insurance carriers require that anyone doing business with them show evidence of a current workers' compensation policy.

Business Interruption

An element of business packages is coverage to help you get past a shutdown of your business due to a direct loss (one that is covered by other elements of your policy). For example, if your office or workshop is damaged by fire, you could collect the current or replacement value of the items and receive some payment for income you lose while the business is unable to operate. The money could help pay for taxes, loans, utilities, and other fixed costs that don't stop even when your business does.

Disability or Death of Owner or Key Person

What if your business is entirely dependent on the health and involvement of a single person: an expert, an artisan, or a salesperson? If that person were to die or become incapacitated, the business might grind to a halt. Some policies in this area amount to specialized life insurance, with the business or the business owner listed as beneficiary.

Types of Insurance Coverage

The insurance industry packages named risks into classes of policies intended to cover various forms of business or business activities.

Commercial General Liability

The basic form of business liability coverage protects (up to policy limits) against damage or loss to property, bodily injury, personal injury (including slander or libel), and advertising injury and related claims.

A good policy also extends to other liabilities, including protection for damages and legal expenses related to an injury caused by a product or service provided by your company, other kinds of product liability, and liability for certain risks you may assume under a contract.

Property Coverage

This sort of policy offers protection against loss or damage to your business property as the result of fire, theft, and certain other situations. (Some policies exclude or limit loss due to floods, windstorms, and other risks.)

Depending on the nature of your business, you may need to extend coverage to protect against loss of property owned by customers and to insure against loss of valuable papers, records, and data stored on computer media.

For most companies, the best type of coverage offers to pay for lost property at replacement value rather than at its generally lower (depreciated) actual value. With the assistance of your insurance agent, make a realistic appraisal of the cost you would face if all of your business equipment, inventory, and vehicles, or the structures that hold them, were lost. If you have $250,000 in potential losses, you should have coverage that comes very close to that amount; one way to reduce your insurance premium is to accept a small amount of the risk yourself by choosing a policy with a higher deductible that is still within your ability to absorb. There is, however, no reason to pay for a coverage limit that is higher than the amount you could collect in the event of a loss.

Business Owner's Policy (BOP)

This insurance package brings together general liability and property coverage in a single policy that usually costs less than individual plans; BOP is generally offered to small and medium-sized businesses that do not have extraordinary exposure to loss.

This sort of policy does not ordinarily protect against errors, omissions, or negligence; a more inclusive professional liability policy should be considered if your business is exposed to those sorts of risks.

Professional Liability Insurance for Errors and Omissions

For professional businesses, including consultancies, accounting, and advisory services, this is somewhat like malpractice insurance. This coverage protects against claims for errors or omissions in your work and for negligence.

Umbrella Coverage and Excess Liability

One way to save money on insurance costs is to extend your overall coverage level by purchasing an umbrella policy. These policies are secondary to basic coverage, adding more available funds after other policies have reached their payout limit.

Business Auto Insurance

If your company owns, leases, or rents vehicles, or if any employees use their own vehicles for business purposes, this sort of policy will protect against liability claims for injury to others or damage to other vehicles and property. The policy can also include collision and comprehensive coverage to pay for damage to your own vehicles and for protection against theft of personal contents.

Legalities and Taxes

As we said in the introduction to this book, every business begins with an idea. Once that business begins to spend and, more important, *earn* money, it becomes an entity that is of interest to local, state, and federal authorities. Regulators will want to regulate, inspectors will want to inspect, and tax agencies will absolutely insist on collecting taxes.

Many of the jobs we write about in this book can begin on the most casual basis, as a sole proprietorship or a general partnership. In these sorts of businesses, the owners put their own money into the operation and pay taxes on their personal income.

We can also hope that our little idea for a business will one day grow into a larger enterprise with multiple employees, assets of its own, and a long and profitable life. In this chapter, we examine the most common structures for businesses.

Form of Business

If you hang up a shingle that says "Paul Revere, Silversmith" (and your name is Paul Revere), you can set up a sole proprietorship and run your business out of your personal checkbook. In some states and localities, you must register the business name with the county where you will conduct business. In addition, banking laws generally require a business certificate to enable you to deposit checks made out to "Paul Revere, Silversmith" into an account, although checks to "Paul Revere" would probably be accepted.

If your birth certificate actually reads "Paul Hickenlooper" (to pick a name at random), and you want to call your company "Paul Revere, Silversmith," you will need to file a *doing-business-as* (DBA) or *fictitious name* form in most jurisdictions.

There are advantages to each of the various forms of business, including sole proprietorships, partnerships, and corporations, that might argue for one or another, depending on the nature of your enterprise.

State and federal laws differ with regard to certain requirements for various business structures: for example, whether a business needs to have workers' compensation insurance, the deductibility of certain expenses, and the filing of tax and information returns.

Be sure to discuss available forms of business with an accountant and attorney. Here is a general description of common options; please don't confuse this section with legal or tax accounting advice.

Sole Proprietorship

This is a business that is owned and controlled by an individual, with all of the profits directed to the owner. In many localities the company must obtain a business license from local government; additional licenses and permits may be required for certain types of businesses.

This is the simplest and least expensive form of business to set up, and the owner does not have to answer to anyone else about operations.

The most significant disadvantage of a sole proprietorship is that the company and its owner are linked when it comes to financial responsibility, liability, and taxes. If the business is unable to pay its bills, creditors can seek to collect from the owner's personal assets. When it comes to taxes, income from the business is treated as personal income of the owner.

It may also be more difficult to obtain bank loans and other types of financing for a sole proprietorship because of the limited resources of the single owner and because the business's success is entirely dependent on one person.

General Partnership

This is a business that is owned and controlled by two or more people, sharing in the investment, management, and profits of the company. There should be a written agreement signed by the partners, spelling out investment obligations, management expectations, and the distribution of profits.

A general partnership has the advantage of additional sources of capital and labor, but it does not relieve the partners of personal responsibility for debts and other liabilities. Since the general partnership is not a separate business entity, salaries, profits, and losses are reported as personal income by each partner.

Limited Partnership

This form of business is owned and controlled by two or more people, who share in the investment and profits of the company, but who give operational control of the business to a general partner or partners.

A limited partnership is a step toward a corporation. Though the partnership is not a business entity of its own, the agreement among the owners can limit responsibility for debts and liabilities to the general partner. The limited partners, who do not exercise control over operations, are personally liable only up to the amount of their investment in the company.

Setting up a limited partnership is more complex than forming a general partnership and should involve a lawyer to draft the agreements.

Corporation

After receiving a charter from the state where it is headquartered, a corporation becomes a legal entity that exists independently of the people who invest in it, manage it, and share in its profits. The corporation, owned by its shareholders, can raise funds through the sale of additional stock; depending on the type of stock sold, shareholders may receive partial, majority, or total control over operations.

Although it is possible to set up a corporation without the involvement of an attorney using do-it-yourself kits and Internet sites, you may benefit from the advice of an attorney, and you'll want to coordinate your efforts with your accountant, in any case.

The principal advantage of a corporation is that its owners (the shareholders) are personally liable only up to the amount they have invested in the corporation.

When it comes to taxes, the corporation reports its own income, expenses, and profits to state and federal authorities and pays its own taxes and fees. Dividends paid to shareholders are generally not deductible from business income, and therefore this income is subject to taxes at both the corporate and personal levels.

Subchapter S Corporation

A Subchapter S corporation passes through the income or loss to the shareholders, as a partnership would (the corporation does not pay taxes on the profit) and provides the liability protection of a corporation.

As an employee of a corporation, you will report salary as personal income on your personal tax forms.

Limited Liability Corporation

As a legal entity that is permitted in most states, an LLC combines some of the tax benefits of a partnership with the limits on liability of a corporation. A lawyer's advice is generally needed for the drafting of agreements among the owners.

On the tax front, shareholders report their portion of the company's profit or loss on their personal tax forms.

Business Licenses

Check with city or county clerks or your attorney to see if you require a local or state business license. Some states require licenses for almost every form of business, while others are more selective. Among businesses that often require licenses are *trades,* such as electricians, plumbers, construction, mining, forestry, and *professions,* including health care, financial services, entertainment, and food preparation and sale.

In some states, businesses operated from a home do not require a license, or they may face less stringent criteria.

Sales Tax on Services and Products

As of 2004, 45 states and the District of Columbia levied sales tax on most products and some services. Some states exempt food and certain services and products from tax. Contact your state department of revenue for details about requirements for your business; your accountant should also be able to advise you.

If you are required to assess sales tax, you will have to register with the state and set up an account for regular deposit of taxes you have collected. In many states, you can obtain an exemption from having to pay or collect sales taxes if you are buying products or raw materials and then reselling them to a retailer. Again, your accountant should be able to help you set up your tax status.

Zoning Issues

In many parts of the country, zoning laws and regulations place limits on the types of businesses that can be established and operated in particular areas. You may be completely barred from opening a business in a residential area or other noncommercial zone, or you may face regulations requiring off-street parking, limits on hours of operation, or other strictures.

Consult an attorney for advice.

CHAPTER 3

Setting Your Price

For many businesses, the most difficult question of all is this: How do you set a price for your goods or services?

At its simplest level, you need to set your prices at a level high enough to allow you to make a profit. That means higher than the cost of materials, supplies, rent, utilities, insurance, legal fees, and accounting costs. Include the cost of breakage, spoilage, or loss. Then add in a margin high enough to pay yourself (and your staff) a living wage.

On one hand, if you set your prices too high, you will receive a higher profit, but your cash flow may be lower because you could lose some business to others.

On the other hand, as salespeople like to say, if you price your product or service too low, you are leaving too much money on the table.

Let's begin by differentiating between *cost* and *price:*

- *Cost* is the total amount of money you need to pay for manufacturing or purchasing a product or service and offering it for sale. Included in the expenses are *fixed* and *variable* costs.

- *Price* is the amount of money you ask a customer or client to pay for a product or service.

Analyzing Your Costs for Product Sales

Begin by conducting a very detailed analysis of all of your fixed and variable costs.

A *fixed cost* is one that does not change no matter how many widgets you sell or services you provide; this is often referred to as *overhead*. For example, if you must rent an office, the monthly payment is a fixed cost of doing business. So, too, is the cost of any basic tools and equipment you must purchase or rent, most insurance, and basic utilities.

> **Most businesses** are born on the back of an envelope, or at best on a yellow legal pad. There are, though, some very useful computer tools you can use to help with your planning. One is Business Plan Pro, from Palo Alto Software (www.paloalto.com) and we have included a few sample screens in this chapter.

If you have any employees, they are a fixed cost if they are on salary and being paid whether or not they sell or perform services successfully.

Business Plan Pro; © 2004 Palo Alto Software, Inc. (www.paloalto.com), reproduced with permission.

A *variable cost* is one that is directly related to sales; it can also be referred to as the *incremental cost per unit*. For example, if you are handcrafting cuckoo clocks, the amount of money you spend on parts and supplies varies based on the number of clocks you put together each month. If you hire and pay workers on an hourly basis, their cost varies with production or services. As an example, if you must purchase $50 worth of materials and spend one hour of time that you value at $50 to assemble a clock, the incremental cost of that clock is $100.

It is essential that you have a realistic accounting of your fixed costs (overhead) and your variable costs (incremental cost per unit) before you can determine your break-even point and build in a profit.

Let's use a simple example with the following two assumptions:

1. The fixed costs of your business, including office rent, equipment, insurance, and utilities, works out to a monthly expense of $1,000.

2. The variable cost for the one model of cuckoo clock you are building, including materials and labor, is $100.

Business Plan Pro
File Edit Insert Format View Tools Help

Break-even Analysis Table

Break-even analysis is an expected component of most business plans, especially for start-up companies. This analysis shows how much revenue you need to meet both fixed and variable costs. By default, everything in this table is calculated for you from numbers in other tables.

The analysis depends on assumptions for estimated monthly fixed cost, average per-unit revenue, and average per-unit variable cost. It assumes a standard month and requires averages for your business overall, not detailed unit pricing or unit costs.

Examples
Break-even Wizard
Table Review
Other Resources
Additional Detail

Table: Break-even Analysis — Full Columns

O6 | 350

	A	O
1	Break-even Analysis:	
2	Monthly Units Break-even	2
3	Monthly Revenue Break-even	$613
4		
5	Assumptions:	
6	Average Per-Unit Revenue	$350.00
7	Average Per-Unit Variable Cost	$150.00
8	Estimated Monthly Fixed Cost	$350

Previous Task   Next Task

Therefore, if you expect to sell only one clock per month, your break-even point is $1,100. Put another way, you'll need to sell that single clock for at least $1,100 or you will lose money on your business.

Let's say you expect to sell 20 clocks per month. Your fixed costs are still $1,000, but your variable costs now total $2,000 ($100 in materials times 20 units.) To break even, you'll need to sell those 20 clocks for an average of $150 each to generate a total of $3,000 for fixed and variable costs.

If you can sell 200 clocks per month, fixed costs remain $1,000, and variable costs reach $20,000; the break-even price for those 200 clocks would have to average $105 each to generate $21,000.

Adding a Markup for Profit

The cuckoo clock example works well because it has the advantage of being based on a single product sold at a specific price. Things become much more complex if you are selling a range of products at varying prices.

Business Plan Pro; © 2004 Palo Alto Software, Inc. (www.paloalto.com), reproduced with permission.

Here is a five-step method to go about determining prices in this situation:

1. Calculate your *fixed costs,* or overhead.
2. Determine the *incremental cost per unit,* or variable cost, for each of the various items you expect to sell.
3. Come up with a realistic estimate of the number of each of the items you expect to sell in a month.
4. Multiply the units times the incremental cost.
5. Add the total to fixed costs. The result is your break-even point.

Here is an example:

1. Your fixed costs are $1,000 per month.
2. Here's the incremental cost per unit for the five products you expect to sell:
   Product A $50
   Product B $75
   Product C $25
   Product D $100
   Product E $10
3. You expect to sell the following numbers of each product per month (based on annual sales divided by 12):
   Product A   5 units
   Product B   4 units
   Product C   10 units
   Product D   2 units
   Product E   10 units
4. Units sold times the incremental cost:
   Product A $ 50 × 5 = $ 250
   Product B $ 75 × 4 = $ 300
   Product C $ 25 × 10 = $ 250
   Product D $100 × 2 = $ 200
   Product E $ 10 × 10 = $1,000
   TOTAL: $2,000
5. Break-even cost:
   Fixed costs $1,000
   Variable costs   2,000
   TOTAL: $3,000

This tells you that you need to mark up your products by an average of 50 percent to break even. (Products that cost you $2,000 to build or buy need to sell for $3,000 to include the cost of overhead.)

One method of setting prices is to determine a standard markup, in the form of a percentage, and apply it to the cost of an item. For example, you might determine that your cost of goods for a cuckoo clock is $40 and your target markup percentage is 50 percent. That means its selling price would be $60.

If you decide that you want your business to generate $500 in profit, you would need to apply a markup of 75 percent ($2,000 in variable costs times 1.75 equals $3,500 in receipts).

To apply a markup, you can multiply the cost by the markup percentage and then add in the cost, or you can add 100 percent to the markup percentage and multiply it by the cost. The result is the same either way.

In some business models, different products or services may have different markups. If one product or service costs much more to inventory, has higher breakage or spoilage, or requires much more expenditure to advertise or sell, you might apply a higher markup. On the other hand, if you are selling some high-priced items you might be willing to accept a lower percentage of profit.

You may also be forced to lower the markup on certain products or services if you face strong competition for sales, or if you are seeking to build market share for a new company or a new offering.

In the end, what matters is that the money you receive for the products you sell in a month, a quarter, or a year is at least equal to the total of the fixed and variable costs.

Depending on your business plan, your personal resources, and your faith in your idea, you may be willing to allow a few months or even a few years to reach profitability.

Analyzing Your Costs for a Service Business

As a consultant or service provider, your primary commodity is your time. In general, your fixed costs will represent much or all of your expenses.

Fixed costs, or overhead, for a service business include rent for an office, the cost of any basic tools and equipment, most insurance, and basic utilities.

Variable costs for a service business are principally the value you place on your own time, plus incidentals such as transportation.

There's not really a markup per se for a service business. You will pay your overhead and generate profits on the basis of the hourly rate you charge.

Business Plan Pro; © 2004 Palo Alto Software, Inc. (www.paloalto.com), reproduced with permission.

Note that a service-only business, such as tutoring or college advising, will have minimal operating expenses, although you must be careful not to overlook the cost in time of preparation for a service, including research, education, and sales of that service. For services-based companies, the markup amounts to the hourly rate you will charge.

When you set your hourly rate, be sure to take into account any helpers you may be paying separately. For example, if you have someone managing your office or helping maintain equipment, that becomes an element of your cost of goods.

No formula can set the value of your time; you can, though, usually find the hourly rate for others performing similar work in your area. You might choose to underprice the competition to build your business, or you may believe that your experience and skills warrant a higher hourly rate than other contenders charge. You can easily adjust your hourly rate downward in slow periods or upward when demand is high.

In some small businesses, labor is a major component of the job but operating expenses and cost of goods are also a major component. For example, a lawn mowing business has fixed expenses, such as the cost of machinery, a vehicle, permits, licenses, and insurance, plus variable expenses, including gasoline, maintenance, labor, and taxes.

CHAPTER 4

Financing a Small Business

It takes money to make money; that's a basic truism of business school. Some enterprises require a lot more cash than others: A car dealership may need millions of dollars to build a showroom and fund an inventory of vehicles to sell. Even a neighborhood snow removal service or lawn mowing enterprise (two of the small businesses we discuss in this book) needs to spend some cash to purchase equipment and supplies and transport them from client to client.

Many of the jobs discussed in this book can be started with minimal investment. However, if you hope to expand to include multiple locations, numerous employees, and more ambitious services, it will be essential that you have enough ready capital for investment. The sources and uses of that money have to be as carefully managed as the rest of the business.

If you will be using your own resources, you should be sure your business and its underlying plan is sound.

Computer partner. Depending on the complexity of your business, you may want to enlist the assistance of a computer business planner. Among the best is Business Plan Pro, from Palo Alto Software. You can learn about that product at www.paloalto.com.

If you will be using someone else's money—a bank, an investor, or a government agency—you'll need to be just as sure of your plan and fully understand the risks of borrowing.

The two basic types of financing are *equity* and *debt.*

Equity versus Debt

Equity financing is an investment in the ownership of the company. Equity can come from your own resources, from family, friends, employees, and customers, or from outside investors, including venture capitalists who seek to buy into businesses that have the potential for growth. Equity investors are generally given a portion of ownership (and control) of the company; looking at it from the point of view of the founder, accepting equity financing from others reduces the percentage of the company that you own and control.

Debt financing is a loan, a liability to the company (and, depending on the form of the business, also to the owner). Sources include banks, commercial lenders, and government agencies, including the U.S. Small Business Administration.

Loans can be used for ongoing operations, for the purchase of equipment, and for short-term uses such as inventory.

Outside investors will usually be very interested in determining and assessing your company's *debt-to-equity ratio.* That formula compares the money you have borrowed, or plan to borrow, to the amount of your own money you have invested in the business. The more money the owner and partners or shareholders have put into the business, the more comfortable an outside lender is likely to be with a request for a loan.

Think of the parallel in buying a home. Most lenders are much more willing to issue a mortgage to a borrower who puts a substantial down payment into the home. The theory is that an owner who is risking some of his or her own money is a more dedicated and trustworthy borrower than someone who is working entirely with other people's money.

Types of Loans

A *line of credit* is somewhat like a personal credit card: The lender disburses funds as they are requested, up to a preset limit. The borrower pays interest (and usually a portion of the outstanding balance) on the amount of funds outstanding at the end of each borrowing period, usually monthly.

An *installment loan* gives the borrower a lump sum of money and sets a schedule for regular payments over a set period of time for repayment.

A *short-term loan* is money advanced for a specific purpose: to pay for inventory, to help a company get past a cash flow problem related to accounts receivable, and so on. The loan is expected to be repaid once the immediate need has been resolved.

A *long-term loan* is aimed at capital spending, including equipment and real estate, and is intended to be repaid from the ongoing proceeds of the company.

Collateral for Loans

From the point of view of the lender, the riskiest type of loan is one that is *unsecured:* The borrower merely promises to repay it. A personal credit card is an unsecured loan, and it generally bears a higher interest rate than is charged for a secured note.

Lenders would rather tie their loans to an interest in something tangible, a *secured* note. For example, if you purchase an automobile, the lender technically owns the vehicle until the loan is paid off; in the event of a default, the lender has the right to repossess the car and sell it off to regain some or all of the money it has loaned.

For commercial loans, banks or other lenders might require that an individual or a company pledge or sign over title to assets to protect their interest in a loan. For example, a company could offer as collateral that portion of any real estate not encumbered by a mortgage, or it could pledge equipment, accounts receivable, and other things of value. An individual could pledge personal real estate, cash investments, and life insurance cash value or death benefits.

For some personal loans, the lender may ask for another party to sign the note. An *endorser* is someone who agrees to pay the loan if the borrower defaults. A *comaker* is similar, with the distinction that the lender can collect from either the maker or the comaker. A *guarantor* is a third party who guarantees to repay the outstanding balance of a note if the maker defaults; the guarantor could be an officer of the corporation or company. In some situations, a government or private program may agree to guarantee the loan to assist a small business in obtaining financing.

Working with the Small Business Administration

The U.S. Small Business Administration (SBA) is an independent agency of the federal government. Its programs include education and direct and indirect programs to help small businesses obtain financing. For information, consult www.sba.gov, or call the district office for the agency: 800-827-5722.

The SBA offers some direct loans as well as loan guarantees that allow other lenders to receive backing on some or all of the money they lend to businesses. The SBA also licenses private lenders to participate in the small business investment company (SBIC) program, a low-level form of venture capital.

Among the SBA's programs are the following:

- *7 (a) loan guarantee.* The SBA's basic program offers guarantees to lenders to entice them to make loans to small businesses that might not otherwise qualify for a loan. Loans are extended for up to 10 years for working capital and for longer periods to purchase equipment and other fixed assets.

- *Certified development company (CDC) 504 loans.* Private lenders can offer loans to acquire real estate or equipment for expansion or modernization; the loans are funded by an SBA-guaranteed note.

- *7 (m) microloans.* Short-term, small loans to small businesses for working capital, equipment, or inventory; the SBA lends money or guarantees loans to third parties that offer funds to enterprises.

- *Surety bond guarantee (SBG).* This program offers completion and contract bonds for small and minority contractors. If a company is unable to fulfill a contract, the surety bond is supposed to pay for completion of the project by others.

CHAPTER **5**

Home Services (Exterior)

1 Lawn Mowing Service

2 Snow Removal

3 Garden Tilling

4 Window Cleaning

5 Deck Cleaning

6 Landscape Designer

7 Deck Construction

8 Storage Sheds, Playhouses, Doghouses

9 Children's Outdoor Playset Installer

10 Low-Voltage Outdoor Electrical Wiring

11 Stonemason and Decorative Brick Worker

Lawn Mowing Service

Description of Job

- Perform basic lawn care, including lawn mowing, trimming around buildings and lawn furniture, and edging.

- Conduct seasonal fertilizing and application of other lawn chemicals, including weed killer.

The Need

Do you have a lawn? You need to keep it trimmed.

It's not just a matter of keeping up with the Joneses; in most communities, laws and regulations require that property owners keep their land reasonably neat. Cutting the grass also helps reduce the incidence of ticks, fleas, and other unwelcome visitors in residential neighborhoods.

That said, not everyone has the time, inclination, or ability to take care of their own lawn. The market for lawn mowing services includes older homeowners, persons with disabilities, and people who just don't have the time to do it themselves.

Challenges

In most parts of the country, lawn mowing is a seasonal job. (In northern climes, lawns generally hibernate at least half the year, from about October through May.) You'll need to pay off the cost of equipment during the growing season . . . and watch it gather dust over the winter. You will also likely have to pay for 12 months of insurance and licenses even if your business runs only 6 months of the year.

Rain helps the grass grow, which is good news, but a particularly dismal summer could result in long periods when lawns cannot be mowed. Similarly, a drought could cause lawns to grow unusually slowly.

Know the Territory

Will you bring your own equipment, or use whatever you find at your client's premises?

Using your client's equipment simplifies your operation in many ways: You won't have to buy a lawn mower and other devices; you will not be responsible for maintaining it and providing gas; and you will not have to transport bulky and heavy machines from your home to your customer's lawn.

On the other hand, the equipment you find may be of poor quality or unreliable. Some homeowners won't have lawn mowers, costing you a job.

Using your own equipment should guarantee you'll have machines you can rely on; you will, though, have to properly maintain the devices. If you bring your own equipment, you'll need to transport the devices to your clients. If you're working on your own street, you may be able to roll the mower down the sidewalk; anywhere more distant will probably require that you use a truck or a trailer with a ramp.

Will you be responsible for removing grass clippings? Are there any local regulations regarding disposal? (A mulching lawn mower may solve this problem, if that's okay with your client.)

Investigate other local ordinances. For example, some towns may limit the hours when noisy power equipment may be used.

Educate yourself on lawn chemicals, including fertilizers, weed killers, and pest control options. Take care to avoid exposure to dangerous substances. Remember, although a manufacturer may claim that a chemical is not harmful when its instructions are followed, you may be exposing yourself to repeated use of the substance as you move from one job to the next.

Not all lawns are the same. If the property is hilly or irregularly shaped, it will likely require more time and effort than a flat, square property.

Lawn mowing is the sort of job that can be done by one person or by a crew. A lawn that takes one person two hours to cut could be done in one hour by a crew of two. Although having a crew may allow you to cut many more lawns, you'll also have to pay additional salaries and benefits, and you'll need more equipment. The principal advantage to hiring a crew is that you may be able to step back from actually cutting the grass yourself and instead earn your income as the manager for your lawn mowing empire.

How to Get Started

Market your services before they are needed. In the best of all possible worlds, you will be able to sign up enough clients ahead of the season to justify purchase of equipment. Place ads on bulletin boards, at gardening supply stores, and in community newspapers.

Ask friends and neighbors for referrals. Offer a discount or a free service for any clients they bring to you.

Draw up a simple but complete agreement with clients listing exactly which services you will be providing and the cost. Include in the agreement whether lawn mowing services will be provided on a regular schedule (weekly, biweekly, on a particular day of the month) or whether the client must call to schedule a visit each time.

Get specific written instructions about any special conditions—a flower bed to be avoided or a section that needs to be hand-trimmed.

Up-front Expenses

Commercial equipment can be quite expensive; you may need to amortize the cost over an entire season, or even over more than one season. A heavy-duty machine can easily cost $1,000, reaching to $3,000 for the most powerful, widest, and most flexible devices.

Investigate buying used equipment from a reliable dealer who will offer a warranty and provide service.

Additional services such as edging and trimming, fertilizing, weed killing, and pest control will require purchasing additional equipment and chemicals.

How Much to Charge

Underlying the charge for lawn mowing services is the amount of time each job requires, plus the cost of fertilizer or chemicals. You'll also need to build into your price the cost of equipment (amortized over its useful life) plus an allowance for maintenance and repair.

You can establish an hourly rate and bill customers for actual time on-site, or you can estimate the time a job will require and then charge a flat rate. Remember that square footage alone is not an adequate indicator of the amount of time required for a job: Take into account the shape of the land, whether it is level or hilly, and any other special conditions. Lawns that are overgrown or wet will take more time and effort to cut.

Offer a discount to clients who sign up for an entire season, which could be in the form of a reduced rate or a bonus, such as a free end-of-season lawn mowing or fertilizing.

Legal and Insurance Issues

Special notes: Check with local authorities about the possible need for a permit to dump grass clippings.

① **Legal**

② **Legal**

③ **Legal**

④ **Accounting**

⑤ **Insurance**

Snow Removal

Description of Job

- Remove snow from sidewalks and driveways of private homes.
- Clear snow from parking lots and entranceways of commercial locations, including retail stores and office complexes.
- Subcontract with local governments to plow public roads and parking lots.

The Need

Snow happens, more so in some parts of the country than others. Many people do not have the time to clear snow, or they may not be physically able to do so.

In some parts of the country, including many rural areas, local governments may hire subcontractors to clear snow on an as-needed basis. Owners of commercial real estate also need to arrange for snow removal at stores and office complexes.

Challenges

In most parts of the country, snow removal is a seasonal job. In the Midwest and Northeast, the snow season generally runs from late November to early April, although storms can come earlier and later; in high mountain areas and certain other locations, including regions in the lee of the Great Lakes, snow can occur almost daily in an extended season.

In any case, you will need to pay off the cost of equipment during the winter season . . . and watch it gather dust over the summer. You will also likely have to pay for 12 months of insurance and licenses even if your business runs only 6 months of the year.

Snowfall, like rainfall, generally follows annual patterns that could result in exceptionally large amounts of snow in one year and a virtual drought the next. Don't base your investment on last winter's storms, which could be unusually heavy or light. You can research typical snowfall amounts and number of storms at area libraries and government agencies.

Know the Territory

Depending on the sort of jobs you seek, you will need equipment ranging from a sturdy snow shovel to a mechanical snowblower to a substantial truck with a heavy plow.

A snow shovel is quite portable, but a snowblower is much less so and will probably have to be delivered by truck . . . which has to be able to get through the snow on the streets.

Will you bring your own equipment, or use whatever you find at your client's premises?

Using your client's equipment simplifies your operation in many ways: You won't have to buy a snowblower; you will not be responsible for maintaining it and providing gas; and you will not have to transport it from your home to your customer's property.

On the other hand, the equipment you find may be of poor quality or unreliable, and some homeowners won't have a snowblower, costing you a job.

Bringing your own equipment should guarantee you'll have machines you can rely on; you will, though, have to properly maintain the devices.

Investigate local ordinances about snow removal. In some areas, snow cannot be pushed into the street. Many areas also ban disposal of snow in catch basins, rivers, or streams because of concerns about pollution from salt and other road chemicals.

Be aware that you may need to make multiple visits to a property if a storm lasts for many hours or if high winds blow snow back onto cleared pathways.

Not all pieces of property are the same. If the property is hilly or irregularly shaped, it will likely require more time and effort than a flat, square property. Dry and fluffy snow is easier to clear than heavy or rain-soaked snow.

Snow removal is the sort of job that can be done by one person or by a crew. A property that takes two hours to be cleared by one person could be done in one hour by a crew of two. Although having a crew may allow you to sign up many more customers, you'll also have to pay additional salaries and benefits, and you'll need more equipment. The principal advantage to hiring a crew is that you may be able to step back from actually clearing the snow yourself and instead make your income as the manager of a snow removal empire.

How to Get Started

Market your services before they are needed. Your goal should be to sign up enough clients ahead of the season to justify purchase of equipment.

Place ads on bulletin boards, at hardware and home center stores, and in community newspapers.

Ask friends and neighbors for referrals. Offer a discount or a free service for any clients they bring to you.

Draw up a simple but complete agreement with clients listing exactly which services you will be providing and the cost. Include in the agreement whether snow removal services will automatically be provided after a certain amount of snow falls, or whether the client must call to schedule a visit each time.

Get specific written instructions about any special conditions—a flower bed to be avoided or a section that needs to be hand-shoveled. Although it will be extremely difficult to promise exact times for snow removal—you can't schedule the storms—find out from clients whether they have particular needs to meet the demands of their jobs or medical necessities.

If you want to run the business on a more casual basis, you can merely load up a truck with a snowblower or plow and cruise the neighborhood looking for desperate homeowners who need help. Be sure to get a firm agreement on the price before you begin work.

Up-front Expenses

Commercial snowblowers can be quite expensive; you may need to amortize the cost over an entire season, or even over more than one season. A heavy-duty machine can easily cost $1,000, reaching to several thousand dollars for the most powerful devices.

A commercial snowplow—just the plow, not the truck—can cost several thousand dollars. Then you'll need a sufficiently heavy truck, with four-wheel drive and a power takeoff to control the movement of the plow.

Investigate buying used equipment from a reliable dealer who will offer a warranty and provide service.

How Much to Charge

Underlying the charge for snow removal services is the amount of time each job requires. You'll need to build into the rate the cost of equipment—amortized over time—plus an allowance for maintenance and repair. If it is necessary to spread salt or sand to deal with ice, you'll need to bill the customer for the cost of those materials and your time.

You can establish an hourly rate and bill customers for actual time on-site, or you can estimate the time a job will require and then charge a flat rate. Remember that square footage alone is not an adequate indicator of the amount of time required for a job: Take into account the shape of the land, whether it is level or hilly, and any other special conditions.

Commercial or governmental customers will likely agree to a contract that includes an advance deposit and a regular billing cycle based on the actual number of storms or billable hours.

For individual customers, some snow removal companies offer two options: an automatic response anytime there is a snowfall of a particular depth (perhaps three inches) or services on an on-call basis. For an automatic response, there is generally an agreement that covers services to be provided and a requirement for an advance deposit representing an amount equal to a typical season's work; refunds are given if there are fewer snowstorms than usual, and additional charges are billable for a particularly difficult winter.

Most snow removal services offer a discount to clients who sign up for an entire season.

Legal and Insurance Issues

Special notes: You may require a commercial license and plate to operate a snowplow in business; some communities may also require a special permit.

① **Legal**

② **Legal**

③ **Legal**

④ **Accounting**

⑤ **Insurance**

Garden Tilling

Description of Job

- Using a power rototiller or similar equipment, turn over a garden patch at the start of a season to prepare it for planting.

- Mix fertilizer, lime, or other garden chemicals into the soil.

- Cut down plants at the end of the season and compost the greens or haul them away.

- Turn over the earth at the end of the growing season to prepare it for the winter.

The Need

Have rototiller, will travel.

Many homeowners love to grow their own little patch of tomatoes, green beans, onions, and flowers. They look great and taste better than anything they'll find in the supermarket. (So what if the tomatoes end up costing them several dollars apiece or if the massive zucchini squash quickly outpace their ability to eat them, give them away, or use them as doorstops?)

For many gardeners, the most difficult part of the process is tilling the earth: breaking it up to a depth of six inches to a foot to allow easy planting and faster growth. Doing it by hand is a major chore, and purchasing a power tiller does not make sense for the casual gardener.

Your appeal is that you will bring a heavy, commercial rototiller or small tractor to their property and make quick work of a job that is beyond their abilities, interest, or equipment.

Challenges

This is a seasonal job, with most of the work coming in the spring; jobs in the fall will be less common. You'll need to amortize the cost of the machine and trailer over a fairly short period of time.

Know the Territory

Tillers come in front-tine, mid-tine, and rear-tine designs; in general, rear-tine machines are the most powerful, and front-tine devices are more maneuverable. Mid-tine tillers claim to balance power and maneuverability. Spend the time to research (and test, if possible) various designs to find the one that suits your needs best.

The horsepower of the engine varies; the larger the engine, the more powerful the churning of the earth and the movement of the wheels. Some designs use the rotating tines themselves to move the machine forward; many commercial designs apply power to a set of wheels that help pull the heavy device forward while the tines concentrate on breaking the earth.

Many lawn tractors with a power takeoff can be adapted to add a tiller; they may have sufficient horsepower to do the job, but may not be as maneuverable as a special-purpose tiller.

How to Get Started

Post flyers and ads at garden centers and community centers. Place ads in newspapers and shopping guides.

Ask satisfied customers to recommend your services to others; offer a bonus or discount for new business they refer your way.

Up-front Expenses

Commercial-grade rototillers cost in the range of $500 to $1,000 or more. Lighter-weight and less capable units intended for casual gardeners sell for as little as $300.

You may be able to find a reconditioned used machine through a dealer or private seller; either way, you will need a reliable source of parts and maintenance.

Other up-front costs include a trailer and hitch and a vehicle capable of pulling the tiller from place to place; you may be able to use a ramp and open-bed of a pickup truck to transport the device.

You'll also need to pay for advertising and promotion.

How Much to Charge

Charge an hourly rate, taking into account the cost of the equipment, wear and tear, gasoline, and your travel time to the site. Add a surcharge for especially distant travel and for especially difficult access to the property. Add the cost of fertilizer, lime, or other garden chemicals tilled into the ground.

Legal and Insurance Issues

① **Legal**

② **Legal**

③ **Legal**

④ **Accounting**

⑤ **Insurance**

Window Cleaning

Description of Job

- Clean windows for business and residential clients.
- Power-wash ground floor and hard-to-reach upper-floor windows.
- Squeegee and hand-finish windows.
- Remove screens, wash them, and replace them.

The Need

Windows get dirty.

Retail businesses and offices need to present a clean and neat appearance to customers, but window washing is probably not in the CEO's job description.

Homeowners also want their houses to appear attractive from the outside and to be able to see the world without having to peer through a glass darkly. They may not have ladders, or the inclination to climb one, and otherwise lack the equipment to do a good job, especially on second-story windows.

Challenges

It can be difficult to gain access to some windows; challenges include narrow alleys, uneven ground, and landscaping. One solution is to use power washers and rotary brushes on lightweight aluminum or plastic poles.

In many situations it will be necessary to enter a house to remove screens from the inside; some homeowners prefer to do that part of the job themselves.

You'll have to guard against causing damage to windows, siding, gutters, and shingles on the house. You'll also have to protect against harming landscaping, pets, and people below. Don't accept a job where the windows or the structure of the house itself are obviously damaged, and skip any job you don't feel you can perform safely.

Watch out for unpleasant surprises, including hornet nests, unfriendly birds, and uneven ground beneath your ladder.

Your insurance carrier—an important component of your business plan—may not want to cover you for any work performed more than 10 feet off the ground. State and federal occupational safety agencies may also have rules and regulations. We recommend you begin your business by limiting your services to ground-floor and second-story windows; once you are off and flying (metaphorically speaking) you can consider expansion to upper levels.

One way to avoid the complications of tall ladders and insurance concerns is to perform second-story cleaning from the ground using a rotary brush on an extendible pole.

Know the Territory

You'll need a ladder, a power washer, squeegees, sponges—and no fear of heights.

Although some homeowners may want to arrange for exterior window cleaning just once a year as part of their spring cleaning, you may be able to build up a clientele of residential and business customers who want to schedule regular sessions throughout the year.

Power washers range from simple rotating brushes turned by water pressure to systems that use compressors and pumps to boost pressure.

You'll use detergents and sometimes special chemicals to remove bug and bird residue. Once the windows have been washed with detergent, you'll apply an ammonia-based glass cleaner or something similar to finish the job without leaving streaks.

How to Get Started

Ask satisfied customers to recommend your services to friends, acquaintances, and businesses; offer them a bonus or a discount for any jobs they refer to you.

Up-front Expenses

A typical window-washing tool kit would include window brushes of several widths and firmness, an aluminum or plastic telescoping water pipe and handle, and a set of squeegees. You'll also need buckets for mixing chemicals and detergents, along with sponges, rags, and chamois. A simple straight-edge razor scraper will help remove labels and crud from glass. For ground-floor jobs, you'll need a sturdy stepladder; for second floors, you can use the extendible pole system from the ground or climb a 12-foot straight ladder or sturdy extension ladder.

Spend the time to learn the safe ways to use a ladder. For example, don't try to use a stepladder as a straight ladder; don't attempt to increase the height of a ladder by standing it on boxes, blocks, or other objects. Place the base of a straight ladder about one foot away from the sidewall of the house for every four feet of its vertical height.

You'll also need a vehicle large enough to carry your equipment. You may be able to lash the ladders and poles to a rooftop carrier on a full-size car or station wagon; once your business has grown, a small van would work better.

How Much to Charge

You can charge by the hour for your services, or give a flat rate per window or for an entire house based on your estimate of the time required to complete the job. Include in your rate your cost for detergents and other chemicals and a portion of the cost of the equipment you must purchase.

Legal and Insurance Issues

① **Legal**

② **Legal**

③ **Legal**

④ **Accounting**

⑤ **Insurance**

Deck Cleaning

Description of Job

- Clean dirt, stains, and mold from wooden decks and balconies.
- Make minor repairs to wood surfaces.
- Apply water sealer and tints.

The Need

Wooden decks, raised patios, and balconies are gracious extensions of the interior of our homes. Yet as part of the outside, they are constantly exposed to rain, snow, and extremes of temperature. They can accumulate dirt and grime and mold.

Cleaning a deck is relatively simple with the proper tools and chemicals, but it's not a job that many homeowners relish.

Challenges

Deck cleaning is typically limited to the warm weather months, and demand may be highest in late spring and early summer.

Some detergents are extremely caustic and may be dangerous to pets and some plants; you may need to protect against overspray and take care in your cleanup after the job is completed. There may be local regulations on the storage and use of these chemicals.

Some decks may already have rot or other damage that should be repaired before cleaning and coating is performed. You may want to have a relationship with a carpenter who can perform such work.

Power washers do a good job of blasting out debris between the cracks and cleaning the surface of the deck, but an overly strong spray can also damage the wood.

Water-repellent coating chemicals need to be applied when temperatures lie within a specific range, and the deck will need to be protected from humans and pets while it is drying.

Know the Territory

Consult a home supply store for advice on the latest chemicals and tools.

A professional deck cleaner uses brushes, power sprayers, detergents, and bleaches to clean wooden decks. Once the deck has been cleaned, the wooden surface is then coated with a water repellent.

Some water-repellent chemicals include a tint to add a bit of color to the wood.

How to Get Started

Post flyers and ads about your services at home supply stores, in community centers, and on neighborhood bulletin boards. You can also place ads in newspapers and shopping guides.

Ask satisfied customers to refer others to you, and offer a bonus when they bring in new business.

Up-front Expenses

You'll need a water hose, stiff brushes, buckets, and chemicals for the cleaning, and you'll need soft brushes for the application of coatings. You should consider the purchase of a power sprayer for cleaning large areas; the sprayer may also be available as needed from a tool rental company.

You'll also need a vehicle to transport your equipment.

Other costs include advertising and promotion.

How Much to Charge

You can charge by the hour, or calculate the cost for the job based on the square footage of the deck. The typical job includes cleaning plus application of a sealant or coating. Decks may require several applications of coating over multiple days.

In addition to the cost of labor, you should also charge for the cost of cleaning chemicals and coating. As a professional, you should be able to purchase supplies at a discounted or wholesale price and resell them to your client at retail rates.

Legal and Insurance Issues

① **Legal**

② **Legal**

③ **Legal**

④ **Accounting**

⑤ **Insurance**

Landscape Designer

Description of Job

- Change a landscape's appearance using trees, shrubbery, and/or flowering plants.
- Maintain a client's garden and plantings.

The Need

Beautifully planted and maintained properties with flourishing shrubs, artfully placed flowers in vibrant bloom, and handsome rolling lawns do not happen by chance.

A great deal of work goes into designing, planting, and maintaining a stand-alone garden or plantings around a house. Unless you were born with a green thumb or have developed one through years of practice, it may make sense to hire a professional landscape designer.

Challenges

You'll need an artist's eye and a gardener's knowledge of plants, trees, and conditions. What kind of plants grow best in your area? How long is the growing season, and what are the extremes of heat and cold, drought and rain? Is the soil in your area too sandy, or does it have a significant amount of clay or loam? How much mulch do you need to use?

How much sunlight does a particular area receive, and what is the exposure of the plot of land you will be working on?

Take the time to meet with your clients and make sure they understand your proposal and its costs. Make certain you are aware of the boundaries of your client's property; if you put a tree on a neighbor's property you may be opening yourself to liability or a financial loss.

Know the Territory

You need unimproved or underimproved land and clients who are willing to pay to have their property professionally landscaped. The best area for this sort of work is likely to be suburbs.

Look for areas with new subdivisions and other recent construction.

Make use of books, magazines, and the Internet to research landscaping schemes and learn as much as you can about plants that thrive in your area.

You will be selling your services to plan and implement changes to the land-scape; you can also sell your time to maintain the health and attractiveness of plants you have put in place.

How to Get Started

You can gain hands-on experience by working as a helper for a gardener or land-scaping company. Some large home supply stores and garden centers offer classes on planting and landscaping.

Post flyers and ads at community centers, in retail stores, and on bulletin boards. Place ads in newspapers and shopping guides.

Make contact with area greenhouses and nurseries, contractors, and real estate agents; ask them to refer business to you and offer them a bonus or commission for doing so. Ask friends, acquaintances, and satisfied customers to recommend your services, offering them a bonus or discount on future work.

This job can be operated in conjunction with a lawn mowing service (covered earlier in this chapter) or separately. If you will not be offering lawn care, make contact with a company that provides this service and seek a reciprocal agreement whereby they will refer landscaping jobs to you and you will recommend them for their services.

Up-front Expenses

You will need your own tools for planting and maintenance, including shovels, trowels, shears, pruners, and weeders. You will be able to rent major pieces of equipment such as earth movers and power shovels, or hire a subcontractor for such work.

You will need a vehicle large enough to carry your equipment. Most nurseries and plant suppliers will deliver trees and shrubs to your work site.

Some landscapers use computer programs to draw plans that show how plants and shrubs will be placed on the property.

How Much to Charge

Most of this sort of work is billed on an hourly basis, plus the cost of any plants and other expenses. You can offer some fixed prices for simple jobs such as creating a flower bed or planting a bush.

Legal and Insurance Issues

① **Legal**

② **Legal**

③ **Legal**

④ **Accounting**

⑤ **Insurance**

Deck Construction

Description of Job

- Consult with clients about design and materials for decks, and prepare detailed plans and a price quote.
- Obtain all necessary permits for construction.
- Purchase materials and build decks.
- Arrange for any necessary inspections after completion and confirm recording of approvals.

The Need

In days gone by, nearly every house had a large front porch where families would sit after dinner and exchange small talk with neighbors and passersby. With the advent of suburbs, the front porch moved to the backyard and became a comfortable wooden deck.

In many parts of the country there is a strong market for new or expanded decks. Construction of a ground-level or slightly raised deck is a relatively simple construction project.

Challenges

Stay close to the ground, at least at the start of this business. Building a second-story or higher deck requires advanced design and the use of lengthy load-bearing girders, beams, or supports, which will greatly increase your exposure to liability claims.

In many localities you will need to obtain a building permit before construction and seek approval from an inspector afterward. You may also have to conform to local regulations about size and design of structures.

The most difficult jobs involve work on soft or sloping ground. You'll also have to deal with extremes of temperature and environment in some parts of the country.

Know the Territory

Learn the basics of deck construction from available books, web sites, and plans. Among important concepts: proper installation of concrete footings or foundations; specification and use of pressure-treated lumber; and proper protection against rot, splitting, and insect infestation.

You'll need to prepare a plan for construction so you can show the design to your customers, seek building permits, and order materials. Pressure-treated and manufactured deck boards come in standard lengths and widths that should be adaptable to most jobs; the simplest and least expensive jobs are built using readily available dimensions.

Advanced designs add railings, benches, and other wooden features. You may also be called on to integrate lighting and electrical outlets into the deck; in most localities you'll need to work with a licensed electrician for such features.

If the plans call for creation of a new exit from the home to the deck, you may want to partner with an experienced contractor or carpenter for that part of the job.

How to Get Started

Place flyers and ads in community centers and home supply stores. Place ads in newspapers and shopping guides.

Make your services known to existing contractors who may refer small jobs to you; you can offer them a commission. Ask satisfied customers to recommend you to friends and acquaintances; offer a bonus or discount for business they bring to you.

Offer to teach a class about small construction projects at a community school; this may yield some publicity and clients.

Up-front Expenses

You'll need commercial-grade tools, including a circular saw, power drill, hammer, levels, safety goggles, and mask. For construction of concrete footings or foundations, you'll need a wheelbarrow and hoses for making concrete.

Building supply companies should be able to deliver lumber to your construction site; you will need a station wagon or small truck to haul your equipment to and from jobs.

How Much to Charge

You should quote a price for the job that includes your time plus the cost of lumber and hardware, including connectors, nails, and screws. Base your price on your cost—if the customer asks for special lumber or other features you need to take that into account.

Your price should include amortization of tools and your vehicle, plus a portion of the cost of insurance.

Legal and Insurance Issues

① **Legal**

② **Legal**

③ **Legal**

④ **Accounting**

⑤ **Insurance**

Storage Sheds, Playhouses, Doghouses

Description of Job

- Specify, deliver, and install predesigned and prefabricated storage sheds, children's playhouses, doghouses, and other structures.

- Custom-build structures to client's specifications, complementing the home design.

The Need

Some stuff just doesn't fit or belong inside your house: lawn mowers, bicycles, outdoor toys, tools, hoses, lawn food, and fertilizer among them. No one wants to go up and down the stairs to the basement (if you have one) carrying the lawn furniture.

A storage shed can hold the stuff of summer and winter in a way that complements your house and adds to the value of your property.

What child wouldn't treasure a private playhouse? What dog wouldn't like a place to call his or her own?

Challenges

Designing and building a stand-alone shed or outbuilding involves most of the same skills involved in constructing a house, albeit on a much smaller scale. You'll need carpentry skills and knowledge of building and engineering practices.

A much simpler solution is to become an assembler and installer of predesigned and cut wooden structures or high-quality metal buildings.

In most localities you need a building permit to erect a structure. In some areas you also have to deal with zoning laws and regulations on design, materials, and colors.

Depending on the soil and type of structure, you may need a concrete slab or other type of foundation.

The contract should state that the client agrees to pay for any changes to the project beyond what is included in the contract.

Know the Territory

Consult town and city authorities to learn about local regulations and practices. Study the homes in your area to determine common architectural styles.

Make contact with suppliers of predesigned and cut wooden structures and with makers of unassembled metal buildings. Establish a wholesale or commercial account.

Find a source for off-the-shelf plans. Many companies offer blueprints and plans that can be customized with trim, color, and other touches.

Make contact with local architects who would be available to draw custom plans for small projects.

How to Get Started

Post flyers and ads at community centers. Some home supply outlets and lumberyards may permit you to post your flyer if you are a commercial customer there.

Place ads in newspapers and shopping guides.

Let other builders and contractors know of your new business; they may refer jobs to you that are too small for their business. Offer a commission or bonus for work they send your way.

Up-front Expenses

You'll need woodworking and assembly tools and a vehicle large enough to transport them. Wood and metal parts and kits can usually be delivered to the construction site by suppliers.

Books and plans are available in bookstores, over the Internet, and through catalogs. Other expenses include advertising and promotion.

How Much to Charge

Based on the specifications agreed to by the client, your contract will specify a bottom-line price for design, delivery, assembly, and finishing of the job. Add any extra charges for building permits, zoning clearance, and inspections.

An alternative way to price a job like this is to perform it on a *cost-plus basis,* whereby the client agrees to pay the actual cost of all materials and other expenses plus a fixed amount or percentage representing your profit. You'll have to build into the profit payment for your time in ordering and assembling the structure.

Legal and Insurance Issues

Special notes: Some municipalities and local homeowners' associations may have regulations about the type and size of outbuildings, and they may also have zoning limits on the percentage of a lot that can be covered by a structure and its proximity to property lines.

① **Legal**

② **Legal**

③ **Legal**

④ **Accounting**

⑤ **Insurance**

Children's Outdoor Playset Installer

Description of Job

- Working with a client, specify a design for a backyard playground or playset.
- Order a unit from a ready-made catalog, or commission a custom unit.
- Prepare the ground with anchors and concrete footings, as appropriate.
- Assemble and install playset.
- Cover ground with foam, rubber, sand, or other safety surface.

The Need

Backyard swing sets have come a long, long way from the days when you hung a rope and a tire from a tree. Modern equipment offers multiple platforms, various types of swings and slides, and design options to reduce the chances of injury.

These complex constructions often require specialized tools and skills for assembly; the ground must be properly prepared and adequate anchors installed. The job may be beyond the skills and interest of the client.

Challenges

You must install equipment exactly to the specifications of the designer.

Some areas may require permits before installation or inspection afterward. In some subdivisions there may be regulations that limit the type or size of backyard equipment.

Some clients may have some very specific needs and wants for their playset based on particular interests or health and safety concerns. Some pieces of land may be uneven or hilly or require an unusual form of anchorage.

Consult an attorney so you understand proper procedures to limit your liability. In theory, if the equipment is faulty, liability for injuries or damage goes to the manufacturer. If owners make modifications or use the equipment improperly, it is their responsibility. However, if you specify, assemble, or install equipment improperly, the liability for injury or damages most likely will fall on you.

Don't agree to a job you feel is unsafe. Don't agree to modify equipment on your own.

Know the Territory

Modern swing sets have the same basic idea as the steel tube and leather constructions of our own childhood, but today, many playgrounds resemble luxury resorts, built with handsome wood or attractive color-coordinated plastic and vinyl.

How to Get Started

Contact commercial vendors of equipment and become a reseller. Learn about predesigned units as well as the availability of custom designs.

Post flyers and ads at community centers and schools. Place ads in newspapers and shopping guides.

Make area landscapers and contractors aware of your availability; offer them a bonus for any business they direct your way. Ask satisfied customers to recommend you to friends and neighbors; offer a bonus or discount for work they refer.

Up-front Expenses

You'll need a set of tools, shovels, and posthole diggers, a wheelbarrow, and equipment to prepare concrete where necessary. Playsets can be delivered to the site by the manufacturer or a trucking company; you may not need a truck of your own.

Other expenses will include advertising and promotion.

How Much to Charge

Charge a fee that is inclusive of purchase, delivery, assembly, and installation. Add costs for ground preparation before and after installation. You can include additional charges for custom work, and add freight and delivery charges.

Legal and Insurance Issues

① **Legal**
② **Legal**
③ **Legal**
④ **Accounting**
⑤ **Insurance**

Low-Voltage Outdoor Electrical Wiring

Description of Job

- Install low-voltage landscaping and driveway lighting.
- Install specialized low-voltage illuminated street numbers, poolside lighting, and deck lighting.

The Need

Nighttime lighting can serve security, safety, and decorative interests. Many homeowners like to show off their landscaping by night with subtle lighting. In other areas, a bit of light helps demarcate driveway edges or winding pathways.

Challenges

The biggest challenge to installers of outdoor lighting is avoiding excess.

Poor design wastes energy and creates "lighting trespass" that bothers neighbors, dangerous glare that can affect pedestrians and drivers, and "lighting pollution" that washes out the view of the dark night sky.

As an installer, you need to work closely with your client and tour the property to design the best system.

You may need to work with a licensed electrician in some localities, especially if you are asked to include high-voltage outdoor area lighting and motion detectors for security.

Know the Territory

This is a job that can be accomplished by anyone with a small amount of landscaping and simple home improvement skills.

In most jurisdictions, use of low-voltage systems does not require the involvement of a licensed electrician; if your client's home does not have a proper exterior outlet or access to an indoor outlet, you will have to engage an electrician to have one installed.

Plug-in lighting systems attach to an outdoor grounded outlet with fault-interruption protection or to an indoor outlet. A transformer reduces line voltage to safer 12-volt power.

Another alternative is the use of solar-powered lamps that use batteries that are recharged by sunlight each day and require no wires to interconnect them.

Consult web sites, catalogs, and home supply stores to learn about available systems and techniques. Contact manufacturers or distributors for samples, catalogs, and photographs of lamps and accessories.

How to Get Started

Advertise in community centers and garden centers. Some hardware stores or home centers may permit you to advertise your installation services in return for an agreement to purchase lights and supplies there.

Send brochures and letters to landscapers, pool installers, and contractors asking them to recommend your services to their clients; you may want to offer a bonus or commission for business they refer your way. Ask satisfied customers to advise their friends, offering them a bonus or discount.

Up-front Expenses

For most jobs, you'll need a power trenching tool; this device can be a single-purpose unit or one that attaches to other equipment, such as a rototiller or a tractor. Short runs may be possible with hand digging.

You'll also need some basic hand tools, shovels, and hole diggers.

Other expenses include creation of a portfolio of samples of available systems and advertising and promotion.

How Much to Charge

You can charge a flat rate for your services based on the number of lamps and the length and complexity of the wiring involved, or you can quote an hourly rate. Add the cost of any lights, wire, transformers, and accessories; you should be able to purchase equipment at wholesale or discounted rates and resell them to your client at retail prices.

Legal and Insurance Issues

Special notes: Some municipalities have ordinances aimed at reducing light pollution, and some subdivisions may have regulations that limit outdoor lighting. Some localities may require a licensed electrician's involvement or an electrical inspection.

① **Legal**

② **Legal**

③ **Legal**

④ **Accounting**

⑤ **Insurance**

Stonemason and Decorative Brick Worker

Description of Job

- Design and install decorative stone and brick walkways, patios, walls, and garden features.
- Build brick and stone custom barbecues.
- Repair and maintain existing exterior stonework.

The Need

Outdoor stonework in the form of walkways, patios, walls, and barbecues can beautify a property and increase its value. Stonemasonry is one of the oldest construction skills, little changed in thousands of years; in modern days it is a craft not often practiced.

Challenges

This is outdoor work, with heavy lifting.

You'll need to lift and place heavy stones, bricks, and tiles and use tools to shape them. You'll also be working with heavy mortar and cement.

In some parts of the country, this is a seasonal job that is available from late spring through late fall.

You may be called upon to design a decorative element or wall or to follow the plans drawn by an architect or contractor.

Know the Territory

Stonework is in demand nearly everywhere, but with different purposes or styles in various settings. In a big city, jobs might include walkways, steps, and small patios. In rural and suburban settings, jobs might include larger patios, outdoor fireplaces and barbecues, and stone walls.

The traditional method of training for stonemasonry is to work as a helper or apprentice to a skilled craftsperson. In some areas, unions offer training and formal apprenticeship programs. You can also learn many of the skills from books, web sites, and educational programs. The International Union of Bricklayers and Allied Craftsworkers has programs around the country and a national training and education center in Maryland to teach basic job skills for brick, stone, tile, terrazzo, and restoration work.

How to Get Started

If you are already trained as a stonemason, advertise your services with flyers at home and garden centers, retail outlets, and community centers. Place ads in newspapers and shopping guides.

Make yourself known to architects, contractors, and landscapers who might recommend your services to their clients; offer a commission or bonus for work they send to you. Ask satisfied customers to recommend you to others; in return, offer them a bonus or discount on further work.

Up-front Expenses

You'll need stoneworking tools, cement and mortar mixing equipment, and landscaping equipment.

You will need a truck or van to transport your tools and equipment. You may be able to have stone, brick, and other materials delivered directly to the site by your suppliers; if not, you'll need a heavy truck with a lift gate or ramp.

Other expenses include advertising and promotion.

How Much to Charge

For a simple job like a barbecue or a brick patio, you can charge an all-inclusive set fee that covers the cost of materials and your time. Another option is to charge an hourly rate plus the cost of materials and supplies.

Skilled stonemasons typically charge $25 to $40 per hour for their labor; unionized workers generally receive a higher rate.

Legal and Insurance Issues

Special notes: Some municipalities and local homeowners' associations may have regulations about the type and size of ornamentation, walls, and fences.

① **Legal**

② **Legal**

③ **Legal**

④ **Accounting**

⑤ **Insurance**

Home Services (Interior)

12 Housecleaning

13 Rug Cleaner

14 Interior Decorator

15 Upholstery and Slipcover Maker

16 Wallpaper Hanger

17 Specialty Indoor Painting

18 Furniture Stripping

19 Furniture Repair

20 Closet Organizer

21 Bookcase and Shelf Builder

22 Indoor Plant Care

23 Custom Silk and Dried Flower Arrangements

Housecleaning

Description of Job

- Clean, vacuum, and neaten homes or apartments.
- Carry out other services as requested by the client.
- Perform turnover cleaning of rental properties.

The Need

Most of us, unless we live in a hotel (or in a dorm room and don't care), are responsible for cleaning our house or apartment. At one time, the idea of hiring household staff was something reserved for the wealthiest among us; today, it may be much less of a luxury and much more of a necessity.

In a two-job family, who has the time to clean the house? For a stay-at-home mother or father with young kids, who has time for anything but the most basic cleanup tasks?

Scheduled or on-demand housecleaning services are very popular in residential areas where one or more family members have jobs outside the home. Additional opportunities exist in tourist areas, where houses and apartments must be cleaned after each rental.

Challenges

Not all houses are the same; not everyone's idea of minimal orderliness is identical; and few people have exactly the same definition of cleanliness.

The biggest challenge is to have a written agreement that specifies exactly what services you will perform, as well as your expectations from the client. Standard services include vacuuming all carpeted areas, washing kitchen and bathroom floors, dusting, cleaning of kitchen cooking surfaces, sanitizing of bathrooms, and general neatening.

The sort of work that is ordinarily beyond basic services includes jobs such as polishing silver, washing window exteriors, and cleanup after parties.

In most cases, you will be working within an occupied home or apartment and trusted not to steal or damage valuable items. You may be given a set of keys or the code for a burglar alarm and must safeguard them. You will need legal protection against liability and may want to seek bonding. You may be asked to provide references.

You may have to work while your client is in the home or apartment; think carefully before accepting a job where you do not feel personally safe.

If you build your company to include additional employees, you should seek references from them and check for criminal records; any problems they cause will become your problems. Your attorney or insurance agent may recommend that you have your employees bonded as a reassurance to your clients.

Know the Territory

Some people have the "clean gene" and some seem constitutionally unable to keep their homes in shape. You know which type you are; be sure you are willing to become a cleaning genie for a stranger.

There are many web sites and books that give special tips and tricks for cleaning.

How to Get Started

Advertise in the local newspaper and in shopping guides. Put a business card at the supermarket, and, if you have access to the bulletin boards at any companies, leave your card there as well.

In tourist areas leave your business card and references with real estate or rental agencies.

Up-front Expenses

You'll need to purchase an arsenal of cleaners, sanitizers, deodorizers, polishes, and other products. Then there are mops, dusters, and the biggest investment: an industrial-strength vacuum cleaner.

You'll also need a traveling case for your products and equipment and a vehicle to transport the whole kit and caboodle.

As a commercial cleaning contractor, you should be able to purchase supplies at a discount or from a wholesaler. Warehouse stores also offer good deals on extra-large containers.

Other costs include advertising and promotion.

How Much to Charge

Housecleaners generally charge by the hour, with the rate including the cost of the supplies you use and a portion of the cost of the vacuum cleaner and other capital expenditures.

For regular clients, you could work out an arrangement whereby they provide all of the cleaning supplies to meet your needs; in that case, you would charge a lower hourly rate.

You can expect to be asked to give an estimate of how long it will take you to complete the job. Make sure you take into consideration unusually large homes or apartments and unusually messy abodes. The frequency of cleaning will also make a difference; dust and dirt accumulate over time and make for more work. You could offer a discounted rate to clients who agree to schedule frequent visits.

Legal and Insurance Issues

① **Legal**

② **Legal**

③ **Legal**

④ **Accounting**

⑤ **Insurance**

Rug Cleaner

Description of Job

- Clean carpets using professional equipment.
- Use specialized tools and chemicals for expert attention to problematic stains.

The Need

Even with frequent vacuuming, rugs and carpets get dirty. If you have children and pets, they get even dirtier.

Although some home centers rent out portable rug cleaners, they are generally the equivalent of a snow shovel in a world of high-powered plows and snowblowers. The best way to get a seriously dirty carpet clean is with professional cleaning equipment and solutions.

Challenges

You must learn to master the use of professional extraction systems and gain a realistic understanding of their capabilities and limitations. Before committing to a job, make sure you carefully inspect the carpet; make note of any existing stains or damage, and make certain your contract agreement with the client does not promise more than you can reasonably expect to deliver.

Take extra care with especially valuable rugs. Oriental, Persian, or antique carpets may need to be hand-cleaned, or they may need to be processed by specialists. You may be able to act as an agent for another company for that sort of job, collecting a commission.

Make sure that your contract agreement limits your liability for damage to valuable rugs.

You will probably have to move furniture as part of the cleaning process; again, take care not to accept liability for expensive antiques and collectibles—ask the client to remove them from the room.

Know the Territory

Many professional equipment vendors offer assistance to their customers in recommending tools and techniques for tricky problems. Some of the most common stains, such as coffee, tea, blood, and urine, are also the most difficult to remove.

You can also offer special services such as carpet protector and carpet deodorizer for an extra charge.

How to Get Started

Place flyers and business cards at home centers, hardware stores, and community centers. Make your services known to area interior decorators and housecleaning services. Contact real estate agents who might be in a position to recommend your services to someone who is selling or buying a house and to clients who rent their house to others.

You should also place ads in newspapers and shopping guides.

Up-front Expenses

Professional carpet cleaning machines start at about $2,000 and go up from there. A typical package includes a power-cleaning wand or head, a powered extractor, at least 25 feet of hose, and various manual wands, rakes, and detailing tools.

The most powerful units are usually mounted in a truck or van, with hoses that run from the truck into the home or apartment; these machines have their own gas-powered engines, run off the vehicle's motor, or attach to an electrical outlet. Expect to pay about $4,000 to $5,000 for truck-mounted equipment. (That sort of device is quicker to set up and more powerful, but may not be appropriate for jobs on upper floors of homes or apartment houses.)

You'll need a supply of detergents and other solutions, including pretreating sprays, spotting kits, rinses, defoamers, deodorizers, and disinfectants.

You'll require a van or small truck to transport your equipment and supplies; if you use a truck-mounted system, you'll need special equipment and hoses plus a power source or connection to the vehicle's engine.

How Much to Charge

You can charge by the hour or by the square footage of the carpet to be cleaned. Be sure to take into account any especially difficult stains or unusual circumstances when giving a price or estimate.

Legal and Insurance Issues

Special notes: In dealing with your client's property, seek to limit your liability for damage or loss to the actual replacement value of items in your possession. You should protect yourself against claims for sentimental value or loss of use.

① **Legal**

② **Legal**

③ **Legal**

④ **Accounting**

⑤ **Insurance**

⑥ **Insurance**

Interior Decorator

Description of Job

- Draw plans to decorate a client's home or office with attention to style, quality, and budget.

- Meet with designers, contractors, and suppliers to draw up specifications.
- Oversee purchases, renovations, and installation.

The Need

Somewhere in the mind's eye of most of us is a vision of the house beautiful and the office spectacular. Yet relatively few of us have the background, the training, or the time to create a handsome environment all at once.

An interior decorator can redo an entire house or a single room. A new baby may be on the way, or a spare bedroom may be due to make the transition to a home office.

Companies need to have attractive spaces for conferences, meetings with customers, and showrooms for products.

Challenges

There is no license required to hang out a shingle as an interior decorator. Instead, you'll have to demonstrate your abilities through examples of plans you have drawn or work you have accomplished.

In addition to a good sense of design and color, you'll need to be knowledgeable about construction, fabrics, styles of furniture, lighting systems, and flooring.

In most cases you will be called on to interpret your client's needs and wants; you'll rarely be given a blank sheet of paper and an unlimited budget. You'll have to be able to work in a variety of styles, from antiques and reproductions to commercial and industrial to ultramodern.

Know the Territory

You can take courses on interior design at community colleges and major universities. There is also a tremendous amount of information about design and decorating in books and on web sites. Consult the sites for furniture makers to learn about their products; many manufacturers offer impressive catalogs to decorators, and some have sales conferences and demonstrations of products.

Become an expert, or attach yourself to a knowledgeable associate who knows about upholstery, carpeting and other flooring, wallpaper and paneling, and other furnishings. Make contact with manufacturers of lighting systems, audiovisual and computer furniture and fixtures, and office presentation equipment.

Plan on attending national or regional interior decorating shows and conventions where manufacturers display their products and conduct seminars.

How to Get Started

Post flyers and ads at community centers and retail stores. Furniture and home supply centers may allow you to advertise your services in their stores if you promise to direct some of your customers to them.

Contact area contractors. They may want to have a model home decorated and in return would allow you to promote your service there, and they may be willing to give your name to any client who asks for a designer. Offer a commission or bonus for work they send your way.

Ask friends and acquaintances to recommend your services; offer a bonus or discount on future jobs for any business they direct to you. Do the same with satisfied customers.

Create a portfolio of jobs you have completed; obtain permission from clients to take photos for the portfolio or for a web site. (You don't have to identify the names and addresses of clients if they prefer anonymity.)

Up-front Expenses

You may have some expenses in educating yourself about furniture and equipment. Other costs include advertising and promotion.

How Much to Charge

Most interior decorators make their income in the form of commissions from wholesale or retail outlets. Depending on the complexity and size of the job, you might also charge the client an hourly or fixed fee for consultation and drawing up a plan.

Legal and Insurance Issues

① **Legal**

② **Legal**

③ **Legal**

④ **Accounting**

⑤ **Insurance**

Upholstery and Slipcover Maker

Description of Job

- Reupholster sofas, chairs, ottomans, and pillows.
- Make slipcovers for upholstered furniture.
- Recover pillows.
- Design and create custom draperies.

The Need

Furniture is big, bulky, and expensive . . . and sometimes it gets cut, scratched, or stained. Then there are times when we fall in love with an expensive sofa for the living room and fall out of love with its color and fabric long before it's paid for.

Normal wear and tear take their toll on furniture, accelerated by the presence of children and pets. Tastes change; perhaps you've gone through your green period and now you find yourself preferring more neutral colors.

The good news is that good-quality furniture does not have to be thrown away.

A reupholsterer removes the existing fabric and decorations to rebuild the piece from the frame up.

Another option is to create custom slipcovers that fit over the original upholstery.

Pillows can be recovered in new fabric to brighten up the furniture and deal with damage and stains.

Upholsterers can also be called on to create custom draperies, working with the same material used in remaking the furniture or in a contrasting or complementary shade.

Challenges

This job requires a sense of design and some specialized expertise, including skills in minor carpentry and working with fabrics. You need to be able to recognize a hidden gem and reject a makeover project when you can see that the end result will please no one.

Consider carefully before working on a valuable antique or collectible; be sure you are not taking on a huge liability in the event of damage or loss.

Know the Territory

You'll find a tremendous amount of resources in books, magazines, videos, and on the Internet. Read decorating magazines and special-interest publications about furniture repair, restoration, and reupholstering.

Local craft stores may offer seminars or classes; area experts may teach classes at community schools.

Make contact with suppliers of fabric and supplies for upholstering. They will offer samples and consultation, and some may provide training for their clients.

How to Get Started

Place flyers and ads at home supply stores, in community centers, at tag sales, in used furniture stores, and on bulletin boards. Place ads in newspapers and shopping guides.

Contact area interior decorators and used furniture stores and make them aware of your services; offer them a bonus or commission for business they bring your way.

Consider teaching a class at a community school for publicity and perhaps to gain clients.

Up-front Expenses

You will need woodworking and heavy-duty sewing and fabric-working tools. Some of the specialty tools you will need as an upholsterer include tack hammer, shears, webbing stretcher, ripping chisel, staple lifter, upholstery needle card, and upholstery pins. To make slipcovers, and for some upholstery projects, you will need a heavy-duty sewing machine. Some jobs may require a serging machine to bind the ends of fabrics.

You may be able to farm out some specialty sewing jobs to others as part of the overall project. You can choose to purchase a truck for pickup and delivery of furniture, or you can contract with a local shipping or moving company for such service.

Other expenses include advertising and promotion.

How Much to Charge

Give the client a bottom-line price that includes the purchase of fabric, stuffing, notions, and other expenses as well as compensation for your time; be sure to carefully consider the amount of time involved in a job.

Another pricing scheme is a cost-plus contract, whereby the client pays retail prices for all material and you add a charge for your labor.

You can also add charges for pickup and delivery of the furniture, if necessary.

Legal and Insurance Issues

Special notes: In dealing with your client's property, seek to limit your liability for damage or loss to the actual replacement value of items in your possession. You should protect yourself against claims for sentimental value or loss of use.

① **Legal**

② **Legal**

③ **Legal**

④ **Accounting**

⑤ **Insurance**

⑥ **Insurance**

Wallpaper Hanger

Description of Job

- Consult with homeowners on wallpaper projects.
- Measure walls and order paper.
- Hang wallpaper and special treatments, including trim and borders.

The Need

Wallpaper is an attractive way to decorate a home, but most homeowners lack the time or the expertise to do a professional job by themselves.

Here's a secret: It's not that hard to do and does not require great feats of strength. You can learn to hang wallpaper in your own home or by working with someone else on a project, and then you can use your skills to start a profitable small business.

Challenges

No two jobs are the same. The shape of walls and their condition will vary greatly. Some wallpaper patterns are much more difficult to match panel by panel. Some wallpapers are heavier or in other ways more difficult to work with than others.

You need to know how to accurately measure walls and how to apply those measurements to standard widths and lengths of paper.

You should also become an expert on wallpaper itself, able to make recommendations to your clients on the best products and to warn them off of a selection that will not work well in their home or that is extremely difficult and expensive to install.

Sometimes the most difficult part of the job is in preparing the walls for the paper. There may be layers of old wallpaper to be removed, rough paint surfaces that need to be smoothed, holes to be filled, and any number of past sins to be covered up.

Any liability you accept should be limited to the value of the paper itself. In general, you should have the homeowner remove any paintings or other wall hangings and move furniture out of the way before you arrive to do the job.

Know the Territory

Visit home supply stores and wallpaper specialists to become familiar with all the different types of coverings. Contact some of the manufacturers and ask for samples and technical advice. You'll find a wealth of information on web sites from stores and manufacturers.

You need to learn which types of paper work best in particular rooms. For example, wallpaper in a bathroom is subjected to a great deal of humidity, and paper in a kitchen needs to resist food and grease splatters. You should learn about different hanging techniques for various types of paper.

An important skill is learning how to match patterns from panel to panel; some wallpaper allows for easier matching than others, and some room designs may make installation much more difficult.

Make contact with wallpaper wholesalers and find out about programs they offer to small businesses. You may be able to direct-order wallpaper on behalf of your clients, offering them a discount from retail prices or building some additional profit into your business by reselling the wallpaper at retail price.

When you purchase wallpaper for a job, make sure the store or wholesaler is willing to take back unopened rolls of paper; you should generally order more paper than you think you will need to account for errors and problems you may encounter.

You may also be able to work out a deal to receive a discount or a commission from a retail store on wallpaper and supplies you purchase on behalf of a client.

Look for information about wallpaper companies on the Internet and in ads (many of which you'll find in women's and home improvement magazines).

How to Get Started

Post ads and flyers at home supply stores, in community centers, and elsewhere. Place ads in neighborhood newspapers.

Make yourself known to area contractors who may need to hire wallpaper subcontractors for new construction or renovations.

Ask friends and relatives to spread the word, and offer discounts or referral fees to satisfied customers who recommend you to new clients.

Up-front Expenses

In addition to advertising and promotion expenses, you will need ladders, buckets, drop cloths, and brushes. You will also need measuring equipment.

Depending on your level of experience, you may want to practice on walls and rooms in your home before seeking outside work.

How Much to Charge

Jobs can be priced on an hourly or square-foot basis; if you charge per square foot, adjust the rate upward if the walls require extra preparation or if there are any extraordinary demands on your time.

In addition to the cost of time, the customer should pay for the wallpaper and supplies, including paste. If you order the wallpaper from a wholesale source on behalf of your client, you can mark up the price to retail prices or slightly below.

Be realistic in any estimate you make on the number of hours the job will require, and don't promise completion of a job by a particular date unless you are certain you will have all of the supplies and the job entails no special effort.

Legal and Insurance Issues

① **Legal**

② **Legal**

③ **Legal**

④ **Accounting**

⑤ **Insurance**

Specialty Indoor Painting

Description of Job

- Design and specify specialty interior painting.
- Apply special effects.
- Finish and clean up interior work.

The Need

There is no law that says interior walls need to be coated with flat, boring eggshell paint.

An interesting alternative for many homeowners is to decorate using techniques such as marbling, stenciling, sponging, strié (dragging), ragging, rag rolling, stippling, distressing, and faux finishing. In most cases, amateurs are not trained or equipped to perform such work.

This sort of job is usually limited to one or two rooms in a house and therefore may be less attractive to a commercial painter; the skills involved are also different from those required to paint a living room off-white.

Challenges

You need to understand and master a range of special techniques and tools. Make sure your clients understand exactly what effect they are requesting.

You can practice many of the techniques in your own home; you might want to create a room—perhaps a den, a section of the basement, or even the interior of your garage—and create examples of the sort of work you are available to perform.

Know the Territory

There are many web sites and books that describe various techniques and tools for specialty painting. Many large home supply and craft stores offer classes on specialty painting. Here are some interesting techniques:

- *Glazing or color washing.* Dilute paints or varnishes to thin them so they can be used to apply a transparent or translucent film of color.
- *Stippling, or pouncing.* This process delivers a sandy or lightly patterned effect using a specialized stippling brush to modify the surface of a glaze.
- *Ragging, or rag rolling.* A second glaze color, of a different hue, is wiped into place with a rag to create a purposely uneven effect.
- *Strié, or dragging.* A glaze is applied to a base color, then a dry brush is dragged over the glaze in a vertical or horizontal direction to create fine lines.
- *Sponging.* A rough sponge is used to apply an uneven finish to a base coat or to a second coat of paint in a contrasting color.
- *Stenciling.* You may hand-paint stenciled designs to a painted wall.

How to Get Started

Post flyers and ads at community centers, in home outlet stores, and on bulletin boards. Place ads in newspapers and shopping guides.

Offer to conduct a class at a community school to get some publicity and perhaps some clients. Buy a table at home decorating and crafts shows to display samples of some of your work.

Make contact with interior decorators and contractors in your area; do the same with commercial painting companies that do not compete with you for specialty jobs. Offer a bonus or commission for business they refer to you.

Up front Expenses

You will need specialty brushes, sponges, stencils, and other equipment, as well as basic painting tools such as ladders, trays, rollers, tarpaulins, plastic sheeting, and masking tape.

You will have to bear the cost of experiments and practice sessions you conduct as well as preparation of a display room or a photo album or web site to show examples of your work.

You'll need a vehicle large enough to transport your equipment. Other expenses include research books, classes, advertising, and promotion.

How Much to Charge

Most painters quote a fixed price for a job, based on a careful estimate of the number of hours it will require plus the cost of paint and other materials. Many specialty paint jobs require multiple applications of wall covering. Some jobs are quoted on a cost-plus basis: a charge for hours of work plus the actual cost of paint and other supplies.

Prices for specialty painting are usually higher than those for standard indoor work because of the extra time, materials, and skill required.

Legal and Insurance Issues

① **Legal**

② **Legal**

③ **Legal**

④ **Accounting**

⑤ **Insurance**

Furniture Stripping

Description of Job

- Clean valuable old furniture.
- Use chemicals to strip furniture of one or more old coats of paint, varnish, or other finishes.
- Prepare furniture for application of new finish.

The Need

Family heirlooms, an old favorite chair, or just a change in decor—sometimes it makes eminent sense to strip an old varnish, shellac, or paint finish from a still-usable piece of wooden furniture. Once the piece has been brought as close as possible to its original raw wood state, it can be restained and refinished.

The process can result in a rejuvenation of a valuable old piece at much less cost than buying a new piece.

Challenges

This is not rocket science, but furniture stripping involves a great deal of hands-on dirty work and the use of caustic and toxic chemicals. You have to work within local, state, and federal regulations on the use and disposal of chemicals and waste materials.

Communicate clearly with your clients to make sure that they have reasonable expectations about the final product. Some finishes can be completely removed, and others cannot. Some modern finishes, including certain polyurethane and acrylic products, are difficult if not impossible to strip.

There are also some environmentally safe stripping solutions that don't require special handling or disposal; depending on the finish being removed, they may be as effective as harsh chemicals.

Use chemically impervious gloves, eye protection, and protective clothing in your shop; make sure there is adequate ventilation to remove fumes.

Make sure your contract with the customer limits your liability for damage or loss of the furniture; don't accept a very valuable antique or an irreplaceable heirloom if your financial exposure is too high.

Know the Territory

The most common methods for stripping furniture are hand stripping, cold tank dipping, and hot tank dipping.

Hand stripping is the slowest, most labor-intensive, most expensive, and generally the safest way to remove a finish. A chemical stripper is applied to the furniture with a brush, and after a specified period of time the solution is removed with rags and brushes; multiple applications may be necessary. Residue is cleaned off with lacquer thinner or other solvents.

For the cold tank method, the furniture is immersed in a tank filled with a chemical stripping solution. After a period of time, the chemical is scrubbed off and residue is washed off with water or a solvent. This method is generally the quickest and least expensive option for commercial users and works best on pieces with just a single coat of finish; homeowners working on just one piece would end up wasting a great deal of costly stripping solution.

The most intense commercial stripping method uses a heated tank of caustic lye which removes many types of finish but may be too harsh for delicate pieces. The lye is washed off using water. A side effect of the use of lye is that it may darken some types of wood. For that reason, most pieces must then undergo a second dipping, usually in a tank of oxalic acid or a similar chemical to lighten the wood and neutralize any leftover lye. Hot dipping is well suited to removing layers of paint from architectural elements of a home, including doors, moldings, and banisters. It can also be used on painted furniture.

Modern chemicals are much easier to work with and less likely to cause any damage to furniture than older methods, but any stripping process has the potential of causing some discoloration or other stress.

The most difficult finish to remove is paint, especially on pieces that have a lot of detail. For example, the paint on flat surfaces of a dresser may come off relatively easily, but it requires a lot of handwork to get the coating off of carved decorations, spindles, joined edges, and interior angles. Some practitioners use sprayers to get a stripping solution into tight spaces and objects as fine and small as jeweler's or surgeon's tools.

The final step may be to return the near-raw wooden piece to the customer for application of a new finish, or you may offer that service yourself. Some furniture strippers partner with expert furniture finishers.

How to Get Started

Advertise your availability at home centers, community centers, and retail stores. Make your services known to interior decorators, auction houses, and used furniture dealers. Place ads in newspapers and shoppers.

Ask satisfied customers to recommend you to friends and acquaintances; offer a bonus or discount for new business they send your way.

Up-front Expenses

The amount of up-front expenses for a furniture stripping business depends on the level of service you plan to provide to your customers. The least expensive setup (and the most expensive service to sell) is hand stripping; considerably more expensive are operations that offer cold and hot dipping.

For hand stripping, you'll need tarps and level work surfaces, a selection of stripping chemicals, a set of brushes of various sizes and firmness, wooden scrapers, disposable rags, and steel wool. You'll also need containers for the safe disposal of flammable rags and other debris, and for disposal of used chemicals.

To protect yourself, you'll need heavy rubber gloves, safety glasses or a face shield, and a strong ventilation system.

For dipping, you'll need several tubs large enough to fully accommodate a piece of furniture and hold caustic chemicals and acids. You'll also need to arrange for safe disposal of large quantities of the solutions.

How Much to Charge

Charge an hourly rate for your time and the use of chemicals, tanks, and tools. You can offer the client an estimate of hours, but be careful not to lowball the price for intricate pieces. Plan on at least 50 percent more time for removal of paint than for shellac or varnish, and add more time for pieces with intricate carvings and inside angles.

If the customer has not already removed hardware such as knobs, hinges, and badges add time or a fee for that service. Add a freight charge for pickup and delivery.

Many companies also add a charge for disposal of hazardous wastes, either as a percentage of the total price or as a flat fee.

Legal and Insurance Issues

Special notes: In dealing with your client's property, seek to limit your liability for damage or loss to the actual replacement value of items in your possession. You should protect yourself against claims for sentimental value or loss of use.

① **Legal**
② **Legal**
③ **Legal**
④ **Accounting**
⑤ **Insurance**
⑥ **Insurance**

Furniture Repair

Description of Job

- Repair broken pieces of furniture.
- Make minor fixes to torn upholstery.

The Need

Things break, and upholstery tears, but a major piece of furniture, a valued heirloom, or merely a favorite couch may be worth repairing to save the cost of buying a new piece.

Challenges

The two principal challenges are deciding whether a broken piece of furniture can be repaired and whether the repair makes economic sense. If the total cost of removal of the item, labor, parts, and return of the piece is appreciably less than the price of a new one, you have business to perform.

Be especially careful if you are working on an heirloom or antique; don't accept a job you are not capable of doing properly, and don't accept liability for an item of extraordinary value.

Know the Territory

You'll need to have basic repair skills and access to dependable specialists for jobs such as welding broken frames, cutting a custom piece of wood or metal, and reupholstering. In a way, this job could be compared to being a contractor on a house: Much of the work consists of assembling a team of capable subcontractors.

Some jobs can be done in the homes of clients; assemble a mobile workshop for house calls. Otherwise, you will need a truck or require that the client arrange for pickup and delivery.

How to Get Started

Advertise your availability at community centers, home and houseware stores, and antique stores.

Up-front Expenses

You'll need a set of basic tools. You can rent many specialized devices or sub-contract out unusual tasks. Other expenses include promotion and advertising.

How Much to Charge

Charge an hourly rate plus the cost of materials; give your clients an estimate of the number of hours a job should require and notify them if the price will change markedly.

Legal and Insurance Issues

Special notes: In dealing with your client's property, seek to limit your liability for damage or loss to the actual replacement value of items in your possession. You should protect yourself against claims for sentimental value or loss of use.

① **Legal**

② **Legal**

③ **Legal**

④ **Accounting**

⑤ **Insurance**

⑥ **Insurance**

Closet Organizer

Description of Job

- Clean up and organize the chaos and clutter of clients' closets.
- Design closet and storage systems to make the most of available space.

The Need

There has to be a special place in heaven for the well organized. Everybody else has to get in a messy line.

Most people are relatively careful about what they put on display in the places visitors can see, but their private spaces behind closet doors may be disasters; or they may be quite disposed to perfect organization but limited by available space.

A professional closet organizer uses planning, furniture, and hardware to come to a home and convert the clutter and disarray of a closet or storage space in the bedroom, kitchen, or bathroom into an efficient, workable area.

Challenges

Your job is to organize your client's possessions—*not* to pass judgment on what you find. Unless your client specifically asks you to make recommendations on items to be thrown out (or donated to charity), sometimes your job is to fit 12 pounds of stuff into a 10-pound box.

Take special care if you are asked to organize collectibles or other items of great value; your agreement should limit any liability if you are asked to handle such items.

Know the Territory

Professional organizers should spend a lot of time at hardware stores, home furnishing stores, and stores that specialize in equipment for the closet and storeroom. A great deal of information is also available online at the web sites of these companies.

You'll need some basic skills in assembling hardware and some common-sense understanding of the laws of physics: Put the heaviest items on lower shelves and make certain shelves are anchored properly to studs.

The first step involves a thorough inspection of the closet or space you are asked to organize. Take measurements and draw a schematic; a digital camera is a good tool that allows you to study the closet when you are back home.

Determine whether any specialty equipment must be ordered: shoe, tie, or belt organizers, jewelry storage, over-the-door pocket organizers.

Make certain the floors and walls are sturdy enough to support the weight of a shelving system.

Determine your client's budget. Systems can range in price from under $100 to more than $1,000, plus the cost of your time in designing the installation, ordering it, installing it, and placing items in their new homes.

How to Get Started

Place flyers and business cards in community centers, supermarkets, and large home supply stores. Paid ads can be placed in shopping guides and newspapers.

Ask friends, relatives, and satisfied customers to spread the word about your availability.

Up-front Expenses

The principal expenses are advertising and research trips to stores to learn about available systems. You can create a picture album of some of your installations, or load digital pictures onto a laptop computer to show at the initial consultation.

How Much to Charge

This job will generally be billed at an hourly rate; no two jobs will take the same amount of time because of different conditions in the home and closet. You should be able, though, to give the client an estimate of the amount of time the job will require.

The initial consultation can be done for free, but the clock should start ticking as soon as you actually begin the measuring and planning of the job. Other billable time includes the installation and finishing of the job.

The client should pay you up front for each piece of hardware as it is ordered.

Legal and Insurance Issues

① **Legal**

② **Legal**

③ **Legal**

④ **Accounting**

⑤ **Insurance**

Bookcase and Shelf Builder

Description of Job

- Produce customized bookcases and shelving units to meet the needs of your client.

- Adapt published plans for bookcases and shelving using a client's specifi-cations and choices of wood and stain.

The Need

Few interior architectural touches are more impressive than built-in or cus-tomized bookcases or shelving in a personal library, den, or family room. There's a big and obvious difference between a store-bought bookshelf and one that has been built exactly to the specifications of a particular space.

Challenges

A customized piece of furniture requires the ability to perform finishing work, several steps beyond a stack of boards separated by cinder blocks. You'll need to be able to work with bevels, curves, and joints and add a high-quality stain and finish or paint job.

Some jobs will require working with unusual and expensive types of wood, which may call for unusual woodworking methods and can eat up profits very quickly in the event of an error during construction.

Know the Territory

Make sure you understand the needs and wants of your customer. Show photos of work you have completed, or use books of plans as examples.

Avoid taking the job based on the *customer's* measurements; visit the home or office to make certain that jobs you prepare in your workshop will fit properly in the intended space.

There are many sources for plans and designs for woodworking, including books and web sites. For large (and well-paid) jobs you can design your own pieces or work with an architect.

If you will be working with unusual species of wood, get some samples from a supplier and test assembly methods, stains, and finishes before you work on the actual job.

Some woodworkers prefer to leave the application of stain or paint to an expert on those tasks; in that case, they can subcontract the completion of the job.

How to Get Started

Post flyers and ads at community centers, retail stores, and home decorating stores. Place ads in newspapers and shopping guides.

Make your services known to contractors and architects; you can pay them a commission for work they refer your way, or they may hire you to do the work and bill their clients directly.

Create a portfolio of work you have produced; it can also be displayed on a web site.

You can also promote your services at craft and holiday fairs. Offer to teach a class at a community school—to garner publicity and perhaps some clients.

Up-front Expenses

You'll need a full woodworking shop and enough space to work on large pieces. You may be able to subcontract some of the work on components of the book-shelves to shops with specialized tools.

Other expenses include advertising and promotion.

You will need a truck to deliver completed items, or work with a trucking company, as needed.

How Much to Charge

Charge a flat rate for completed bookcases and shelving based on your estimate of the amount of time required and the cost of the materials. You can add fees for painting or staining, plus the cost of delivery and installation.

Legal and Insurance Issues

① **Legal**

② **Legal**

③ **Legal**

④ **Accounting**

⑤ **Insurance**

Indoor Plant Care

Description of Job

- Water, feed, and tend to live plants in offices, stores, malls, lobbies, and private homes.
- Inspect a client's premises and make recommendations for the purchase of greenery.
- Install new plants, or change plants or flowers for seasonal or holiday displays.

The Need

Indoor plants can beautify almost any space in offices, stores, lobbies, and public areas; they're also a graceful addition to homes and apartments. Yet relatively few of us have a green thumb . . . or the time and inclination to tend to plants in our places of business or homes.

The basic services of an indoor plant specialist include care, feeding, and maintenance of plants on a regularly scheduled basis. You can also offer to design new plantings, providing installation only or making seasonal and holiday changes.

Challenges

You'll need to be, or become, an expert on all sorts of indoor plants; there are many books and web sites that can help you. Although you may be quite able to tend to a plant that lives in a greenhouse or a protected corner of your home, your clients (or more precisely, the plants of your clients) will exist in a threatening world: They may not receive proper light or temperature conditions, and they likely will be subject to accidental or intentional abuse from visitors.

Among the challenges you'll be called on to deal with are these:

- Matching plants to the available lighting in an office, public place, or home
- Managing proper watering and fertilizing schedules
- Dealing with plant diseases and insect infestations
- Repairing damage caused by visitors who touch or cut plants

You should also be aware of which plants are poisonous if eaten by children or pets. For installations in a doctor's office, you might want to submit a list of plants unlikely to activate allergies for approval by the medical staff.

Know the Territory

You can perform much of your research over the Internet at web sites about plants; there are also many excellent reference books about selection and care of greenery.

Visit area greenhouses and garden specialists to learn about available plants, fertilizers, cleaners, and tools. One or more of these stores may be the place you shop for plants and supplies, and they should be glad to partner with you.

How to Get Started

Post ads and flyers at greenhouses, garden supply stores, and home supply stores.

Place ads in area newspapers and shopping guides.

Ask friends and relatives to spread the word about your availability; offer a bonus to clients who refer new business to you.

Contact the reception desk, office manager, and maintenance departments of large businesses in your area and offer your services. Send letters to the office managers of doctors, lawyers, and other professionals in your area. Do the same with managers of area restaurants.

Up-front Expenses

Your expenses include advertising and promotion, reference books, and appropriate gardening, watering, and fertilizing supplies.

How Much to Charge

You can charge by the hour or use a flat rate per plant after you calculate the amount of time required for each. In addition to hourly charges, you bill for fertilizer, cleaners, and replacement of plants that are dead or dying.

If you design and install new plantings, you should charge by the hour, plus the cost of new plants.

Legal and Insurance Issues

① **Legal**

② **Legal**

③ **Legal**

④ **Accounting**

⑤ **Insurance**

Custom Silk and Dried Flower Arrangements

Description of Job

- Prepare and assemble flower arrangements to clients' specifications.
- Create custom wreaths and decorations.

The Need

Flowers, flowering plants, and lush foliage will beautify any room. But expensive long-stemmed roses will last only a week; Christmas poinsettias may struggle to make it to the new year, and even a hardy zebra plant will wither and die if not cared for properly.

Unless you have unlimited resources and time, one solution—done properly—is to use high-quality artificial plants made of silk and other material. (Strike from your mind's eye any thought of cheap plastic carnations; a well-made artificial plant sometimes requires lengthy, closeup examination to confirm it is not the real thing.)

Another answer is the use of well-prepared and properly arranged dried flowers.

Faux foliage can generally be placed in any light and temperature variation, and can be created or ordered in almost any hue. A client may want a centerpiece to match the color scheme in the dining room; a bride may want a bouquet that will last longer than the ceremony.

A wreath of dried sunflowers offers a welcome addition to the front door all summer and fall, and an attractive artificial or dried flower wreath brightens any indoor holiday setting.

Challenges

Even artificial plants need a bit of care; they'll need to be dusted and occasionally wiped with a damp rag. Dried plants may fade over time and become more brittle, but if not abused will probably last longer than other decorations.

You'll need an artistic eye, good judgment of quality, and a sense of style. It's important to understand how to harmonize and avoid clashes and to have an appreciation of size and proportions.

Make sure you fully understand your client's hopes and wishes before you commission any custom pieces or place orders.

Know the Territory

Become familiar with suppliers of artificial and dried flowers. Area decorating companies may sell silk and other artificial flowers at wholesale prices to professionals; you'll also find many sources on the Internet.

Dried flowers can also be ordered online or from catalogs and are generally available from local sources, including hobbyists and professional flower growers.

Many large cities have a wholesale flower district where you can find both artificial and dried arrangements.

You'll also need to suggest appropriate containers for the arrangements; among popular materials are wood, ceramic, brass, and silver. Some designs benefit from accent pieces such as ferns, feathers, ribbon, and other types of fabric.

How to Get Started

Advertise your availability through flyers and ads at community centers, schools, home supply stores, and other retail outlets. Take out ads in newspapers, shopping guides, and local decorating and women's magazines.

Teach a class at a community school or college. You will get some publicity and maybe a few clients.

Consider renting a table at local craft or holiday shows.

This type of business also works well as a virtual company, taking orders through a web site and through catalogs.

Up-front Expenses

Principal expenses include advertising and promotion. You should also prepare a portfolio with photos of actual and suggested arrangements.

You'll need some basic hobbyist tools, including shears and blades, and a supply of floral foam to serve as the base for the display.

How Much to Charge

Price your work at a flat rate per piece, taking into consideration the cost of materials, shipping, and the amount of time required to complete it.

Legal and Insurance Issues

① **Legal**

② **Legal**

③ **Legal**

④ **Accounting**

⑤ **Insurance**

CHAPTER 7

Home Services (Specialty)

24 Handy Person

25 Errand Runner

26 Vacation Home Caretaker

27 Vacation House Watcher

28 House Painting

29 Chimney Cleaning

30 Pool Service

31 Firewood Delivery

32 On-Demand Trash Removal

33 Christmas Tree Service

34 Small Engine Repair

Handyperson

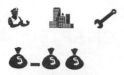

Description of Job

- Perform almost any *minor* repair or maintenance chore for homeowners.
- Be available on short notice for urgent jobs.
- Supervise subcontractors and licensed plumbers and electricians.

The Need

Have you heard the old joke about the definition of *homeowners*? They're people who sleep in their own bed at night but live at the hardware store!

Every house needs care. Older houses need repairs to essential systems, from leaky sinks to broken light switches. New homes need to have curtains and shades hung and minor landscaping; some homeowners need help in assembling gas grills or putting bicycles together. Houses in between new and old need all sorts of touch-ups, refurbishments, and installations.

Even the most handy of homeowners may not have time to work around the house—or may just need help from time to time. Examples of jobs include changing smoke detectors, caulking windows and bathtubs, touch-up painting or staining, changing locks, replacing light fixtures, installing garage door openers, driveway sealing, repairing screens, and installing weather stripping.

Challenges

A handyperson is capable enough to do almost any job around the house and smart enough to know when to call in an expert. It is important to know when to draw the line; unless you have the qualifications, you should not perform substantial work on electrical, plumbing, heating, or cooling systems. (That doesn't mean you can't change a light switch, hang a chandelier, fix a leaky faucet, change the filters on a heating system, or make simple adjustments to an air conditioner.)

You also have to know your own abilities; don't promise something you are not capable of completing in a professional manner.

You should be able to assist your client with your own list of plumbers and electricians and other professionals for more complex jobs, and you should be willing to take on the role of contractor to supervise their work.

You'll have to learn how to keep more than one client at a time happy. One customer may think that his or her blocked rain gutter is more important than someone else's broken storm door.

Know the Territory

You'll need some natural skill as a handyperson, augmented by experience. Read books on home repair, visit hardware and home centers, and consult Internet web sites for information about projects. (Some home centers offer free classes on projects.)

Get to know area tradespeople.

How to Get Started

Make people aware of your services through ads and flyers placed in home centers, hardware stores, and community centers. Include postings at area senior centers, as older homeowners are a large market for handyperson services.

Place an ad in local newspapers and shopping guides. Church and club bulletins are also helpful.

Contact area licensed professionals to find out about their services and to let them know about your availability. They may be able to steer some simple jobs your way in return for calls from your client for their services.

Up-front Expenses

You'll need a basic set of tools. Complex and/or expensive tools can often be rented for particular jobs. A good collection of home repair books and access to the Internet will be of great value.

Up-front expenses include advertising and promotion.

How Much to Charge

Bill for jobs on an hourly basis; add charges for any hardware or supplies you must purchase, plus the cost of any rented equipment.

If you will be on call for a number of jobs, it's good business practice to ask for an advance payment equal to several days' worth of work; your actual hours will be subtracted from this retainer.

Legal and Insurance Issues

Special notes: In dealing with your client's property, seek to limit your liability for damage or loss to the actual replacement value of items in your possession. You should protect yourself against claims for sentimental value or loss of use.

Discuss with the attorney any prior legal problems you may have encountered and seek advice about whether they need to be disclosed to clients.

① **Legal**

② **Legal**

③ **Legal**

④ **Accounting**

⑤ **Insurance**

⑥ **Insurance**

Errand Runner

Description of Job

- Stand in for clients to perform any reasonable assignment on their behalf when they cannot do it for themselves.
- Perform other tasks within the home, as appropriate.

The Need

Robinson Crusoe had his servant, Friday. Batman had Robin. Sherlock Holmes had his sometimes-confused but always well-meaning stalwart Dr. Watson.

For most of us, it's not feasible to hire a household staff to attend to our every need, but there are certainly many instances when it would be absolutely wonderful to have a man Friday or a gal Friday to help us do the things we don't have time for, or that must be taken care of in places we can't be.

One of the reasons our lives have become so complicated is that there are fewer stay-at-home moms and greater distances from extended family that served as supports in the past.

A man or gal Friday can be hired to perform just about any task. A typical set of jobs includes:

- Accepting deliveries
- Delivering packages to the post office
- Supervising service calls on appliances or meeting a plumber in the home
- Meeting the cable guy or the telephone repair person
- Answering correspondence and returning phone calls
- Picking up dry cleaning and laundry
- Taking a vehicle for service
- Assisting in the organization and conduct of a party
- Organizing closets, basements, and attics
- Organizing book and music collections
- Setting up and maintaining a personal filing system for important papers

Challenges

You'll need a flexible schedule and a willingness to take on just about any reasonable request. Don't agree to perform a task that is beyond your skills or experience, and be careful about accepting liability beyond your agreement and insurance coverage.

This sort of job is appropriate for someone who is highly organized and dependable, someone who enjoys solving problems.

Ask your clients to tell neighbors that you will be in their home while they are away; this should prevent neighbors from calling the police to report a burglar. (It may also help you recruit new clients.)

Know the Territory

This sort of job is in greatest demand in areas where homeowners and renters commute to work or are otherwise out of their homes for much of the day. You might also be able to find assignments from seniors and others who may be housebound or who cannot easily get about.

You should have a good knowledge of the map of your region and be able to make pickups and deliveries. You should feel comfortable dealing with tradespeople and repair specialists. You will be representing the client and should not sign off on a repair or maintenance job if it has not been done properly.

How to Get Started

Post flyers and business cards on bulletin boards at community centers, super-markets, and schools. Place ads in local newspapers and shopping guides. Ask satisfied customers to recommend your services to others.

You should collect references and letters of recommendation from previous customers.

Up-front Expenses

The principal expenses are for advertising and promotion. If you are called on to use your own vehicle for pickups and deliveries, you may need to purchase addi-tional insurance for that purpose.

How Much to Charge

Charge an hourly rate for your services, plus a mileage fee for driving. If you are asked to pay for any services on behalf of your client, you should be immediately repaid.

If you will be working on a regular basis for a client, ask to be put on a retainer; subtract actual hours worked from the balance and give your client a regular accounting.

Legal and Insurance Issues

Special notes: Discuss with your attorney any prior legal problems you may have encountered and seek advice about whether they need to be disclosed to clients.

If you will be transporting clients or their children—not something to be taken lightly—you will need additional insurance.

① **Legal**

② **Legal**

③ **Legal**

④ **Accounting**

⑤ **Insurance**

Vacation Home Caretaker

Description of Job

- Watch over a summer or vacation home when the owner is not there.
- Supervise maintenance, including lawn mowing, snow removal, winterizing.
- Check for storm damage and represent the homeowner in any emergency repairs.
- Prepare the home for the arrival of the owner.

The Need

The wonderful thing about owning a vacation home at the beach, by the lake, or near a ski resort is the warm spot it occupies in your mind even when you are many miles away.

The difficult thing about owning a vacation home is the load of worries that will afflict you because you are not there to attend to them. Vacation property is often very expensive, and homes are often in isolated locations or in areas where there are few if any year-round residents.

Homes are subject to break-ins, vandalism, storm damage, and power outages (which could cut off heating in the winter).

The job of the caretaker is to be the owner's representative and watchdog.

This job does *not* include overseeing the rental of vacation property, which is a much more complex operation usually undertaken by management companies that handle advertising, booking, billing, maintenance, cleaning, postrental inspections, and other functions.

The job includes making regular visits to the home to check for unexpected incidents, including storm damage and problems with heating systems.

The owner may ask you to supervise scheduled maintenance of the house, including servicing of the furnace, air conditioner, electrical, and plumbing systems. You may also be asked to act as the owner's representative in overseeing painting, remodeling, or expansion of the home, reporting on progress and problems. (Some caretakers send digital photographs over the Internet to their clients.)

You'll be responsible for lawn mowing and snow removal, either as tasks you perform yourself or hire others to do.

Finally, a caretaker may be asked to prepare the house before the season begins, which may include a thorough cleaning.

Challenges

A competent caretaker accepts responsibility for the house as if it were his or her own. The caretaker will have possession of keys to the property, which must be safeguarded from loss or theft.

You must demonstrate dependability; if you will be unable to personally supervise the homes of your clients for any extended period of time, you will need to have a trustworthy substitute fill in for you. If you are contracted to oversee a property on Cape Cod, you can't spend the winter on the beach in Florida without making arrangements that satisfy the needs of your client.

It is also very important that you have a good relationship with your clients, a strong understanding of their needs, and an explicit contract that spells out your responsibilities and the authority granted to you by the owner. If a pipe freezes in the winter, you should be able to hire a plumber and a cleanup crew without having to wait to speak with your client.

Your client or you should notify neighbors that you will be acting as caretaker for the property so that they do not mistake you for an unauthorized visitor. Leave your card with the neighbors; they may be able to serve as an extra pair of eyes, and they may end up hiring you to watch their homes.

Know the Territory

One of the best tools of a caretaker is an up-to-date Rolodex of dependable electricians, plumbers, carpenters, landscapers, snow removal companies, and cleaning services who will respond to your call on behalf of your client.

You should have a working knowledge of home systems and repairs.

How to Get Started

Contact area electricians, plumbers, landscapers, contractors, and rental agents to let them know of your services. Ask them to let their own clients know about you; in return, you can promise to engage them for any necessary work.

Place ads on community bulletin boards, in stores, and in newspapers. Ask friends and acquaintances to spread the word about your availability.

Up-front Expenses

Expenses are principally for advertising and promotion. Any travel and services provided are billed to your client.

How Much to Charge

Most caretakers charge a fixed rate for devoting a minimum number of hours each month to scheduled visits to the home, inspections, and supervision of scheduled services such as landscaping. Additional charges are levied (by the hour) for supervising emergency repairs, renovations, and construction.

The contract with the client should include payment of a month or two in advance as a retainer, with regular monthly billing.

Legal and Insurance Issues

Special notes: Discuss with your attorney any prior legal problems you may have encountered and seek advice about whether they need to be disclosed to clients.

① **Legal**

② **Legal**

③ **Legal**

④ **Accounting**

⑤ **Insurance**

Vacation House Watcher

Description of Job

- Make regular visits to a vacant home to check on doors, windows, heating and plumbing systems, collect mail or packages, and make the home appear occupied.
- Contact the homeowner in the event of an emergency, or arrange for emergency service without further authorization, if necessary.

The Need

Some people are comfortable going away from home for weeks at a time and simply locking the front door, holding their mail at the post office, and stopping the newspaper. Others want—or need—more protection and security.

In many neighborhoods it may be common practice to ask a neighbor to look in on your home when you are away. Unfortunately, not everyone knows their neighbors well enough to ask for this sort of help, or it may be a situation where homes are too far away from each other for a neighbor to be of much assistance.

The job of the vacation house watcher includes regular visits to the home to look for obvious signs of problems—broken windows, open doors, frost or humidity on the windows, and exterior damage. The client may also give you a key to the house and ask you to check the interior.

Other tasks include taking steps to make the house appear occupied. These would include turning on different lights in the house, or adjusting timers within. You could move garbage cans or lawn furniture from one place to another each time you visit.

Challenges

By charging for your services you will be accepting a great deal of responsibility; make sure you have a written contract that lists specific tasks and gives you permission to enter the home. You will likely be given a set of keys and possibly the entrance code for a burglar alarm. (Ask your client for a temporary code, or ask that the code be changed after you have completed your assignment.)

You need to be flexible enough to increase the number of visits you make to a home in the event of a severe cold snap or storm.

Make sure you know where your client is going. Obtain a telephone number, cell phone number, and e-mail address. You should also obtain the name of another family member or a friend of the client who is specifically authorized to give permission for repairs or special services in case of an emergency. The agreement should also list the name of your client's insurance company and local agent.

Be sure to limit your activities at the client's property and within the house to those that are appropriate and approved. As tempting as it might be to host a pool party or watch the Super Bowl with some buddies on the big-screen TV, you could be opening yourself to an expensive liability lawsuit.

You should not take a job that endangers your safety or requires you to travel at times or to locations that make you uncomfortable. Your agreement should also include language stating that in case of a general evacuation in the area because of a storm, fire, or other reason, you will follow the instructions of officials.

Know the Territory

You should get to know your client, and allow the client to get to know you, in order to establish a level of trust. Ask for a full tour of the house and point out anything that bothers you, such as unlocked windows or doors, unlocked safes, or guns.

Ask to be introduced to neighbors so that they know you will be visiting the property; you can use the opportunity to advertise your services to them at the same time.

How to Get Started

Post ads and business cards in community centers, stores, and newspapers. Ask friends and family to let others know of your availability. Ask for referrals from satisfied clients.

Collect references from satisfied customers.

Up-front Expenses

The principal up-front expense is advertising. You will be reimbursed by your client for any out-of-pocket expenses.

How Much to Charge

House watchers would likely charge an hourly rate for visits to the house. If the location is at some distance from your own home, you can ask for reimbursement for mileage, or request payment for your time in driving to the client's property.

The best arrangement is advance payment for expected time, plus an agreement for payment for unanticipated time and expense in case of an emergency.

Your agreement should specifically state that the client will directly pay any outside contractors, such as plumbers, electricians, or carpenters, who come to the house for emergency services.

Legal and Insurance Issues

Special notes: Discuss with the attorney any prior legal problems you may have encountered, and seek advice about whether they need to be disclosed to clients.

① **Legal**
② **Legal**
③ **Legal**
④ **Accounting**
⑤ **Insurance**

House Painting

Description of Job

- Work with client to choose appropriate paint and method of application.
- Prepare interior or exterior surfaces for painting or repainting.
- Make minor repairs to wall surfaces, as needed, or arrange for repairs by a contractor.
- Apply paint with brush, rollers, or spray.
- Clean up the home.

The Need

Painting is a dirty job, but someone has to do it. Some homeowners will tackle a small job like slapping a fresh coat of paint on their bathroom walls, but repainting the entire interior of a house or its exterior siding, trim, and decks may require the time, expertise, and equipment of a professional.

Challenges

Some jobs are much more complicated than others. Among difficulties requiring extra time, materials, and equipment are cathedral ceilings, multicolor rooms, textured applicators, and fancy trim.

You will need to be able to recognize the type of surface to be painted and match it to the appropriate type of paint and method of application.

For a bathroom or kitchen, you may need to use mildew-resistant glossy paint that cleans easily; bedrooms and common rooms may call for more subtle shades in a flat or nongloss finish. Do interior walls already have one or more coats of paint, or are some covered with wallpaper? Is the underlying surface drywall, plaster, or wood?

Is the home empty, with no carpeting or hardwood floor in place, or will you need to move and cover furniture and protect floors and rugs?

In some areas, many painters belong to a union. You may have to apprentice with the union or join as a full member to be considered for many business jobs—and perhaps some house-painting assignments if a contractor or government agency is involved.

Know the Territory

The best way to obtain experience in this sort of work is to work as a helper for a professional painter or assist a knowledgeable do-it-yourselfer on a major job. In other words, don't start a business as a housepainter and expect to learn on the job; the risk of damage to the home or its contents, or inefficient use of time and materials, is too great.

There is a great deal of information available on the web sites of paint manufacturers and in books. Manufacturers of paint sprayers and other equipment may offer training sessions.

In most jobs, the homeowner is asked to remove paintings, drapes, and other wall decorations; the painter is responsible for moving and covering furniture and protecting carpeting and other flooring. Other tasks include taping trim and windows to protect them from overpainting and removal of outlet and switch covers.

Modern water-based paints are much easier to clean up for interior jobs; for exterior work, the choice is either latex (water) or oil (alkyd) base. Floor enamel, available in acrylic latex and polyurethane formulas, is often used in areas that receive a great deal of traffic or are exposed to extremes of weather; floor enamel can be used on wood, concrete, and metal.

How to Get Started

Post flyers and ads in community centers, retail outlets, and bulletin boards. Place ads in newspapers and shopping guides.

Make contact with contractors, real estate agents, and cleaning services; offer a bonus or commission on work they bring your way.

Up-front Expenses

You will need ladders, high-quality brushes, roller applicators, paint trays, tarpaulins, plastic sheeting, painter's masking tape, mixers, and other tools. For some jobs, especially interior painting of new or otherwise empty homes, you may need a commercial paint sprayer. (It may be possible to rent a sprayer, as needed.)

Some painters work with high-powered portable lighting rigs to help them in their work. If you use a paint sprayer, you may need a breathing mask and eye shield.

You will need a vehicle large enough to carry your necessary equipment and supplies.

Other costs include advertising and promotion.

How Much to Charge

Most painters quote a fixed price for a job, based on a careful estimate of the number of hours it will require, plus the cost of paint and other materials. Some jobs are quoted on a cost-plus basis: a charge for hours of work plus the actual cost of paint and other supplies.

Legal and Insurance Issues

- ① **Legal**
- ② **Legal**
- ③ **Legal**
- ④ **Accounting**
- ⑤ **Insurance**

Chimney Cleaning

Description of Job

- Inspect fireplace chimney, firebox, smoke shelf, and damper for blockages, cracks, and buildup of hazardous substances.
- Mechanically clean interior of the flue.
- Remove ash, creosote, and other substances dislodged during cleaning.
- Assist the homeowner in obtaining necessary repairs from a qualified mason.

The Need

A crackling blaze in a fireplace warms the soul and the body. Yet over time, the interior of a chimney can become inefficient and dangerous due to the buildup of creosote and other substances or because of blockages caused by leaves and nests. Cracks and other damage to the flue can divert carbon monoxide, smoke, or flames to the house itself.

The less frequently you use your fireplace, or the shorter the period of time a fire is permitted to burn at full heat, the more often the flue should be inspected and cleaned. A cold chimney causes more of the smoke to condense on the flue. People who damp down a fire by closing fireplace doors or shutting off the flow of oxygen from a vent usually send more partially burnt solids up the chimney, which results in a more rapid buildup within the flue.

Experts recommend that homeowners who light fires three or more times a week during the winter season should have a chimney cleaning and inspection once a year; if homeowners burn unseasoned wood in a fireplace, twice-yearly cleaning may be necessary.

Challenges

Some jobs are much more complex than others: exceptionally steep and high roofs; chimney designs with twists and turns; adverse environmental conditions, including severe weather, bird and rodent nests, and insect infestations.

You'll be working at heights and in a dirty environment. You'll also be entering the clean homes of clients and be responsible for keeping dirt away from carpeting and furniture.

The bulk of work may be seasonal, as homeowners prepare to use fireplaces in the fall of each year.

Make sure your insurance coverage offers protection against claims for liability in the event of a subsequent fire or structural problem.

Know the Territory

The basic work of the chimney sweep is to clean the flue, but the job also involves inspection and careful protection of the interior of the home from the ash and dirt. Here are the steps in a typical job:

- Climb ladders to the roof and gain access to the chimney.
- Inspect the fireplace, firebox, smoke shelf, damper, and flue for blockage, buildup, cracks, and other damage.
- Seal the front of the fireplace with plastic to prevent soot and dirt from entering the house. Put protective drop cloths on the floor to prevent damage to carpeting and flooring.
- Brush the interior of the flue and other components from above. After

sweeping, shovel out large debris and then vacuum the firebox, damper, and smoke shelf.

- Give the homeowner a written report on the condition of the chimney with recommendations for repair.

How to Get Started

Chimney cleaning is not regulated in most states and localities. In some areas, though, licensing may be required. Several national groups offer certification to members who complete specified education and training. A credential from one of these groups, such as the Chimney Safety Institute of America, may help you in selling your services and in obtaining insurance.

Place flyers and ads in home supply stores and community centers. Make your services known to firewood suppliers, contractors, housecleaning companies, and real estate agencies. Ask them to recommend you to their clients; offer a commission for business they refer to you. Ask satisfied customers to recommend you to friends and acquaintances, and offer a bonus or discount for new business that results.

Make contact with masons and chimney repair specialists. You should be able to refer your clients to them for necessary repairs and maintenance; they may be willing to recommend your services to customers whose chimneys need cleaning.

Up-front Expenses

You'll need a basic chimney sweep's kit, including at least one extension ladder to reach the roof, a set of chimney rods and brushes, short-handled brushes, a powerful shop vacuum with crevice tools and extension hoses, and buckets and cans to haul away ashes and debris. You'll also need drop cloths to cover carpeting and plastic sheeting to seal the front of fireplaces while the flue is being brushed.

You'll need a station wagon or small van to transport your tools and equipment.

Other expenses include advertising and promotion.

How Much to Charge

Depending on local costs and the difficulty involved in gaining access to the roof and the interior of the flue, chimney cleaning rates are generally in the range of about $60 to $150. Inspections are usually billed in the range of $40 to $60.

Legal and Insurance Issues

Special note: Make sure your insurance coverage offers adequate protection against liability claims that result from damage that may occur after you have completed your inspection and cleaning.

① **Legal**

② **Legal**

③ **Legal**

④ **Accounting**

⑤ **Insurance**

Pool Service

Description of Job

- Prepare private swimming pools for seasonal openings.
- Clean the surface of pools and filter traps on a regular basis.
- Test water quality and make adjustments to chlorine and other chemicals in the system.
- Coordinate with pump and filter service companies for necessary repairs.
- Prepare pools for winter closing.

The Need

A backyard swimming pool is a great comfort and (for some) a huge chore. The cleanliness and chemical balance of the water in the pool has to be regularly maintained, and the surface of the water and its filter traps have to be cleared of leaves and debris.

Many homeowners hire a service to make scheduled visits to keep their pools in good health during the season and to close them down for the winter and reopen them in the spring.

Challenges

Although the basics of treatment and filtration systems are very similar from pool to pool, you will have to deal with variations in machinery and conditions at each client's home. You will also be responsible for keeping a close eye on health conditions in the water, taking into account such factors as number of children using the pool, trees and plants in the immediate vicinity, and the average ambient temperature, which also affects the temperature of the water (except in the case of heated pools, which maintain water temperature above the average ambient temperature). Pollutants that affect water quality may include anything from cosmetics to runoff to rainfall.

Know the Territory

Among the assignments for a pool service are:

- Checking the chlorine (or other sanitizer) level to ensure that it's at a level sufficient to keep unhealthy bacteria at bay
- Determining the water balance for proper levels of pH (acidity or alkalinity) and hardness, adding chemicals to adjust the balance
- Checking total dissolved solids and adjusting filtration settings
- Cleaning both the surface of the pool and the filter traps
- Delivering a preseason treatment to sanitize the water, adding winterizing chemicals at the end of the season

Most pools use chlorine as their principal chemical to sanitize the water. When chlorine is added to water, it reacts to form a weak form of hydrochloric acid and hypochlorous acid that kills microorganisms. The acids eventually break down to harmless compounds.

While chlorine in the pool water is harmless to most swimmers, pool attendants face a hazard when they are adding the full-strength chemical. Be sure to read and follow the directions carefully, and especially avoid mixing the chemical with other solutions. Avoid breathing in chlorine gas, which can be fatal; wear protective gloves and eye coverings.

From time to time, it may be necessary to add other chemicals to deal with algae, cloudy water, and other conditions that might arise.

How to Get Started

Place flyers and ads in community centers and home supply stores. Place ads in newspapers and shopping guides.

Ask satisfied customers to recommend you to friends and acquaintances; offer a bonus or discount for any business they bring your way.

Up-front Expenses

You will need a basic set of nets and scoops to clean the surface of the pool, as well as traps and a simple tool kit to work with some compartments and valves of the filtration system. To test the quality of the water, you'll need a test kit that uses special chemicals and reagents; some advanced testers are electronic.

Your client will need to provide chlorine and other chemicals or pay you for supplying them as needed. You will need a station wagon or small van to carry your tools.

How Much to Charge

You can set a fixed fee for regular service, based on an estimate of the amount of time required. If you provide any chemicals, bill for them at retail rates; you should be able to purchase supplies at wholesale or discounted prices.

Add a fee for winterizing a pool; this usually involves adding special chemicals and installing a pool cover. Similarly, at the start of the season you can charge a separate fee for removing the cover and giving the pool a preseason treatment.

Legal and Insurance Issues

Special notes: Some insurance carriers have very stringent underwriting conditions before they will issue policies for people who work with dangerous chemicals.

① **Legal**
② **Legal**
③ **Legal**
④ **Accounting**
⑤ **Insurance**

Firewood Delivery

Description of Job

- Pick up and deliver seasoned firewood to clients in rural and urban settings.
- Consult with clients about specialty woods for particular effects.
- Stack wood and protect it from rain and insects.

The Need

If you have a fireplace or a woodstove, you need a reliable source of good-quality firewood. Especially if you live in a city, it may be very difficult to find and store wood.

City dwellers may need frequent deliveries of small quantities of wood, and they may need to store it inside. Quality wood for inside storage is dry and free of insects.

Rural and urban dwellers may be able to accept deliveries large enough to last a full season; they may not have a truck for pickup of the wood and may not have the time or inclination to properly stack and store the wood.

Some buyers may have needs or wants for wood of a particular species. Owners of woodstoves may need logs that are shorter and thinner than those used for a large fireplace.

Challenges

You will need to obtain a reliable source of quality wood in large quantities. The wood should be insect- and disease-free, and should be seasoned about one year after cutting to reduce the water content.

The wood will need to be cut into usable lengths and split to allow easy lighting and efficient burning; in the best situation, this work will be done by the wood wholesaler you deal with, leaving you to concentrate on resale and delivery.

Know the Territory

The preferred products for fireplaces and woodstoves are hardwoods and specialty fruitwoods.

Hardwoods, such as oak, maple, and elm, catch fire easier, burn more efficiently, and produce more heat than most other species. Specialty fruitwoods have properties similar to hardwoods and can add aroma to the room; used in a cooking stove or a wood oven, they add flavor to foods. Fruitwoods include apple, birch, cherry, and peach.

Typically, a full cord of hardwood yields about the same heat as 200 gallons of heating oil or 4,000 kilowatts of electricity. The heat from wood depends on its density, resin, and moisture content.

Softwoods give a fast-burning, crackling blaze but deliver much less heat and may produce resins and creosote that could cause a dangerous condition in chimneys and stovepipes.

Freshly cut trees have as much as 60 percent moisture content by weight; logs containing that much water will not burn well—if they light at all. After a year of seasoning, the moisture content of wood generally falls to 25 percent or less. Wood seasons faster if it has been split and then stacked off the ground in a manner that allows flow of air in and around the logs.

A full cord of wood is defined as 128 cubic feet, which typically measures four feet high, four feet deep, and eight feet long when stacked. In two-foot lengths, a full cord typically includes about 600 logs and weighs about two tons.

In some areas, wood sellers offer *face cords,* which are only two feet deep and amount to 64 cubic feet, basically, this is a half cord.

Wood is best stored outside where fresh air can help it continue to season; it should be covered only when it is raining. If wood is stored indoors, it should be cleaned of insects and stored in a rack or shelving that allows circulation of air.

There are four ways to sell wood, at increasing levels of difficulty; the price to the customer climbs accordingly:

- Self-serve pickup at a wood lot
- Delivery of orders to a client's property
- Delivery and proper stacking of wood outdoors on a client's property
- Delivery and stacking of wood inside in apartments and condos, including carrying wood up stairs, where necessary

How to Get Started

Post ads in community centers. Place ads in newspapers and shopping guides.

Ask satisfied customers to recommend your services; offer a bonus or discount for any business they refer to you.

Up-front Expenses

You will need to purchase or lease a heavy-duty truck and pay for licensing, maintenance, and repair. You may need a ramp and hand truck or cart to transport wood.

Other expenses include advertising and promotion.

How Much to Charge

Many states regulate commercial wood sellers by defining *quantities* of wood (this to protect consumers); most use a standard cord size or cubic footage. In some places dealers are prohibited from selling by undefined "rack," "pile," or "truckload" sizes.

Prices for firewood vary by location and by difficulty of pickup and delivery. A typical price for a full cord of hardwood delivered and stacked in a rural or suburban area would be in the range of $200 to $250; a half cord might range in price from about $125 to $150. Special-order fruitwood can be as much as 50 to 100 percent more costly.

To determine your price, start with your wholesale cost of wood. Add to it the expense of owning or leasing a truck, travel to the woodlot, time to measure and load an order, travel to the customer, and time for unloading and stacking the wood properly. You should increase your price to cover extra time when you are required to carry wood into a home or apartment.

Legal and Insurance Issues

① **Legal [1]**
② **Legal [2]**
③ **Legal [3]**
④ **Accounting [4]**
⑤ **Insurance [5]**

On-demand Trash Removal

Description of Job

- Pick up appliances, furniture, boxes, and other large items and deliver them to the town dump or trash collection center.
- Assist homeowners and renters in clearing basements, attics, and closets of unwanted items.

The Need

As comedian George Carlin once said, a house is just a place to keep your stuff. If you didn't have so much stuff, you wouldn't need a house.

If you've lived in a house for any length of time, you know that, over time, it increasingly fills up with extra furniture, old appliances, boxes of magazines, and other stuff. The basement may also become cluttered with cans of paint, solvents, insecticides, and other dangerous chemicals.

The job of the on-demand trash pickup service is to help people move bulky or restricted items from their homes or apartments to dumps or trash collection centers.

Challenges

Among the requirements for this sort of job: a strong back, a truck or van, and observance of local ordinances.

Some municipalities are very strict in regulating use of their facilities and require local residents to obtain a sticker. Others may not require identification from individuals, but may have separate regulations for commercial dumpers. If you are bringing items to the dump, recycling center, or trash collection center on behalf of someone else, you may need to obtain a commercial license from your local government.

The municipality may charge a fee for the disposal of large items such as appliances, tires, and furniture.

Most municipalities have strict regulations about the disposal of hazardous substances, including paint and chemicals; in some areas, there are designated days when such material is accepted, and there may be a fee for disposal.

Be specific about what sort of jobs you are willing to accept. Will you carry items up or down stairs?

Know the Territory

You'll need to know the hours of operation for dumps and understand local regulations on disposal of large items, appliances, and hazardous chemicals.

How to Get Started

Advertise your availability in local newspapers, at community centers, and by word of mouth. Your vehicle will become a portable advertisement for your services; keep business cards and flyers handy as you load and unload.

Up-front Expenses

You'll need a vehicle. Other expenses include advertising and promotions.

How Much to Charge

This job is usually billed by the hour, plus a mileage charge to and from the dump. The hourly rate should reflect the cost of any necessary permits. The mileage rate should be high enough to pay for a portion of repair and maintenance for the vehicle plus gasoline and licenses. The client is also responsible for payment of any special fees for disposal of large items and hazardous chemicals.

Legal and Insurance Issues

Special notes: You may need a special commercial permit or license from a municipality. Discuss with your attorney any prior legal problems you may have encountered and seek advice about whether they need to be disclosed to clients.

- **Legal [1]**
- **Legal [2]**
- **Legal [3]**
- **Accounting [4]**
- **Insurance [5]**

Christmas Tree Service

Description of Job

- Select a Christmas tree to the exact specifications of the client.
- Deliver and set up the tree in client's home.
- Remove the tree from client's home on request and dispose of it properly.

The Need

A fresh, perfectly shaped, fragrant pine tree is at the heart of some of our best Christmas memories. Yet most of us also have horror stories of the scrawny one that wouldn't fit into the tree stand and immediately began shedding needles.

Even before that stage, there is the problem of finding the time to go out and choose the perfect tree, strap it to the top of the car, and lug it up the stairs and into the house or apartment.

The job of the Christmas tree specialist is to locate, purchase, and deliver a tree that exactly meets the specifications of the client; this may involve trimming and shaping it. After Christmas, the specialist comes back to remove the tree and dispose of it properly.

This sort of service may be especially popular in cities where residents don't have easy access to a vehicle to transport a tree.

Challenges

It is very important to establish a good relationship with a nursery or tree supplier. You want first choice of the best trees of various species and shapes, and you want cooperation in trimming branches and cutting it to an exact height.

Your arrangement with the supplier will be built on your ability to buy in volume.

It is also critical to have good communication with your client. You can post pictures of various types of trees on a web site, or include photos in brochures. Make sure your client measures the height of the room properly.

Know the Territory

Learn all you can about the types of trees available in your area. For example, Scotch pines hold their needles longer than most varieties, and Virginia pines have a very strong scent.

How to Get Started

Post flyers and ads at community bulletin boards and in stores. Place advertisements in local newspapers, shopping guides, and church bulletins.

Up-front Expenses

You will need to own or rent a vehicle large enough to pick up trees from the supplier before Christmas and retrieve them at the end of the holiday season.

Other expenses include advertising and promotion.

How Much to Charge

The simplest way to charge for this sort of service is to set a fee based on the size and variety of the tree; in addition to marking up your wholesale or discounted cost for the tree, add in your time plus mileage for pickup and delivery and retrieval after the holiday. Depending on the neighborhood and the level of service you provide, you should be able to mark up the price of a tree by $50 to $100.

Increase the price of the tree if you need to travel a great distance for pickup or delivery or if the tree must be carried up stairs.

You can add the cost of a tree stand if you will be supplying one.

Legal and Insurance Issues

① **Legal**

② **Legal**

③ **Legal**

④ **Accounting**

⑤ **Insurance**

Small Engine Repair

Description of Job

- Repair small engines on lawn mowers, all-terrain vehicles, chainsaws, and generators.
- Provide scheduled maintenance including installation of filters, oil changes, and tune-ups on small engines.

The Need

We love our power tools and toys: lawn mowers, riding tractors, weed whackers, chainsaws, snowblowers, go-carts, and many other devices that use small gasoline engines. Though these engines are essentially similar to highly reliable automobile engines, they are by necessity much smaller, lighter, and constructed of much less expensive components.

The compromises that come from small size and low cost usually mean that these engines require regular attention and adjustment, and parts may wear out quickly.

A small engine repair business can be done at your workshop, which allows you to keep all of your tools and spare parts right at hand. However, another attractive opportunity exists for mobile repair service, where the workshop travels to the customer and work is done on-site. The advantage to the client is that a cumbersome lawn mower or snowblower does not have to be carted away to a shop for repair.

Challenges

Set the boundaries for the types and sizes of engines you will work on. The simplest and most common are air-cooled, one-cylinder, two- or four-cycle gasoline engines. More complex engines are (like most automobile engines) multicylinder, water-cooled plants.

Complexity of repair and inventory of parts goes up dramatically when you come to engines with belts, generators, and power takeoffs. You'll need some special expertise to take on outboard motors and mission-critical systems such as emergency electrical generators.

Be aware of local ordinances that might limit your ability to work in residential neighborhoods, and many jurisdictions have strict regulations regarding the disposal of engine oil and other chemicals.

Know the Territory

You'll need a strong background in engine repair and the ability to quickly research techniques and parts for unusual jobs.

When a customer calls for repair or maintenance, obtain full information about the device: manufacturer, model number, and serial number. Note that half a dozen or so companies manufacture the majority of small engines, and those engines are used to power dozens of other brand-name devices. For example, power units from companies like Tecumseh engines and Briggs & Stratton are used in a wide variety of equipment.

You should be able to stock a basic collection of engine parts and lubricants for a wide variety of engines; have a list of sources from whom you can special-order unusual components, as needed.

Some jobs are more complex than others, and in some cases you may need to order replacement parts from a supplier before work can be completed.

How to Get Started

Advertise your availability through sporting goods, home and garden, and other retail stores. Post ads and flyers on community bulletin boards and in schools.

Your mobile van, if you have one, will become a portable billboard for your services. Be sure to keep a supply of flyers and business cards at hand while doing repairs in someone's driveway or garage; the neighbors may come knocking.

Ask satisfied customers to recommend your services to friends and neighbors, and offer them a discount or bonus for new business they bring you.

Up-front Expenses

You'll need to invest in a library of technical manuals for the most common engines. You'll need a set of small engine tools and you'll need basic parts and supplies, including spark plugs, engine oil, filters, and gaskets. Based on your customer's description of the type of engine and its model number, you may be able to purchase parts as needed.

If you will be operating a mobile repair service, you'll need a vehicle large enough to carry your tools and supplies. You should be able to work with a small van or a station wagon; you can add a trailer hitch and a small trailer if you need to transport an engine or an entire machine back to your workshop.

Other expenses include advertising and promotion.

How Much to Charge

Charge by the hour, plus the cost of parts (marked up from wholesale) for standard repairs. For basic maintenance, you can set a flat fee for particular classes of engines—for example, for a tuneup of a lawn mower or chainsaw.

Legal and Insurance Issues

① **Legal**

② **Legal**

③ **Legal**

④ **Accounting**

⑤ **Insurance**

Parties, Entertainment, and Special Events

35 Party Planner

36 Children's Event Organizer

37 Party and Special-Event Rentals

38 Catering

39 Visiting Chef

40 Specialty Cake Baker

41 Prepared Custom-Meal Service

42 Freelance Bartender

43 Entertainer

44 Holiday Decoration Service

Party Planner

Description of Job

- Plan and manage personal events such as a child's birthday party, a special occasion such as an anniversary, graduation celebration, adult's birthday, retirement party, or reunion.

- Plan and manage business events such as cocktail parties, product introductions, fund-raisers, open houses, retirement parties, and holiday parties.

- Design an event that meets your client's needs, wishes, and budget.

- Develop a network of reliable and professional service providers such as caterers, servers, bartenders, entertainers, and setup and cleanup crews

- Stay abreast of appropriate locations for events that will be held outside of your client's residence or place of business.

- Write an inclusive contract for your services that properly spells out all that you will provide.

- Budget accurately and maintain records for proper billing.

The Need

A truly successful social event doesn't happen by accident. We're not talking about inviting a few of your best friends over for pizza and beer to watch the Red Sox break the curse of the Bambino. A party planner has the creativity, the sense of organization, and the contacts to put together dozens of details, from location to theme to food and drink to entertainment . . . and even the morning after the night before.

Here are just three of many reasons party planners are needed:

1. Putting on a good party requires creativity, and many people are willing to pay for good help.

2. Planning and putting on a party requires a great deal of time and effort, and individuals and companies may not be able to do it themselves.

3. Many people are not comfortable with all of the details that may go into mounting a successful event.

You'll probably know that this is the job for you if you've put on more than a few successful parties of your own, but remember that as a professional party planner you'll have to deal with someone else's expectations, needs, budget, friends, and business associates.

The biggest difference between a party or event you set up for yourself and one that you do for a client is this: You are not the host and not a guest. It is your job to exceed your client's expectations and spare your client from all of the headaches.

Challenges

This is *not* your party, and you *can't* cry if you want to. The headaches are all yours. The client is always right, even when he or she is wrong.

You are there to interpret and suggest, but not to impose your sense of style on an event if the client disagrees. Don't take on a job that you can't do well. If the job is too complex or too large or not possible, walk away from the contract. It's much worse to have a failure—and a bad reference—than to forgo a job.

Expect to be asked to put on a champagne-and-caviar reception on a beer-and-pizza budget; you'll need to know costs and be able to steer your clients to realistic expectations.

If a caterer delivers a bad meal, the entertainer fails to show, or the tent company provides a leaky covering, it's *your* headache.

Spend the time to learn about available caterers, locations, entertainers, setup crews, furniture and equipment rentals, and other services you may need.

Read your local newspaper carefully to learn about social events and parties in your area. Consider the newspaper coverage as part of your research about what kind of events are put on and how they are set up.

Visit the locations for events you might manage. Tour facilities when they are empty and ask if you can return during—or just before—scheduled events they may be putting on. Obtain price lists and advance calendars that let you know when facilities may already be booked.

Ask for references from any service provider you may want to make part of your team. Talk to more than one company in each of the categories you will be working with.

Gather a database of prices for all of the available services from service providers. Collect menus from caterers and restaurants you will be working with.

Establish and maintain a list of names, phone numbers, cell phone numbers, e-mail addresses, and other information for all of the service providers you may need to work with. Your black book will become the heart of your operation.

Get to know some of the other party planners in your area; you may find it valuable to partner with them on a particularly large or complex event, and they may do the same with you someday.

How to Get Started

Start spreading the news. Let your friends and acquaintances know you are in the business. For parties for individuals, post flyers on bulletin boards in markets, at sports clubs, and in schools to let people know your availability. Include your phone number and web page address.

For parties for businesses, start by asking your friends and acquaintances about the sorts of events they see at work, and ask for the names of the people in charge. Create a professional letter, including your qualifications, and send it out.

Advertise in shopping guides and newspapers. Set up a web page to advertise your availability. Ask clients for permission to list them as references or to include pictures or descriptions from events you've staged for them.

Maintain a portfolio of photos and details of all of your parties and events to show to prospective clients.

Carefully prepare a questionnaire and checklist for your client. Send it on ahead of your first planning meeting, or go over it line by line with the client. This will help you determine exactly what the client wants to have at the party and will be the basis of your bid for the job. Make a professional appearance when you consult with your client. Wear business clothing; bring business cards and supporting material.

Follow up after your initial contact. Some people take a long time to make a decision, and your continued expression of interest may get you the job. If you are not selected for the job, be polite and ask the reason. Was it price? Was it a service you did not offer? Ask the client to keep you in mind for a future event.

Don't go out of your way to lose money, but you might want to take on a job or two on a break-even basis or at a minimal profit when you're getting started to help you build a reputation and some references.

Up-front Expenses

Initial expenses include advertising and promotion. You may also have to bear the costs of research trips to visit locations and service providers.

How Much to Charge

There are three ways to set your prices for this sort of business: (1) Charge a flat fee for your services; (2) offer a cost-plus contract in which the client agrees to pay all agreed-upon expenses plus a specified percentage; or (3) provide an all-inclusive contract in which the client sees only the bottom line.

Whichever way you choose to establish your rates, it should be based on an estimation of how much time you will need to devote to the job. If an event is going to require 40 hours of work by you, and you determine that you need to receive $25 per hour to pay the costs of running your business and generating a profit, then your contract should either (in this example) consist of a flat fee of $1,000, a cost-plus figure that produces about $1,000 for you, or an all-inclusive amount that is marked up by $1,000.

Make certain your contract is properly drawn. If the client makes a change to the requirements that results in a higher cost, the contract should be written in a way that allows you to increase your charge accordingly. Similarly, you should seek written contracts or bids from your suppliers with full details about their responsibilities and products.

Legal and Insurance Issues

Special notes: Consult your insurance agent about specialized insurance to protect you once you begin putting on large events. You'll want to especially watch for liability issues. In addition, your client might want to know about insurance that protects against such things as cancellations and unanticipated expenses because of rain, snow, extremes of temperature, or other acts of God.

① **Legal**
② **Legal**
③ **Legal**
④ **Accounting**
⑤ **Insurance**

Children's Event Organizer

Description of Job

- Be the organizer and majordomo of a party or special event for children.
- Meet with parents (and child where appropriate) to discuss activities, entertainment, and food.
- Develop a budget and a plan for the event, including contingencies for weather.
- Supervise the event.

The Need

If you think that putting on a wedding reception for a hundred guests or planning a formal cocktail party for the boss and the board of directors is stressful, you obviously have never been in charge of a birthday party for 12 six-year-olds.

Adults look for the quality of conversation, food, and drink. The younger set wants to be entertained constantly, fed often, and generally allowed to run wild. (Well, yes, so do the adults, but sometimes they can be reasoned with, and their temper tantrums are usually easier to head off.)

Events for children can be held at the home of their parents, which may be the most comfortable and least expensive but also brings problems of breakage, bathrooms, pets, and neighbors; or they can be held at parks, amusement areas, sporting arenas, theaters, restaurants, and other venues.

The job of the children's event organizer is to know the territory, understand children, and be willing to take on the challenge of throwing a party for the pint-sized.

Challenges

You should be able to see things from a child's point of view. The party has to be fun, and the guest of honor is going to expect to earn bragging rights that will last at least until the next friend's party.

Many parties for youngsters are based on a theme, and you have to keep current. Harry Potter may be just so *yesterday* by the time of your event.

Among the challenges: goodie bags, piñatas, lawn games. Do you need to rent a clown or a pony? Is the client's backyard an appropriate and safe location? How far into the house can the children venture? What happens if it rains?

Meet with the parents first to understand their expectations and limitations; then include the child to hear his or her expectations. (If the party is to be a surprise, the parents will have to be able to speak on behalf of their child.)

Be sure that the parents have a realistic idea of the number of guests they intend to invite. Twenty kids in a three-room apartment with one bathroom is not going to be pleasant; six kids in a formal dining room may meet a kid's definition of boring. Make a presentation that includes area amusement parks, museums, restaurants, and theaters that will host a party.

Explore themes for home parties. If the child is a fan of *The Wizard of Oz*, suggest decorating the client's home with a yellow-brick road into the Emerald City.

Avoid unnecessary exposure to liability. We'd suggest staying away from trampolines, bounce houses, and anything else that increases the risk of children being hurt. Even a pool party involves potential danger unless it's heavily supervised. Your contract should limit your exposure to liability, especially for any danger that already exists at the home or party location.

Know the Territory

Contact area theme parks, museums, arenas, theaters, and restaurants that cater to children, and find out about their programs for parties. You'll also need to meet and check out clowns, magicians, balloon artists, singers, and other entertainers you may engage.

You have to know what's hot and what's not in the fickle world of children and match the age group of the party to the right theme.

How to Get Started

Post flyers and ads at community centers, schools, and retail outlets, including party supply stores. Retailers may be willing to allow you to advertise at their stores if you promise to shop for supplies there. Place ads in newspapers and shopping guides.

Ask friends and acquaintances to spread the word about your services; offer a bonus or a discount on future services for business they send your way. Do the same with satisfied customers.

You can also contact companies in your area that plan holiday events (Fourth of July, Christmas, and the like) for their employees; offer your services to organize separate entertainment for the children.

Up-front Expenses

The principal up-front expenses are for advertising and promotion.

How Much to Charge

Charge by the hour for your planning and supervision of the event, and add the cost of any supplies you must purchase or rent; you should be able to buy at wholesale or discount prices and resell at retail prices.

Your client can pay entertainers and food providers directly, or those services can bill *you,* in which case you can use a cost-plus basis for billing for your hours, adding a markup to other costs.

Legal and Insurance Issues

    ① **Legal**

    ② **Legal**

    ③ **Legal**

    ④ **Accounting**

    ⑤ **Insurance**

Party and Special-Event Rentals

Description of Job

- Set up an inventory of party furniture and entertainment equipment for rental to individual and business clients.
- Act as a broker to use the equipment of other companies, as needed.

- Establish contacts with other suppliers of unusual equipment for rent.
- Deliver and set up equipment at client's location.
- Pick up and clean equipment after the party.

The Need

Most of us put on a big bash only a handful of times in our lives: weddings, major anniversaries and birthdays, graduations, and the like. Very few of us have a garage full of folding chairs, banquet tables, umbrellas, audio equipment, and other elements of a successful party.

A business may want to throw a party to celebrate a product introduction or a holiday, but is not likely to have tables and chairs and other equipment for guests.

The job of the party and special-event rental company is to maintain an inventory of portable furniture and equipment, or establish and maintain relationships with other companies who can supply necessary equipment as needed.

Most of the jobs for this sort of business will occur in places other than hotels, banquet halls, or church basements. Those locations will likely have their own chairs, tables, and equipment, or they may have master contracts with major companies.

As a start-up company, you will be looking for jobs in nontraditional locations: perhaps a wedding on the beach at sunset or a graduation party in someone's own backyard.

Challenges

If you will be offering your own equipment for rent, this sort of business can involve a large investment. You will also have to clean and maintain the furniture and equipment.

The peak periods for special events and parties include summertime and holidays. At other times of the year there may be much less business, and competition with other suppliers may reduce prices and profits.

However, if you will be working as a broker, you can let others make the investment and earn your profit as a percentage of the rental charges plus any other fees you might assess the client directly.

Know the Territory

Learn as much as you can about the party and special-event calendar in your area; read the social pages of the newspaper as though they were a scouting report. Check the prices for rentals from competitors to help you draw up your business plan.

Check wholesale supply companies for chairs and tables and other items you will be buying in quantity. Be on the lookout for restaurants or hotels going out of business or disposing of surplus equipment.

Contact major rental companies and seek an arrangement as a broker. In doing so, you will be similar to party planners who offer their services in return for a percentage of the rental fee or the markup. Bill yourself as a specialist who can provide just about any piece of furniture and equipment—or an entire lawnful of them—from your various sources.

How to Get Started

Post flyers and ads at community centers, on church bulletin boards, and in stores. Place ads in local newspapers and shopping guides, including special wedding and holiday sections.

Make your services known to party planners and caterers; offer to share commissions or a finder's fee for business they direct to you. Ask satisfied customers to recommend you to friends and acquaintances; offer a bonus or discount for new business. Send letters to corporate event planners.

Up-front Expenses

If you will be establishing your own inventory, there will be a substantial up-front investment. Among the items you'll need are chairs, chair covers, tables, umbrellas, a dance floor, and a portable bar. You'll also need linens.

For meals, you'll need to provide utensils and china service. You may be able to partner with a caterer who will bring serving trays and equipment for the food preparation.

If you will be operating as a broker, you will need to create a catalog of available items.

Other expenses include advertising and promotion.

How Much to Charge

Rental companies generally charge a flat rate for each piece of furniture or equipment, taking into account the cost of equipment and depreciation. You can offer packages of blocks of tables, chairs, and other furniture at a discounted rate. Add a fee for delivery and pickup.

If you will be functioning as a broker, seek a discount from the owner of the furniture or equipment and mark the prices up to the retail rate.

Legal and Insurance Issues

Special notes: You'll want insurance on your equipment; don't expect to collect if a single umbrella is stolen or if a table breaks, but you should be covered in case the tent burns down or the beach floods, resulting in the tragic loss of hundreds of folding chairs.

① **Legal**

② **Legal**

③ **Legal**

④ **Accounting**

⑤ **Insurance**

Catering

Description of Job

- Prepare meals to a client's specifications.
- Offer a range of theme and gourmet menus for special occasions.

The Need

A good caterer brings excitement, elegance, and professionalism to any gathering, large or small.

In a business setting, there is often no choice but to bring in a caterer for a meeting or social event. Offices and halls may not have a kitchen on-site, and in any case, cooking for the CEO and important customers is not generally part of the job description for the head of marketing.

For private parties and gatherings in a home, hiring a caterer relieves the hosts of the responsibility for shopping, preparing, serving, and cleaning up. Although the host may be quite capable when it comes to preparing a family dinner, producing a full spread of appetizers, entrées, salads, and desserts for a roomful of people may be well beyond a reasonable assignment.

Other social settings where catering is appropriate include fund-raising events, cocktail parties, and after-theater gatherings.

Challenges

You have to know your way around your own kitchen and be able to work in a client's facility if needed. You'll also need to be very well versed in the rules of proper food handling, including the storage and transportation of raw ingredients, the handling of cooked food, and the proper temperatures to protect prepared dishes on the buffet line.

In most jurisdictions you'll also have to obtain a license or otherwise work closely with health departments.

If you will be providing food within hotels or convention halls, you may need to work with some of their unionized employees. If you will be delivering food to offices or other businesses, you will have to meet their professional standards.

Caterers generally offer both preselected combinations of dishes and customized menus to meet the requests of their clients. You must be able to adapt your recipes to fit the number of guests at the event.

In some cases, the caterer is involved in the actual serving of the food. In other instances, the caterer delivers the food—completely cooked or one or more steps short of completion—to a serving crew provided by the client, a party planner, or a meeting hall.

Know the Territory

Build a library of your specialties. Take photos and collect testimonials from satisfied customers. For very large gatherings you may be called on to provide some samples of your cooking for evaluation.

A vast collection of recipes and cooking techniques available is on the Internet, as well as in newspapers and cookbooks.

Get to know area businesses, hotels, and convention centers. Read the social pages of local newspapers to learn about major events held on an annual basis, and make contact with the sponsors.

How to Get Started

Advertise in newspapers and shopping guides. Post flyers and ads on community bulletin boards.

Offer to teach a course at local schools or colleges as a way to get some publicity and perhaps some clients.

Up-front Expenses

You'll need a kitchen with large, commercial-grade preparation and cooking equipment. Depending on local regulations, you may have to purchase and use special equipment to measure temperature of raw and cooked food and to maintain it within a safe range.

You'll also need appropriate containers to transport finished food from your kitchen to the client; depending on the formality of the event, the same containers might also be used for serving.

You'll need a vehicle to transport your prepared food to your client and pick up any equipment you leave behind; when you first start your business, you may be able to rent a van on an as-needed basis for jobs.

You'll need to stock your kitchen with basic ingredients, spices, and flavorings. You'll also want a library of cookbooks and reference books.

Additional costs include advertising and promotion.

How Much to Charge

Most caterers have a standard selection of offerings, with prices based on the number of guests at the event. The cost of a dish should take into account the price of ingredients and the amount of time required to prepare it. Simple baked or steamed lobster is relatively easy to prepare but expensive to purchase; a fancy dessert may use some very basic ingredients but require a great deal of time and attention in the kitchen.

If the client asks for dishes not on your standard list of offerings, you'll need to research the cost carefully.

Add charges for delivery and for the cost of containers that are not reusable.

If you will be working during the party itself to assist in serving and cleanup, add an hourly charge for your time.

Legal and Insurance Issues

① **Legal**
② **Legal**
③ **Legal**
④ **Accounting**
⑤ **Insurance**

Visiting Chef

Description of Job

- Plan and prepare a gourmet or theme dinner at a client's home.
- Select and serve appropriate wines.
- Serve meal to guests.
- Clean up kitchen.

The Need

For a formal dinner party or an extraordinary gathering of friends and family, one very special option is to hire a professional cook to come to your home to prepare and serve a meal. A visiting chef delivers a customized gourmet or theme dinner to your exact order, leaving you free to be a guest at your own party.

Challenges

You will need the skills and background of a professional chef, with some additional flexibility to be able to work in unfamiliar kitchens and with sometimes unusual requests. You may have to work with less-than-optimal ovens, with utensils and pots that are less than commercial quality, and in limited space.

You'll need to be able to put together an entire meal, including appetizers, entrées, and dessert. In most situations, you'll also need to have some knowledge about the selection and serving of wine.

Depending on the size of the job and your own experience, you may need to experiment with unusual dishes in your own kitchen before cooking them for your client.

Know the Territory

Spend the time to meet with clients to discuss menu and ingredient choices. Tour the kitchen you'll be working in to learn about your working area.

You can offer menus of available, tested recipes or ask for requests and suggestions from your clients. Be sure to discuss any special ingredients they may want, and ask about allergies and special diets.

Plan on shopping for ingredients on your own, from suppliers you know and trust. You should be able to perform some of the prep work on dishes in your own kitchen and finish them on-site. In some cases, you may want to subcontract desserts to a professional pastry chef and arrange for just-in-time delivery to the home.

You should work with a knowledgeable wine merchant to match libations to menu items (and to your client's budget). Do the same with suppliers of gourmet cheese, meat, and other specialty items.

You may need a helper for food preparation, serving, and/or cleanup.

How to Get Started

Post flyers and ads in community centers, schools, and retail outlets. Place ads in newspapers and shopping guides.

You may be able to advertise your services at area gourmet food stores, butcher shops, and liquor stores; offer a commission or bonus for business they refer to you, and do some of your own shopping there. Ask friends, acquaintances, and satisfied customers to recommend your services; offer them a bonus or discount on future services in return for business they send your way.

Make contact with area party planners, chambers of commerce, and other groups whose members might be active in the local social scene.

You could teach a cooking course at a local community school for publicity and perhaps some clients.

Up-front Expenses

You'll need specialty pots, pans, and cooking utensils. For unusual dishes you may need specialty oven pans and serving platters. You may also need to purchase and maintain some basic and unusual ingredients.

You should build a library of cookbooks and reference books; a great deal of information is also available on the Internet.

Other costs include advertising and promotion.

How Much to Charge

There are two common ways to bill for your service for this sort of a job:

1. *A set charge* for each dish prepared, taking into account the amount of time required and the cost of ingredients. You'll need to adjust the price based on the number of guests you will be feeding.

2. *An hourly rate* for planning, preparing, cooking, serving, and cleaning up, plus an additional charge for the cost of ingredients and supplies. You should be able to purchase wine, gourmet ingredients, and other supplies at wholesale or discount prices and bill your customers at retail rates.

Additional expenses include delivery charges for special ingredients or equipment and an hourly charge for a helper for food preparation or serving.

Legal and Insurance Issues

Special notes: Your attorney should be able to advise you about any local health codes that might be involved and about any regulations on the resale of alcoholic beverages (it might be necessary to have the client deal directly with a liquor store).

① **Legal**
② **Legal**
③ **Legal**
④ **Accounting**
⑤ **Insurance**

Specialty Cake Baker

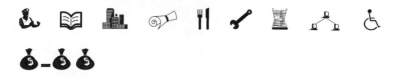

Description of Job

- Create custom edible works of dessert art for celebrations and special occasions.
- Produce unusual image cakes and theme designs.

The Need

We are almost all blessed or cursed with a sweet tooth, and there are few better ways to mark a special occasion than with a cake. However, there are cakes . . . and then there are very special cakes.

The specialty cake baker produces extraordinary cakes to the exact needs and wants of the client, customizing flavors, fillings, styles, shapes, and decoration.

A child may want a cake in the shape of his favorite superhero or her beloved pop star. You could score points with a serious sports fan by making a cake in the shape of a football stadium or a baseball diamond.

A corporate gathering could celebrate a sales meeting with a cake formed and decorated to look like its latest product launch.

A custom wedding cake could include decorations and elements that make reference to the story of the bride and groom.

One of the newest touches in cake decorating is the *image cake,* which uses a computer-scanned photo or a digital image to control a special printer that applies food coloring to icing to re-create a picture on a cake. Similar effects can be created freehand by a capable painter using edible inks.

Challenges

The primary skill is the ability to bake a cake and decorate it with an artistic touch. You'll need to fully communicate with clients about how much chocolate is needed to satisfy a chocoholic, how much carrot goes into a proper carrot cake, and the exact specifications for frosting and decorations.

You'll also need to become an expert on state and local health codes related to the preparation, sale, and delivery of food. In some localities you need a license for commercial sale of food and may have to follow strict regulations about cleanliness, supplies, and storage of finished goods.

Depending on the regulations, you may be able to perform baking in your own home or you may have to create a separate area; you may be able to use your personal utensils and other equipment or you may need to segregate them from items used for commercial work.

You'll also need to know about food allergies (peanuts are a somewhat common problem, and some clients may insist on food prepared without whole eggs, wheat, or certain other ingredients); and you'll need to understand state and federal definitions of *low fat* and other terms that may impact your business.

Be very specific about the size and dimensions of your cake, and give precise and reasonable estimates of serving portions. If you say your cake will serve 20, it is not your problem if 40 show up with plate in hand.

Know the Territory

You can't become a specialty baker without having spent more than a little time in front of an oven. Develop a collection of tried-and-proven recipes (and know how to scale them up or down for different sizes of groups).

Special shapes for cakes can be accomplished by using shaped baking tins or by carefully sculpting sheet cakes.

Image cakes can be created using freehand artistic skills or with the aid of some high-tech equipment. For freehand work, you can use an overhead projector or a slide projector to display a photo or drawing on a plain frosted background; special airbrush equipment can spray food coloring onto the surface.

The high-tech solution is to use a computer scanner to copy a photo or image into a digital file, or to directly import a digital photograph. The resulting file can be edited using a digital image program such as Adobe Photoshop. Once the file has been prepared and sized to fit the cake, you can use special edible inks and an ink-jet printer to apply the image to a thin, edible carrier sheet that can then be put on an iced surface.

Finished cakes can be picked up by a customer or frozen and packed with dry ice for shipment anywhere in the country. (Again, you'll have to follow regulations about preparation and shipping of foodstuffs.) Frozen cakes are usually shipped in insulated coolers for overnight delivery; products shipped in this way can be sent to homes or businesses, but some carriers do not deliver to post office boxes or overseas locations.

How to Get Started

Start locally by advertising your services on bulletin boards at community centers and schools. Place ads in newspapers and shopping guides.

Make contact with area party planners and caterers. Offer a commission for jobs they send your way.

Ask satisfied customers to recommend you to their friends and acquaintances; offer a discount or bonus for business they refer to you.

Rent a table at wedding and holiday shows to display photos and actual examples of some of your work. Consider offering a "sample day" where, by appointment, customers can try some of your cakes.

Up-front Expenses

To begin, you'll need a commercial or high-quality consumer oven plus mixing bowls, baking pans, pastry bags for filling, icing tools, and other utensils. You'll need to invest in basic ingredients and store them properly.

For formal cakes, you'll need elegant presentation platters and cake plates.

To create image cakes, you can choose to draw pictures freehand using a food-grade airbrush system with food coloring. The high-tech solution requires a computer and scanner to create digital files from photographs or an Internet connection capable of accepting digital images sent directly by customers; you'll also need image-editing software such as Adobe Photoshop. Finally, you'll need an ink-jet printer, a supply of edible food color ink, and special edible transfer sheets that can be laid on top of an iced cake.

Ink-jet printers range in price from about $150 to $350; ink and edible frosting sheets cost about $2 to $4 per cake.

You will also need delivery boxes for local customers and shipping containers and access to packaged dry ice for cakes that will be sent by air freight.

How Much to Charge

In most situations you can set a fixed price for creating specific types of cakes at particular sizes. Add a fee for special icing or decorations and/or for special ingredients such as costly marzipan, fudge, or liqueur.

For local customers you can include charges for slicing the cake and renting display dishes and utensils. For customers out of your area, add to the price charges for packaging, dry ice, and shipping.

Prices for custom cakes deserve to be somewhat higher than for off-the-shelf offerings from commercial bakeries or out-of-the-box cakes from supermarkets. However, keep in mind all these competing prices your customers will find if they shop around.

Typical prices for customized sheet cakes start at about $20 to $25; image cakes typically cost about twice as much. Fancy multilayer cakes can rise in price to hundreds of dollars.

Legal and Insurance Issues

Special notes: Make sure you are aware of any legal requirements in your area regarding the preparation of food.

An insurance agent can offer counsel about commercial insurance or riders to your homeowner's policies to cover business use of your kitchen (providing such use is permitted in your locality).

① **Legal**
② **Legal**
③ **Legal**
④ **Accounting**
⑤ **Insurance**

Prepared Custom-Meal Service

Description of Job

- Prepare custom meals for clients, either refrigerated or frozen for future use.
- Provide meals to meet specific medical or dietary needs.

The Need

We all like to eat, but not all of us have the time or the talent to cook full meals every night. Many solve this dilemma by purchasing expensive restaurant meals, fatty and otherwise unhealthy fast food, or pricey and less-than-satisfactory mass-produced frozen food.

Another solution, though, is for busy people to hire a custom chef to stock their freezer with a week's worth of meals created to meet their tastes and needs. A custom chef may also be asked to produce meals that meet specific medical or dietary needs, including low-fat, low-calorie, low-carbohydrate, low-sodium, high-protein, gluten-free, and vegetarian menus.

Here's the enticing pitch: Every day when you come home from work, or when older kids come home from school, there's a delicious meal—chosen from a menu of offerings—waiting in the freezer or the refrigerator. If you're on a diet, it will be that much easier to keep on the straight and narrow because the meal has been prepared to your specifications by a professional chef.

In most cases, the custom meal service delivers several days' or a week's worth of food at one time. The food is labeled and instructions are provided for reheating.

Challenges

You'll need to be a good cook and to be able to work within the bounds set by your client. It will be important to take note of allergies and strong preferences. For example, people who are allergic to peanuts can react to food prepared anywhere near nuts or with peanut-based oils; vegetarians won't want meat products used in the preparation of their food and may not want you to use pots and pans that have contained meat products for other clients.

In some areas, you may have to follow local or state health codes and food preparation and storage regulations.

Don't take on jobs to provide highly specialized foods, such as kosher dishes, unless you fully understand the strict conditions involved.

You will likely need to deliver food to your customers (or arrange for others to do so) and must meet their schedules. In some arrangements, food preparers may be given a key to the house to stock the freezer; another arrangement is to place a large freezer in a garage or basement and give access just to that area.

Know the Territory

You'll need to be a good cook, but equally important is the ability to cook to the exact needs of your client. You are, in effect, cooking for an audience of one or two or a small family.

You will also need to fully understand the intricacies of diets. If a client is on a strict medical diet, ask to meet with a dietitian or nurse to discuss needs. For other diets, ask the client to provide books and information about its requirements.

Meet with your clients initially to go over their diet and preferences; they may provide specific recipes or leave that up to you. Once you've delivered a few meals, you can check with clients to adjust the style or ingredients to meet their preferences.

How to Get Started

Meet with area dieticians, nurse's aides, and other health care providers and make them aware of your availability. Be prepared to offer references.

Post flyers and ads at community centers, schools, and supermarkets. Place ads in newspapers and shopping guides.

Ask friends and acquaintances to spread the word about your business; offer a commission or bonus for business they bring your way. Do the same with satisfied customers, giving them a discount or a free meal for new business.

Up-front Expenses

You will need a suitable, reliable oven; proper utensils, pots, and pans for food preparation; and appropriate storage and delivery containers. You can purchase one-time-use containers that can be reheated in a conventional oven or a microwave.

A great deal of information is available on the Internet, and you should build up a library of cookbooks and reference books. You'll also need a supply of basic ingredients, spices, and flavorings.

Other expenses include advertising and promotion.

How Much to Charge

One way to charge for this sort of service is to create price bands (ranges) based on the cost of ingredients and the amount of time required to prepare a particular dish. Within each band, adjust the price based on the number of portions ordered.

For example, band A might include basic, relatively inexpensive meals like lasagna, casseroles, and stews. Band B meals might feature meatloaf, steak tips, turkey, and chicken dishes. Luxury band C would include roasts, fresh fish, shrimp, and expensive cuts of meat.

You can add a charge for delivery, or work it into the price. Consider offering a discount for steady customers.

Legal and Insurance Issues

Special notes: Make sure you are aware of any legal requirements in your area regarding the preparation of food.

An insurance agent can offer counsel about commercial insurance or riders to your homeowner's policies to cover business use of your kitchen (if such use is permitted in your locality).

① **Legal**

② **Legal**

③ **Legal**

④ **Accounting**

⑤ **Insurance**

Freelance Bartender

Description of Job

- Tend bar at private parties and functions.
- Work with setup and cleanup crews at large parties.

The Need

At a simple gathering of half a dozen close friends, you can go into the kitchen and take a beer from the refrigerator or pour your own drink from a setup on the countertop. For larger parties or more formal affairs, hiring a professional bartender is a nice touch.

Here's one compelling sales pitch: Let the hosts be guests at their own party.

Challenges

You mix a mean margarita, and your Singapore sling is practically world famous. That's half the job. Are you also able to play the role of the sociable bartender among strangers?

Know the Territory

This job requires some specific knowledge; there are numerous books of recipes for mixed drinks that can help you prepare. If you are going to be asked to pour wine, learn enough about the varieties and vintages the host will be offering to be able to describe them to guests.

Not everybody throws large parties, and not every neighborhood supports formal gatherings in the home. This sort of job is more likely to be needed in affluent or professional communities.

When you meet with clients, you need to be absolutely clear about the services you will provide—and those you will not. You should be firm in your intent to follow liquor laws; refuse service to underage guests; limit service to guests who drink too much.

Your contract agreement should be specific about hours and services and include a release from liability for incidents related to alcohol served at the party.

The host should supply the beer, wine, and alcohol for the bar, and there should not be a charge to guests for service; state and local laws may require a license if you are involved in the resale of alcohol. (Consult your state alcohol licensing agency or a civil attorney for details about necessary permits or licenses if you want to get involved in resale.)

Your agreement should also specify the supplies you'll need for the party: glasses, utensils, ice buckets, ice, sodas and mixers, napkins, and cleanup necessities. You may want to work with a party supply company to rent glassware; make certain that responsibility for any breakage passes through you to the host.

Your role may be limited to working at the bar, or you may be asked to be a member of a setup or cleanup crew.

Determine the host's expectations for your attire; should you wear your brightest Hawaiian shirt, or rent a tuxedo?

During the party, remember that you are working; you are not a guest. Don't sample the alcohol at the bar, and keep your involvement with guests on a professional level.

How to Get Started

Advertise your availability to professional party planners and caterers.

Post flyers at liquor stores and on community bulletin boards.

Ask friends and acquaintances for referrals.

Up-front Expenses

You'll need a few basic recipe books for exotic drinks, and perhaps a reference guide to wine.

You should keep on hand a neat outfit of black pants or skirt and a white shirt as a basic wardrobe for the job; if the contract specifies a tuxedo or special uniform, you can purchase or rent the outfit.

How Much to Charge

This sort of job is paid on an hourly basis; be sure to include setup and breakdown time in your price. If you are asked to wear a special uniform or a tuxedo, you can add a charge to cover your costs, including cleaning expenses.

If you are asked to contract with a party supply company for glassware or to provide a cleanup or serving crew, you should add a charge for your time spent to obtain these outside services.

Offer references from hosts who have employed you in the past.

Legal and Insurance Issues

Special notes: The host should release you from responsibility or indemnify you in the case of lawsuit if a guest is injured or causes injury or damage as a result of intoxication.

① **Legal**

② **Legal**

③ **Legal**

④ **Accounting**

⑤ **Insurance**

Entertainer

Description of Job

- Put on shows at nightclubs, coffeehouses, and other public venues.
- Perform at parties and private functions.

The Need

Here's your chance to showcase your talent—and earn some money—as a singer, comedian, juggler, musician, magician, or dancer.

Although performing at the halftime of the Super Bowl or exhibiting your talents as the latest television idol are worthy goals, there are a lot more jobs for entertainers at private parties, conventions, fund-raisers, weddings, municipal celebrations, and business functions.

Challenges

The biggest challenge for a performer is to keep it professional.

Present yourself honestly to prospective clients, and be sure you understand their expectations, even as they appreciate your demonstrated abilities.

Be very specific about your act, including length of the show and its content; you don't want to talk dirty at a church function and you don't want to sing children's songs at a retirement party.

For musical acts, define the specifics, including the number of sets and break times. Indicate the need for any special equipment, including amplifiers, microphones, and spotlights, and spell out who is to provide them. In general, musicians acts are responsible for bringing their own instruments. If a piano is available on location, make certain it is of acceptable quality and has been properly maintained.

In some circumstances, you may find that unionized workers at hotels, convention centers, and businesses are guaranteed certain jobs, including setup, operations, and cleanup. Your client should handle all of the negotiations and costs for such workers, specifying that in your contract.

Know the Territory

Private parties can be held anywhere; the best way to get jobs is to spread the word before, during, and after any gigs you land. We have been to parties where the hired band passed out flyers and business cards to guests.

To get a corporate job, of course, you'll have to have big businesses in your area. The same goes for convention centers and hotel functions.

Does your town have an annual celebration or an upcoming historical celebration?

How to Get Started

For private parties, post flyers in community centers, churches, and recreational centers. Place ads in community newspapers. Ask friends and relatives to spread the word.

For professional gigs, contact bars, nightclubs, and lounges in your area and ask if they book talent.

Seek out facility and booking managers at convention centers and banquet halls; many large hotels also have convention facilities. Send letters and proposals to the marketing and human resources departments of large employers, offering entertainment for office parties, holiday celebrations, and sales campaigns.

Prepare videotapes, audiotapes, and other supporting materials as a portfolio of your work. Offer copies of references and testimonials from previous clients. Be prepared to audition for jobs. You can also invite prospective employers to attend a show you give elsewhere; be sure to obtain permission to bring a visitor.

Up-front Expenses

Costs include advertising and promotion.

Your contract should specify any setup you expect the client to provide—a stage, a stool or chair, spotlights, and the like. In most cases, you will have to provide your own musical equipment; some locations have amplifiers and speakers, but you can't count on that—and if the client promises to provide them, you should check out the quality beforehand to make sure it is acceptable.

You will probably have to transport equipment to the location.

How Much to Charge

Most entertainment jobs are paid a flat rate, taking into account the number of entertainers and the hours they will be performing.

Some gigs at lounges and bars may promise payment as a percentage of the house's receipts—as a portion of admission charges, bar sales, or both. You may want to include in your contract the right to examine the books or to have a representative do so.

Legal and Insurance Issues

① **Legal**

② **Legal**

③ **Legal**

④ **Accounting**

⑤ **Insurance**

Holiday Decoration Service

Description of Job

- Plan outdoor holiday decorations in consultation with clients.
- Set up lights and displays; purchase and repair elements as needed.
- Remove holiday decorations and store them according to client's instructions.

The Need

For some people, the year revolves around Christmas. These people light their houses brighter than O'Hare Airport, install more plastic elves and reindeer than Macy's, and buy garlands by the truckload.

Anyone responsible for the setup of a spectacular, complex outdoor display knows that it takes a tremendous amount of time and effort to do it right. Then come January, it all has to be taken down and put away until the next season.

A holiday decoration service offers the expertise, time, and equipment to help busy people create, set up, and maintain a holiday display.

Challenges

You'll need to know more than a little about architecture, engineering, wood-working, and electrical devices. Not that you'll have to build a house, design systems, or make changes to the wiring layout, but you will be standing on stepladders, stringing wires, and plugging electrical components into mains.

Outdoor wiring needs to be of better construction than cheaper indoor sets, and you'll need to be aware of wattage loads and ground fault interrupters. You may need to construct frames for lighting and displays, or hang them from elements of the home.

This job is obviously tied to the holiday season. Setup may begin around Thanksgiving, and dismantling may be requested just after New Year's Day. In addition to the economic impact of a short season, you may have to deal with cold weather and snow in many parts of the country.

Know the Territory

Spend the time to become familiar with electrical circuits. You'll also need to learn about ways to protect outdoor wiring from the effects of rain, snow, and cold weather; outdoor outlets need to be properly grounded, and wiring must be protected from the elements.

The laws of physics limit acceptable loads on electrical circuits; extension cords are rated for a specified wattage that decreases as their length increases.

In most cases you will be responsible for maintaining the display while it is in service.

Some localities may have laws or regulations limiting the brightness of outdoor displays or prohibiting sound systems. Some neighborhoods may have regulations limiting displays to cut down on traffic.

How to Get Started

Post flyers and ads in community centers, home supply stores, and retail stores. Place ads in newspapers and shopping guides, especially in special preholiday advertising sections.

Contact stores that specialize in sales of Christmas decorations; they may be willing to post flyers for your services or recommend you to customers seeking this sort of assistance. Do the same with specialty Christmas shops; offer to purchase supplies there, to pay a bonus or commission, or both.

Contact area businesses that hang holiday decorations and offer your services.

Ask friends and acquaintances to recommend you; in exchange, offer a bonus or discount on future services. Do the same with satisfied customers.

Up-front Expenses

You'll need a basic tool kit with a hammer, screwdrivers, and various hangers. For electrical devices, a continuity tester and ground fault tester will be valuable. You'll also need one or more ladders and a vehicle to carry your equipment.

Create a portfolio of pictures, digital images, and videos of work you have performed for other clients.

Other expenses include advertising and promotion.

How Much to Charge

Charge by the hour for your labor, plus the cost of lights and any other devices you purchase; you should be able to buy materials at wholesale or discounted prices and resell them at retail prices.

Another way to bill is on a cost-plus basis. Compute the hours of work, the actual cost of materials purchased, and a preagreed percentage of profit.

Legal and Insurance Issues

① **Legal**

② **Legal**

③ **Legal**

④ **Accounting**

⑤ **Insurance**

Personal Services

45 Personal Shopper

46 Personalized Gift Basket Maker

47 Travel Planner

48 Historical Tours

49 Personal Fitness Trainer

50 Sports Trainer

Personal Shopper

Description of Job

- Provide special expertise in shopping for unusual items.
- Assist clients who are not able to shop for themselves because of disability or illness.
- Research and purchase gifts for business clients to present on special occasions.

The Need

There are only 24 hours in each day. Subtract a full day of work, getting the kids off to school and back home, making dinner, and, if you're lucky, eight hours of sleep, and there's not much time left over for shopping.

Senior citizens and people with physical infirmities may not be able to get out of their homes to shop for food, necessities, and gifts.

Businesses purchase gifts for clients and to honor employees for significant personal milestones.

Then there are those people whose vision of the levels of hell include one specifically devoted to being trapped in a shopping mall.

The personal shopper gets to know the client and the market, and efficiently shops for (and often delivers) items ranging from groceries to furniture, appliances, and supplies.

Challenges

The personal shopper puts the emphasis on the *personal,* promising a sharp focus on the client's needs and careful shopping to fulfill them. You will not succeed if you deliver the wrong items at the wrong price.

Make sure you fully understand the needs and wants of your client. If you are asked to go to The Gap and buy a pair of size 8 cropped jeans, you can't substitute relaxed-fit khakis from Wal-Mart.

On the other hand, if you are asked to research and find the highest-quality set of kitchen knives, your client may ask you to present a list of recommendations with prices.

A third option would be for a client to give you a general description of a type of product and ask you to use your judgment in finding it and buying it without further consultation.

Wear appropriate clothing for the stores in which you shop, and act professionally in all of your dealings, since you are representing someone else.

In some situations, you may be given a key to a house and asked to deliver groceries and place them appropriately in the refrigerator, freezer, or cupboard.

You will be in competition with shopping sites on the Internet, although not everyone feels comfortable (or has the time) for that exercise, and again, your pitch should emphasize the personal attention you will deliver.

Know the Territory

You're probably interested in this sort of job because you consider yourself to be a good shopper for yourself. However, make sure you don't limit yourself solely to stores that meet *your* needs; you should spend the time to learn about retail outlets, grocery stores, and specialty shops in your area. You should also become familiar with shopping on the Internet and by mail order.

This sort of assistance is most likely to be popular in areas with professionals who do not have the time to shop for themselves or in localities with many senior citizens who are unable to get out on their own.

How to Get Started

Advertise your availability in community and senior citizen centers. Place ads in area newspapers and shopping guides.

Ask friends and relatives to spread the word, and offer satisfied customers a bonus if they refer new clients to you.

Send letters of introduction to the human resources departments of major employers in your area, offering to shop for gifts for employees and customers of the company.

Up-front Expenses

The primary expenses here are for advertising and promotion. You should have access to the Internet for research, shopping, and promotion.

How Much to Charge

The simplest and most transparent way to charge for this sort of service is to levy an hourly charge plus the actual cost of purchases; keep copies of all receipts and maintain accurate records of your time. If you use your vehicle for shopping, add a mileage charge to the bill.

Legal and Insurance Issues

① **Legal**

② **Legal**

③ **Legal**

④ **Accounting**

⑤ **Insurance**

Personalized Gift Basket Maker

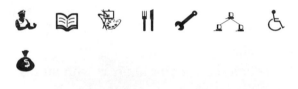

Description of Job

- Create customized gifts for friends and family of your clients.
- Work with corporate marketing departments to produce and deliver customized gifts and promotional items for their customers.

The Need

We give gifts for many reasons—out of love, appreciation, thanks, and self-promotion, and just as no two people are exactly the same, it is extremely difficult to find the perfect gift on the shelf of a store.

Personal gift baskets can be assembled for many occasions:

- Holiday greetings
- Birthday, wedding, anniversary, childbirth
- Thanks for a favor
- Welcome, housewarming
- Congratulations on graduation, engagement, promotion

Businesses, too, may want gift baskets for a variety of reasons:

- To promote a new product or service
- To congratulate an employee on a business accomplishment
- To congratulate an employee on a personal event

The professional gift basket maker sells knowledge of the market, expertise in assembling a customized collection of items, and packaging and delivery skills.

Challenges

The keys to success in this job are a combination of creativity, detective work, and knowledge of the market.

Most basket makers start by developing a set of generic baskets that can be customized, then move on from there to totally custom jobs that involve extra time and expense.

You'll need to find a reliable source of products to include in the basket and establish a wholesale or discount relationship with the supplier. This will allow you to resell your baskets for a price that includes a markup to retail prices.

Know the Territory

For generic baskets, spend the time to think about local products, local traditions, and local sensibilities. In New England, most people are infatuated with the Boston Red Sox, and a baseball-themed basket is sure to be a hit. In the South, a NASCAR basket would likely have more appeal.

Other common offerings include chocoholic collections, barbecue fixings, coffee or tea, packaged cheeses, desktop doodads and toys, stuffed animals, and holiday-themed assemblages. Dog lovers may be thrilled with a basket of toys and treats for their best friend; puzzle fans will be happy to receive crossword books, logic games, and the like.

Clients are generally invited to request small adjustments to the contents of generic baskets—substituting dark chocolate for milk chocolate, for example, or picking a particular sports team.

Most gift basket makers also offer customized consultation at a higher price. Here you will meet with the client or consult on the telephone to find out details about the interests of the recipient and the reasons for the gift.

Is the recipient a sports fan? A lover of opera or rock and roll? Is the person deeply involved in community affairs or historical projects? Any details should lead a creative mind to the proper collection of gifts.

For corporate gifts, make sure you are aware of any company guidelines that might steer you away from baskets with religious, political, or overly personal themes. If you are being asked to assemble baskets to support a new product or service, learn as much as you can about the introduction and see if it is possible to include a sample of the product or a clever gift that ties into the new offering. (For example, we received a gift basket from a theme park announcing a new water ride. Included was a beach towel, a tube of sunscreen, a pair of sunglasses . . . and a media kit.)

Make certain you know the client's budget for gifts and the deadline for delivery.

How to Get Started

Place flyers in community centers; advertise in shopping guides and newspapers. Establish a relationship with gift shops, gourmet food stores, and other locations where you might shop for supplies, and ask them to post your flyer or business card; in return you could promise to buy some of their products when appropriate. Ask friends and relatives to spread the word.

This sort of business does not necessarily have to be limited to your local area. It would work well in conjunction with a web site. Visitors could send you e-mails or call you to discuss jobs, or you could request that they send you a phone number where you could call them. For web site sales, you would probably need to establish a credit card merchant account.

Up-front Expenses

The principal up-front expenses are (1) researching stores and web sites for available products and (2) the cost of advertising. If you choose to set up a web site, you'll need to arrange for hosting and a credit card merchant account.

Very little in the way of inventory would be needed, although you may want to set up some sample baskets and photograph them to display on your web site or in an album you show to customers.

How Much to Charge

Generic baskets would be sold at a fixed price plus the cost of shipping or delivery. You should make arrangements to purchase products at wholesale or discounted prices whenever possible, marking them up to retail price as part of your profit.

If you are called on to custom-design a basket for an individual or a corporate client, you can charge on a cost-plus basis (the cost of the elements in the basket plus an agreed-on fee or percentage), or you can bill at an hourly rate.

Legal and Insurance Issues

Special notes: Shipping alcohol, including beer, wine, and hard liquor, can be very complex and may require state licenses and observance of federal laws. For simplicity's sake, we'd recommend starting with other products. If you feel it necessary to offer alcohol, consult an attorney for advice.

① **Legal**

② **Legal**

③ **Legal**

④ **Accounting**

⑤ **Insurance**

Travel Planner

Description of Job

- Research and design a vacation trip based on the wants and needs of a client.
- Work with travel suppliers to put together the best-priced package for your client.

The Need

A good travel agent—someone who gets to know you and your interests and is an expert on travel and destinations—is hard to find. Always keep in mind how traditional travel agents earn a living: They are paid commissions by travel providers. The higher the price tag on the package they sell, the more they receive in commissions and perks (such as free trips for themselves).

We're not saying that travel agents are dishonest, that they don't provide a valuable service, or that they don't deserve to earn a living for their investment of time. It's just that they may not always deliver the best deals.

By contrast, a travel planner works directly for the customer and is paid by the hour for research and expertise. One reason this sort of business is viable is the tremendous amount of information available over the Internet. Travel planners can shop for the best airfare, car rental, hotel or cruise accommodations, and every other element of a trip through Internet web sites, easily comparing offerings of different providers.

The travel planner can also produce customized itineraries with information about museums, attractions, and restaurants for each day of a trip.

Challenges

This is a job tailor-made for someone who is capable of focusing on the hundreds of little details involved in a trip. You must also be comfortable using Internet search engines and travel portals.

You'll also need to spend the time to get to know your clients well. Find out their interests and experience in travel. Determine if they require five-star hotels or would be perfectly happy with clean, safe, inexpensive bed-and-breakfasts.

Find out your client's budget for the trip. As a travel planner, you have no incentive to boost the cost of the trip to increase your commission; however, you might want to present your client with several alternatives at different price points.

Know the Territory

It certainly helps if you are an experienced traveler yourself. You'll need to keep current by reading travel guidebooks and magazines and searching Internet web sites regularly.

Learn how to use travel portals like Expedia.com, Travelocity.com, and Priceline.com. You can conduct research without actually booking tickets on any of these sites.

You should also keep current on terrorism and health warnings posted for certain parts of the world.

How to Get Started

Announce your services on bulletin boards in community centers and schools. Advertise in newspapers and shopping guides. Ask your friends and relatives to spread the word; offer a bonus to satisfied customers who refer new clients to you.

Up-front Expenses

The principal expenses are for advertising and promotion, plus setting up a computer with access to the Internet. You should also purchase a library of guidebooks and maps.

Investigate purchasing computer software that allows you to print out detailed driving instructions and maps for day-to-day itineraries.

How Much to Charge

Charge by the hour, and add in the documented cost of related phone calls and guidebooks or maps.

Planning a trip may require 6 to 10 hours and include a visit to your client's home for an initial session plus a final visit to present the options.

Legal and Insurance Issues

    ① **Legal**

    ② **Legal**

    ③ **Legal**

    ④ **Accounting**

    ⑤ **Insurance**

Historical Tours

Description of Job

- Research historical, cultural, or entertainment history of a district or town and design a tour.
- Write an informative and entertaining spiel.
- Promote and conduct excursions highlighting history and significant events

The Need

Hundreds of locations in the United States and elsewhere have the magic combination of an interesting past . . . and a steady supply of tourists.

Historical tours on foot are very easy to set up and run; tours by van or bus require greater up-front expenditures and complexity. The tours can be lectures about local history, or they can be attached to a theme: Haunted Graveyards of Tarrytown; Federal Architecture in Washington, or Walking in the Steps of Herman Melville in New Bedford.

Tourist magnets like Boston, Philadelphia, New York, and Washington, D.C., are obvious markets for this sort of enterprise, although many well-established tours already exist in those areas. (If you have an especially creative idea, you still may be able to find a niche.)

Many other markets that draw lots of visitors remain relatively untouched, such as Nantucket, Miami Beach, Richmond, Atlanta, Cincinnati, Los Angeles, and San Francisco.

Your audience will primarily consist of visitors, including people who have traveled from distant corners of the United States and from other countries, but a well-done tour can also draw local residents who want to know more about their own backyard.

Challenges

In urban settings, the most intimate way to bring your story to life is a walking tour. Make sure the people in your group are aware of what is expected of them physically. Your advertising should indicate the approximate length of the tour in time and distance, the existence of significant hills, and other details such as uneven pavement. Can someone negotiate the entire trip in a wheelchair?

Another way to conduct a tour is to use a small van or a tour bus. Be aware that this adds a great deal of expense and complexity to your operation; you'll need to buy or lease a vehicle, obtain a commercial license, and sign up for commercial liability insurance. You'll also need a place to park the vehicle before, during, and after the tour. (One way to reduce the complexity is to work with an existing bus or limousine company that can provide equipment and driver.)

Know the Territory

Any tour begins with thorough research. Consult local historical societies, libraries, and knowledgeable old-timers for information. Seek second and third sources for any stories or facts you might seek.

Don't embellish stories to make them more dramatic, and make sure you have your facts straight; you don't want to be tripped up by a client who knows the story better than you do. If your account includes elements that may be legends or otherwise unprovable, say so; that might make your tour even more interesting.

Take special care to avoid plagiarizing someone else's work; no one can own a copyright on facts and events, but they can protect their own expression of story in print, a movie or video, or other form of publication. You might be able to receive permission to use material researched by others; if so, be sure to obtain written permission.

Any good teacher also has to have some acting ability. Some tour guides dress up as someone from the past or assume some of that person's characteristics. You might conduct nighttime tours by lantern. Some guides arrange for accomplices to appear at particular locations along the way.

Look for ways to expand your offerings and times to allow you to conduct several tours a day, or prepare a full week's lineup. You may be able to sell packages that include several tours.

Part of your research will include information about seasonal trends among visitors. Is your locality most popular in the summer, with few visitors in the winter? Does the mix of visitors change with the season? Are senior citizens (who may be good customers, albeit with special needs) more common in the spring and fall? Are families with young children more plentiful in the summer?

How to Get Started

Advertise your tours at convention centers, visitor's bureaus, tourist offices, and hotels and guesthouses. Distribute special discount cards and flyers around town, with numeric codes for different locations, which will allow you to pay commissions to business owners or hotel concierges who steer visitors your way.

Place ads in local newspapers aimed at tourists.

In addition, don't forget that your tours advertise themselves; if people who are not part of the tour seem interested in what you're saying, give them a card inviting them to come along another time.

Up-front Expenses

Expenses include research books and materials, costumes, and props. You might want to purchase a small battery-operated amplifier to increase the volume of your voice.

Other expenses include advertising.

How Much to Charge

Price tours at a fixed rate, and offer discounts for children and senior citizens. (If the tour is not appropriate for youngsters, make sure that is clear ahead of time.) You might offer a discount to visitors who sign up for more than one tour and a reduced rate for organized groups that book more than 8 or 10 tickets at a time.

Decide on your policy if just a couple of people show up for a tour instead of the usual 15 or 20; in general, it is best to go ahead with the tour rather than risk endangering your reputation. You will also need to set refund policies regarding cancellations or abbreviated tours due to rain, snow, or extremes of temperature.

Legal and Insurance Issues

Special notes: If you will be using a van or bus on the tour, consult an insurance agent to make sure you are properly covered for liability. The vehicle will most likely require commercial plates, and you may need a special driver's license and insurance policy to transport people in a commercial operation.

In some localities, tour guides must apply for a license.

① **Legal**

② **Legal**

③ **Legal**

④ **Accounting**

⑤ **Insurance**

Personal Fitness Trainer

Description of Job

- Develop a customized workout schedule for your client to improve cardio-vascular health and strength.
- Help clients improve technical skills for golf, tennis, and other sports.
- Assist a client in an exercise-based weight loss program.

The Need

Why would people hire a stranger to stand over them with a verbal whip, pushing them to get into shape and stay that way?

First of all, because many of us need a whole lot of motivation to work out regularly. A personal trainer provides structure and a schedule; the workouts themselves will follow a plan based on efficiency of time and effectiveness.

Second, a well-prepared trainer will personalize a training program to take into account a client's specific needs as well as any health conditions and injuries.

Perhaps most important, a properly educated personal trainer is capable of monitoring clients' medical conditions as they perform their workouts.

Challenges

Your success as a personal trainer may depend more on your personality and communication skills than on your technical skills and background. Clients will want to feel comfortable with you in the somewhat intimate setting of a workout.

If you will be working with clients in their homes, you should offer suggestions on equipment, but be prepared to work with whatever they have available.

You will be in competition with health clubs, gyms, television workouts, and videotapes. Your response should be to emphasize your highly customized service.

Although trainers should not offer medical advice or take on any of the roles that should be done by a nurse or doctor, you should be able to offer certain limited emergency assistance and be ready to contact a doctor or ambulance if necessary.

Know the Territory

A personal trainer is a bit of a luxury, perhaps not as much as a personal cook or chauffeur but nevertheless a service more likely to be in demand among people with above-average discretionary income.

Make a survey of available health clubs, gyms, and community centers to find out about their programs. Look for ways to present custom programs that are complementary to their offerings.

Some health clubs may allow you to work with a client at their facility; they may charge you a fee or ask for a percentage of your earnings. The advantage of such an arrangement includes access to a wider range of equipment than you might find at the home of your client or at your own studio.

An appropriate background for a trainer includes education or experience in physiology, athletic training, health sciences, or similar fields. Although there is no requirement that a personal trainer have a license or any professional certification, you should explore possible affiliation with one of a number of national organizations.

How to Get Started

Advertise your availability in community centers, stores, and schools. Some health and athletics clubs may allow you to post flyers or business cards in their facilities. Place ads in newspapers and shopping guides.

Ask satisfied clients to refer you to others; offer a discount or bonus for new business they bring you.

Up-front Expenses

Most personal fitness trainers do their work in the homes or health clubs of their clients and do not need to set up a studio of their own.

Start-up costs include books and research materials about general training and specific sports, plus the expenses of advertising and promotion.

How Much to Charge

Trainers charge by the hour. If there is more than one person in the group, you should adjust your rates to take that into account.

Legal and Insurance Issues

Special notes: An attorney may recommend that you have clients disclose any health conditions and remove liability for those problems. Some trainers may ask clients to provide a letter from a physician clearing them for fitness training.

① **Legal**

② **Legal**

③ **Legal**

④ **Accounting**

⑤ **Insurance**

Sports Trainer

Description of Job

- Provide personal coaching and instruction to a youngster with major-league dreams.
- Serve as a personal pro to an adult who wants to take his or her game to the next level.

The Need

Sports and athletic competition are an intrinsic part of our society, and few of us will deny the wish to reduce our handicap, improve our average, or step up our skiing skills from blue square to black diamond.

In addition, youngsters may be able to cash in on a high school sports career with a college scholarship by elevating their game skills a notch or two.

Enter the personal trainer, who provides instruction and coaching on specific sports and skills and helps you avoid injuries or work through them.

Challenges

The main qualification is not necessarily the ability to hit a major-league fastball, to drive a golf ball like Tiger Woods, or to smash a serve like Venus Williams. Instead it is the ability to teach people how to make the most of their talent.

It is also important to understand the mental side of the games we play. Your students have to be able to withstand the pressures and challenges of big games.

You'll need to understand the demands put on our bodies by sports and athletics and to work with doctors and physical therapists to help your clients get the most out of themselves while staying healthy.

Sports trainers must be careful not to offer medical care or therapies beyond their experience and background. However, they should be able to work with doctors and therapists; they should be prepared to provide emergency CPR and stabilization of injuries and to work with ambulance crews when necessary.

Know the Territory

Necessary proficiencies include the specific skills of sports such as baseball, soccer, football, tennis, golf, swimming, diving, skiing, and track and field. You'll also need training in the prevention of sports injuries and management of warm-ups, stretching, cooldowns, and general cardiovascular exercise. Most sports trainers also provide massage and manipulation as part of physical therapy regimes, or work in conjunction with therapists.

You may want to—or need to—show credentials such as certification from a national or regional accrediting group (such as the Professional Golf Association). You should also offer your qualifications and references for other sports.

Depending on the sport, you may work with clients at their homes or at athletic facilities, including gyms, health clubs, batting cages, swimming pools, skating rinks, golf courses and driving ranges, tennis courts, and ski hills. If you will be instructing or coaching a client at a commercial facility, you may need to make arrangements with the management, which may levy charges or require a percentage of your fees.

How to Get Started

Advertise your availability through community bulletin boards, at high schools and grade schools, and in newsletters. Make yourself known to coaches and organizers of sports leagues and facilities, and contact summer day camp directors.

Place ads in school newspapers, community newspapers, and shopping guides. Post flyers and ads at sporting goods stores.

You can also promote yourself by offering clinics for groups of players.

Up-front Expenses

Build up a library of reference books about sports and athletic training. You'll need your own sports equipment if you will be accompanying your clients to golf courses, tennis courts, ski hills, and the like.

Other expenses include advertising and promotion.

How Much to Charge

Bill for your services on an hourly basis, plus the cost of any greens fees, lift tickets, or admission tickets for sports or athletic facilities.

Legal and Insurance Issues

Special notes: An attorney may recommend that you have clients disclose any health conditions and remove liability for those problems. Some trainers may ask clients to provide a letter from a physician clearing them for fitness training.

① **Legal**

② **Legal**

③ **Legal**

④ **Accounting**

⑤ **Insurance**

Children, Family, and Pet Services

51 Babysitting

52 Babysitting Agency

53 Children's Night Out

54 Vacation Child Care

55 Dog Walking and Vacation Pet Visits

56 Pet Sitter and Doggie Day Care

57 Elder Companion

58 Elder Care Consultant

59 Genealogical Research

60 Family Biographer

Babysitting

Description of Job

- Provide scheduled care for a child, or a small number of children, for a set period of time in the home of the client.
- Accept limited responsibility for feeding and other services within the home of the client.

The Need

If you are a parent, you understand the need for adults to get away from their children every once in a while. It may be for only a few hours to go out to dinner and a movie; it may be short-term scheduled care when the mother or father has a medical appointment or other needs.

Other situations include emergency babysitting for a working parent when a sick child is unable to go to school. Some babysitters are also called on to take care of children at the end of the school day before the parents return from work.

In this modern day, many parents no longer live near family members who might be available to watch children when needed, and suburban neighborhoods don't offer the same sort of support system that used to be found in the higher-density cities.

This job is *not* the same as working in a day care center, which is intended for large numbers of children on a regularly scheduled basis and located away from the children's homes.

Challenges

On some levels, babysitting is the most basic of temporary jobs, something that has been the entry-level job for millions of high school girls and the occasional boy.

Today, though, even this simple job has taken on new challenges, including exposure to legal liability for the care of the child and caretaking of the home. (We discuss this again in the section about legal and insurance issues.)

To reduce your exposure to liability, avoid situations where you will be asked to pick up or deliver a child by car, and don't accept children into your own home.

You must, of course, be good with children. It is also essential that you can be depended on to arrive when promised and flexible enough to be available on reasonably short notice.

Let your clients know if you will be available only for nights and weekends or if they can reach you on weekdays for emergency coverage.

Obtain from your clients full information about where they will be and how you can reach them if needed. You should also get the names and phone numbers of other relatives or guardians in case of emergency. Finally, you should have a signed form authorizing you to grant permission for emergency medical treatment if the need arises.

Parents should also provide full information about allergies and special medical conditions. They should fully explain rules of the house regarding television time, food, bedtime, and so on.

Know the Territory

Although most babysitting is still performed on a very casual basis, if you're going to be performing this service as a business you should protect yourself from liability.

Your best qualification is your reputation in the community. A young person should be able to offer references from teachers as well as parents they have helped previously; older people should offer references from happy clients.

If possible, visit the home and meet with the parents and the child before you take your first job as a babysitter; this will reduce the surprises for the child . . . and for you.

Make sure you know the rules for yourself, as well. Are you welcome to raid the refrigerator, or are you expected to bring your own meal? Do the parents expect you to clean up after the children eat?

How to Get Started

Post flyers in schools, community centers, and supermarkets. Place ads in local newspapers and shopping guides.

Ask family and friends to spread the word about your availability. Send letters to the human resources departments of major employers in your area. Do the same with school nurses.

Up-front Expenses

The principal up-front expense is for advertising and promotion.

How Much to Charge

There is usually a standard rate for babysitting in your area. You can add a premium for emergency calls and for jobs that continue late into the night.

Legal and Insurance Issues

Special notes: Your contract should identify any safety and security responsibilities of the client and limit your liability for accidents, errors, and omissions.

You should also obtain a signature on a document granting you permission to authorize emergency medical treatment for the child if necessary.

If you are making yourself available to care for a sick child, make sure it is clear who is to pick that child up from school. Most schools will not release a child to anyone but a parent unless they have written authorization.

Be very cautious about accepting a job that requires you to pick up or deliver a child by car; if you do, make sure your insurance agent is aware of it and that your insurance covers you for this kind of responsibility.

① **Legal**

② **Legal**

③ **Legal**

④ **Accounting**

⑤ **Insurance**

Babysitting Agency

Description of Job

- Manage a team of responsible, carefully checked babysitters who are available on call.

- Work with area hotels, resorts, and convention centers to provide babysitting services to visitors.

The Need

Every parent knows the feeling: trapped at home with a child night after night. Yet good babysitters are hard to find, especially on an irregular basis.

Even parents on vacation with their children yearn for the chance to go out for dinner at a place where the butter is not shaped like mouse ears and the waitress does not arrive with crayons as well as a menu.

A babysitting agency provides sitters who go to the homes of clients or to hotel rooms. This is *not* a day care situation where parents bring children to a home or a commercial setting involved in a wide range of complexities and risks.

Challenges

Two very specific sets of skills required are these: First of all, you need to be able to recruit, investigate, and manage a team of babysitters and oversee their scheduling, billing, and payment. The babysitters themselves need an abundance of patience, resourcefulness, and responsibility.

For this sort of job, do not agree to accept children into your own home or a commercial setting, and do not agree to pick up or deliver children by car.

Set up a very specific contract that lists the responsibilities you accept and those you do not; seek an attorney's assistance. The agreement should include full information about the child and his or her parents or legal guardians. Here is some of the information you should seek:

- Name, home address, and phone number of either parents or guardians. If they are not known to you, ask to see a driver's license or other form of government identification and make a record of the ID number.
- Cell phone numbers if available.
- Names and phone numbers for other family members or guardians you can call if the parents are not reachable.
- Full information on where the parents or guardians will be while you are in charge of the child. Obtain the phone number of the restaurant or other location where they will be.
- Any details about special medical concerns or allergies of the child.
- You should also obtain a signature on a legal form granting you or your representatives the right to obtain emergency medical treatment for the child if needed.
- Any special rules of behavior for the child.

Know the Territory

This sort of job works well in areas with a large number of professional and white-collar families and in locations that are home to hotels and resorts catering to families.

You'll also need to know the backgrounds of sitters you add to your team. Ask for references and resumes. Ask whether they have a criminal record.

If you want to be even more professional—or if your local market demands this—you can insist that job applicants consent to be checked for possible criminal records through an agency or through a cooperative area police agency. Seek the assistance of an attorney in drawing up a consent form for such an investigation, and be sure you understand the privacy rights of applicants.

A medical permission form also establishes you as a professional. The form should grant to the temporary guardian permission to authorize medical and dental care as recommended by a qualified doctor, dentist, or other medical practitioner.

In some areas, this sort of business may require a special permit or license.

How to Get Started

You'll need a reliable supply of babysitters. For this sort of clientele, you should set your sights higher than high school kids. Instead, recruit college students by placing ads on bulletin boards at student unions and in dorms; tap senior citizens by posting ads at senior centers; and enlist teachers by posting ads in administrative offices and lounges of schools.

Place ads for clients in neighborhood newspapers. Post notices in community centers and at cooperative area retailers, restaurants, and theaters. Make contact with area hotels and speak with concierges and managers to make sure they are aware of your services; you may want to offer a commission to the hotel in return for a listing in the information guide placed in rooms.

If there is a convention center in your area, contact management and ask to be included in information provided to visitors. Again, you may want to—or be asked to—offer a commission.

Up-front Expenses

Most of the expenses for a babysitting agency involve recruiting and managing your team of sitters and advertising for clients.

You'll also need to set up a scheduling system and perform basic accounting functions.

How Much to Charge

Babysitting is priced on an hourly basis. Be clear in your contract how many children are included in the basic rate; a sitter who is being paid to watch two children cannot be expected to have their friends over to the house for the same rate.

The agreement should also specify whether the babysitter is to serve any meals and, if so, whether there is an additional charge for that function.

Legal and Insurance Issues

Special notes: Consult an attorney for advice on criminal background checks, medical permission forms, liability, and other pertinent issues.

Many clients are likely to pay cash for services rendered, which means you will have to collect funds from the babysitters in your service. Consider signing up with a bank or other service provider to accept credit cards for payment; this will allow you to bill clients immediately after services are rendered and help you in maintaining tax records. If you accept credit cards, you will also be in the stronger position of owing payment to your representatives instead of the other way around.

Since the babysitters in your agency are not likely to be full-time employees, you might want to treat them as independent contractors (workers for hire) in which case they are responsible for their own tax payments and benefits.

1. **Legal**
2. **Legal**
3. **Legal**
4. **Accounting**
5. **Insurance**

Children's Night Out

Description of Job

- Organize care and entertainment for children for a specific period of time.
- Provide temporary care for parents on vacation or traveling for business.

- Offer a regular program of activities for parents seeking a night off from their youngsters.

The Need

Even parents have rights and needs.

How does this sound for a typical family vacation for a mother, father, and two young children? Rise at 7 A.M. for a frenetic breakfast, then spend all day at the beach, the ballpark, or at a theme park. Lunch comes in a cardboard box and the paper napkins double as coloring pages for the kids. By dinnertime the kids are running on 220 volts while the parents would do just about anything for an hour or so of quiet and a dinner where the butter pats are not shaped like mouse ears.

Alternatively, it may be a matter of business necessity: Mom and dad are on the road for a business convention and both are expected to be at a formal reception that night . . . and the kids are not invited or expected.

Even in the comfortable environs of home, a little bit of safe separation between parents and children is almost certainly good for both.

A children's-night-out program is short-term care for children, usually for a specified period of time and often with a particular theme: a movie night, a costume ball, a pizza party, video games, or live entertainment by a magician, clown, or small theater group. The program can be presented to tourists on a one-time basis or to locals on a regular schedule.

Challenges

The biggest challenge—one that takes precedence over anything else—is provision of a safe location and adequate supervision for young children.

Unless you are running a regularly scheduled program, you will not know most of the children in your care, and few will have friends with them.

You should set very specific age limits and stick to them; if you will be accepting very young children, set a policy about whether you will welcome only toilet-trained clients. You will also want to avoid mixing very young children with young teens; neither group is likely to be happy to be included with the other.

The simplest plan would also exclude any transportation of the children; have the parents bring the youngsters to your location and pick them up at the specified time. Providing pickup and delivery or planning to take your charges to another location would require a van or bus approved for the transport of children, a licensed driver, and appropriate insurance.

Parents should be asked to fill out a form with full details of where they will be, as well as cell phone numbers and other contact information. Obtain the name of another close family member or a trusted friend of the parents as an additional contact. Your contract should include language that permits you to secure emergency medical treatment for the child if necessary. The parents should be asked to provide information about any medical condition or allergies the child has.

Most child care operations also reserve the right to refuse a child who is obviously sick.

Know the Territory

If your area has schools, resorts, convention centers, or theme parks, you should have a good market of clients.

You'll need to find a location for the program, preferably near parents' homes or their hotels. The facility will have to be childproofed and will likely have to pass inspection from local or state regulators.

One possible solution: Run the program in a ballroom or convention room at a hotel, in cooperation with the management there. The hotel will likely ask for a rental payment for the use of the room or a percentage of your take; you should encourage the hotel to think of your program as a guest service that may encourage adults to use their restaurants and other facilities while their children are properly cared for.

How to Get Started

Spend the time to get to know about convention centers, resorts, hotels, and other attractions in your area that may bring in visitors. Get to know hotel concierges and convention planners who might refer business your way.

Place flyers and business cards on bulletin boards at community centers. Some restaurants and theaters may be willing to allow you to post your flyer at their establishment.

Contact some of the day camps in the area and ask them to recommend your services to parents looking for child care in the evening.

Place ads in community newspapers.

Up-front Expenses

Expenses will include advertising and promotion as well as any licenses and inspections required for child care facilities. You will have to obtain special business liability insurance—not all carriers will write policies for child care operations. If you are running your center at a hotel or on someone else's property you will likely require worker's compensation coverage.

You will probably have to hire assistants; consult with an accountant about whether they need to be salaried or can be engaged on a work-for-hire basis. They may also be required to have worker's compensation coverage.

You may have to invest in some toys, games, TVs, and VCRs.

How Much to Charge

You can charge a flat rate for a specified period of time or an hourly rate with a minimum charge. The rate should include snacks or a meal.

Make it clear to clients that your facility is licensed and insured.

Parents must be advised beforehand of late fees if they pick up their children later than promised or if you are forced to keep the center open later than its official hours.

You should ask for payment by credit card or cash; there is some risk in accepting a check from someone not known to you.

Legal and Insurance Issues

Special notes: Your contract should cover other issues, including legal guardianship of the children. (You should not release a child to anyone other than the parent or legal guardian without advanced written permission.)

① **Legal**

② **Legal**

③ **Legal**

④ **Accounting**

⑤ **Insurance**

Vacation Child Care

Description of Job

- Take up temporary residence in a client's home and accept responsibility to care for children while the parent or parents are traveling.

- Prepare meals, perform ordinary housecleaning, and maintain the security of the home.

- Get children to school and other scheduled appointments.

- Be ready to arrange for emergency medical services and home repairs, based on permissions and instructions given by parents.

The Need

Working parents are sometimes called on to travel for business. Even loving parents sometimes need a break from their children for a long weekend or an out-of-town trip. On occasion, a husband or wife may be able to take along a spouse on an extraordinary business trip.

If they are lucky, some parents can count on family or close friends to take care of their children when they travel, but it is increasingly common for young families to be hundreds or thousands of miles away from the extended family. The worst case of all is a single parent with young children and no family or friends available to help out.

Challenges

Taking responsibility for young children is not an easy job. If you have children of your own, you already know that. If you don't have kids, sit down and talk with someone who does. Make sure you are emotionally, physically, and mentally up to the task.

Decide whether you are willing to accept the additional responsibilities and demands of taking care of an infant or whether you prefer to accept only children who are old enough to attend school. Some children may require special medical care or have physical disabilities or other special needs; be sure you understand the situation and decide whether you are capable of caring for them. You're not discriminating against them if you feel you are not able to give them the help they need.

It may be possible to take this sort of job while maintaining a full-time or part-time job elsewhere, although you will need the same sort of flexibility that any parent requires, including being on call for emergencies for your surrogate family. One good career mix: a school teacher who will work more or less the same hours as his or her young charges.

Will you be expected to use your own car, or will the owner provide permission to use a family car? If so, you should obtain written permission to use the vehicle. Ask about insurance coverage and the registration.

Know the Territory

The job description for parent, and surrogate parent, includes a sense of structure tempered with a great deal of flexibility; also required is the willingness to accept responsibility for supervision and care—and a nearly bottomless well of patience.

You'll begin with the basics: getting the kids up in the morning, getting them dressed, fed, off to school, met after school, fed again, focused on homework, and back to bed. Mix in after-school activities, sports, playgroups, and pets.

Then come the weekends and holidays, when the kids may be home all day or may need to be shuttled about to sports, to clubs, and to play with friends. Finally, there are unexpected responsibilities that cannot be planned: illnesses, accidents, and problems with the house.

The key to success in this sort of job is to spend enough time with the parents and the children to learn all the rules and responsibilities before you take over. Among the questions you need to have answered:

- Are you expected to be at home all of the time when the children are there, or are they old enough and responsible enough so you can take a few hours to do some personal business?

- What is the schedule for wake-up calls, meals, and bedtime?

- Are there any foods the kids are not allowed to eat? Any significant allergies?

- What sort of food will be stocked in the house? Will there be prepared meals in the freezer? Will you need to shop for food? What sort of a budget will you be given for food?

- Are there any significant medical conditions or special needs you will have to deal with? Will you be expected to administer medication or deal with doctors or other providers?

- Are the children allowed to spend time at the houses of friends? Are friends allowed to come over to the child's house?

- What is the schedule for the traveling parents? What are their cell phone numbers? How can they be reached at hotels or conferences?

- Who are the available next of kin and relatives, and how can they be reached? What are the names of responsible friends and neighbors, and how can they be reached?

- What sort of housekeeping tasks will you be asked to perform?

- Are there any pets? What responsibilities will the children have for their care?

Before you accept a job, you should ask the parents to do the following:

- Give you a letter granting you permission to authorize necessary emergency medical care, and providing full details on health insurance (including an insurance card or a photocopy of the card) and the names of family doctors, dentists, and other health care providers
- Provide a to-whom-it-may-concern letter granting you permission to enter their home and reside there
- If it's part of the deal, give you written permission to use the family car, along with its registration and insurance information
- Notify neighbors, schoolteachers, and others that you will be in the home while the parents are away

How to Get Started

Post flyers at schools, community centers, and retail stores. Place ads in newspapers, school newspapers, and shopping guides.

Contact the principals of area schools and ask if they would keep your name on file as a child care resource. They may not be willing—or able—to make recommendations, but they might pass along your card. Ask friends and neighbors to recommend your services; offer a bonus or commission for work they send your way. Do the same for satisfied customers.

Up-front Expenses

The principal up-front costs are for advertising and promotion.

How Much to Charge

Charge by the day for each day you are in the house; typical rates range from about $100 to $200 per day.

The client is responsible for stocking the refrigerator and kitchen and providing a pool of cash for additional food, if needed, and for school lunches, allowances, and the like. If you use your own vehicle for shopping or transportation, you should charge a reasonable mileage rate.

Legal and Insurance Issues

Special notes: Your contract should identify any safety and security responsibilities of the client and limit your liability for accidents, errors, and omissions.

If you are making yourself available to care for a sick child, make sure it is clear who is to pick that child up from school. Most schools will not release a child to anyone but a parent unless they have written authorization.

Your attorney can give you blank forms that grant permission for you to obtain emergency medical care, drive the family car, and identify you to police and other authorities as having permission to live in people's home while they are away.

An insurance agent can advise about necessary liability coverage and offer suggestions about proper coverage if you will be driving children in your own car or in the family vehicle.

① **Legal**

② **Legal**

③ **Legal**

④ **Accounting**

⑤ **Insurance**

Dog Walking and Vacation Pet Visits

Description of Job

- Help pet owners care for their significant others when they can't be there themselves.
- Take dogs for exercise and bathroom breaks.
- Provide a bit of human companionship for lonely pets.
- Maintain fresh food and water for indoor pets.
- Change litter boxes and clean up pet "accidents."

The Need

Three out of ten households include a pet—with cats slightly outnumbering dogs—and those that do greatly benefit from the companionship and fun provided by their animals. Yet most of us lead increasingly complex lives, and we can't always be there to take proper care of our pet's needs.

Dogs must be taken for walks several times a day. Cats need fresh food and water and someone to play with for a while, even if they don't want to admit to needing a human around the house. Goldfish, birds, hamsters—and other critters that qualify as pets—need a bit of help on a regular basis.

The job of a pet service provider is to help keep furry, scaly, or feathery friends healthy and happy when their owners are unable to be there.

Here are some ways this job can be set up:

- You come to a client's home or apartment on a regularly scheduled basis to attend to the pet. This sort of arrangement might be for someone who has a full-time job outside the home or someone who is going away on an extended trip.

   Owners or a caretaker may be there to let you into the house, or they may make other arrangements whereby you can gain access. What does that mean? They might give you a key, leave a key in a hidden location, or give you the combination to a lock or alarm system.

- You could arrange to be on call for a client and respond as needed. For example, someone might call you to say that he or she is going to have to work late tonight, or has been called out of town unexpectedly. You have previously agreed to be available within whatever reasonable advance notice time you have set.

Challenges

You have to be able to get along with animals. In our experience, some people make animals feel quite secure, and others set off growls and hisses from the most docile puppies and kittens. You know which type you are.

You have to be flexible and dependable. Your clients and their pets are going to rely on you; one missed appointment may cost you a client.

You have to demonstrate your trustworthiness. If you are given the keys to someone's house, that person can't accuse you of breaking in; however, if something goes missing, you will automatically become a prime suspect.

Make certain you understand the ground rules; if you're going into the refrigerator for Fido's food, that doesn't mean you're entitled to make your own dinner. It means you're not entitled to use the swimming pool or the big-screen TV unless the owner specifically agrees to that.

Agree to a price list for services and a billing schedule. If possible, obtain an advance payment that covers the first week's or month's services, and always bill in advance. As a businessperson, it is preferable for you to owe money or services to your client than to sweat out receipt of payment after you've done your job (or the pet has done his).

Know the Territory

Research, understand, and obey all local ordinances that affect your business. Many areas have pooper-scooper laws that require dog owners and their representatives to clean up after their animals. There may be regulations against walking multiple dogs as a pack, and there are usually laws against excessive barking.

Consult with your insurance broker to make certain you have proper coverage to protect you from liability claims. Are you covered if a dog you are walking bites someone? Does your auto insurance protect you if you are driving to a client to conduct business?

Maintain a locked cabinet or safe for customers' keys. Avoid putting names or addresses on the keys in case they are lost or stolen; use the pet's name or a code that makes sense to you, and store your clients' names and addresses in a separate, secure location.

Ask your clients to advise friends and neighbors that they have employed you and given you permission to enter their house.

Make an appointment to meet with prospective clients before you make your first solo visit. Meet the pets and spend some time with them to make sure you are comfortable with each other.

Make certain you understand the animal's feeding schedule and allowable treats. The owner should always provide the food. Ask for the name and phone number of the animal's veterinarian, and obtain written permission from the owner to call for medical help if you feel it is needed. If the animal is receiving medication, make sure you understand the schedule and any special instructions.

For dog-walking services, determine if this animal plays well with others. Some pet service providers walk several dogs at the same time, which allows for a bit of socialization and maximizes your profit. But it may not be possible if the dog will not cooperate or is much larger or more aggressive than the others in your pack. Some dog owners may prefer that their dog socialize with others, while others may not want their pet exposed to diseases.

How to Get Started

Add any special circumstances, services, and concerns to your business plan. Determine the going rate for these services in your area. Among the ways to do this: Ask friends if they have ever engaged someone for this sort of job and the price they paid. You could also ask what they think such services are worth. Call the local animal shelter or veterinarian and ask whether they know of others doing this sort of work; they may even offer suggestions on the price of services they don't perform.

Draw up a simple agreement that lays out the services you propose to provide, the responsibilities you are willing to accept and those for which you do not accept liability, a price schedule, and the terms for payment. This may not fully stand up in court, but at least you will have something in writing that covers any verbal agreement you make with a client.

Start spreading the news. Put up posters and flyers on apartment building bulletin boards, in supermarkets, and near parks and other areas where owners exercise their pets. Ask your friends and neighbors. Ask animal shelters or veterinarians to put a notice in their waiting room. Some pet stores will also allow you to put up a small poster. Purchase a small ad in a neighborhood newspaper; the best place to buy an ad is in a publication that has similar ads.

Up-front Expenses

The principal expenses are for advertising and promotion.

How Much to Charge

Rates vary by location, with higher prices in major metropolitan areas, although you should also factor in your costs if you need to drive a great distance to meet a pet in a rural setting. A typical price for a 15-minute quick check on a pet or a short walk ranges from $10 to $15; a 30-minute walk is generally priced from $15 to $20, and a full hour of exercise is priced from about $20 to $30 in most areas.

If you intend to walk packs of dogs as a standard service, you may want to list a higher price for solo walks.

Some pet service providers give volume discounts; for example, they might offer a 10 to 20 percent reduction for a prepaid punch card that entitles the pet owner to 15 visits. Other providers offer lower rates for visits more than once per day.

You might also offer a bonus if customers refer new business to you, especially if the clients live nearby, which will save you time and money.

Legal and Insurance Issues

① **Legal**

② **Legal**

③ **Legal**

④ **Accounting**

⑤ **Insurance**

Pet Sitter and Doggie Day Care

Description of Job

- Care for dogs, cats, and certain other housetrained pets in your home while their owners are away on vacation.

- Maintain a doggy day care center for animals unable to be left at home alone while their owners are at work.

- Take responsibility for emergency medical care as well as basic needs for animals.

The Need

Sometimes you've just got to get away, and you can't always bring your furry best friend with you. Pet sitters can care for animals for extended periods of time, or they can operate a day care that allows owners to drop off a pet in the morning and pick it up at the end of the day.

Some animals may become neurotic or dangerous to themselves or others if they are left alone in a home, and many animals are terrified of animal shelters, a place that may be filled with the odors of other animals that are ill or frightened. A pet sitter offers a comfortable and personalized alternative to boarding a dog or cat at an animal shelter and removes the worry and liability that would come with asking someone to come into your home to visit and care for your pet.

Challenges

You'll begin with a high comfort level with dogs and cats, of course. You'll also need a living space that is large enough to safely handle multiple animals, and a nearby location to give them exercise is a must, too.

Be sure to obtain full information on where the owners will be while you have their animal in your charge, and obtain written permission from them to obtain emergency medical service if required.

You should not accept an animal you feel is dangerous to you or others, and you should not accept an animal that is ill.

Know the Territory

Big cities are more likely to have small dogs that are comfortable with life in apartments. Rural settings may have large dogs that expect to have acres of land to roam.

If you are in a rented home or apartment you'll need the permission of your landlord to house pets. Even if you own your own home you'll need to be observant of local zoning and health laws that might limit the number of animals permitted in a home, even on a temporary basis.

Your neighbors may object, especially if some of the animals are noisy or messy.

How to Get Started

Advertise at pet supply stores, supermarkets, and community centers and in shopping guides and newspapers. Ask friends and family to spread the word, and offer a bonus to clients who refer new business to you.

Up-front Expenses

The principal expenses will be for advertising and promotion. You may have to install fencing on your property and internal gates to keep pets separated or away from places they should not venture. You'll also need some feeding and water bowls.

How Much to Charge

Charge a fixed rate per day or half day. Owners should supply food and any special treats.

Set your prices with awareness of what the area's animal shelter charges; you may want to underprice its rates, or set a higher price for a higher level of service.

Legal and Insurance Issues

① **Legal**

② **Legal**

③ **Legal**

④ **Accounting**

⑤ **Insurance**

Elder Companion

Description of Job

- Provide companionship and security for elderly people in their homes.
- Communicate with family about health and welfare conditions.

The Need

With the benefit of advanced medical care, people are living longer. It is also less common these days for their children to spend their adult lives in the same community where they were born; in fact, many of us end up living hundreds or thousands of miles from our birthplace. In addition, many couples are having children later in life. Among the effects: the "sandwich generation" of adults who are raising their own children and worrying about the welfare of their aging parents at the same time.

The role of the elder care companion is to provide company for senior citizens living alone and to help the family know about the living conditions and health of their elderly loved ones. Some clients might ask the companion to call them during or after each visit to report on the situation.

Challenges

The elder care companion might bring lunch, play cards, or help explain a television show or movie. The companion might provide some light housekeeping, such as vacuuming and dishwashing.

The job stops short of providing medical care, dispensing medications, offering physical therapy, bathing, or other jobs for which training or licensure is required. In some localities, you may require a license or permit.

This sort of job requires a great deal of patience and understanding, and you must have the ability to observe your older charges and to report on their condition to their children or other relatives. In some circumstances, you may need to call doctors or other medical professionals to report on new or ongoing conditions.

Know the Territory

There is a need for this sort of work just about everywhere, but the parents and their children may be living in completely different areas.

How to Get Started

Spread the word about your availability in community centers, in senior centers, in church newsletters, and in area newspapers and shopping guides. Seek to post flyers and business cards at health care stores and pharmacies, including those that sell and rent medical equipment for the home.

Contact area doctors and let them know of your services; they may be willing to recommend you to their patients or their families.

Be prepared to give personal references.

Up-front Expenses

Your principal expenses will be for advertising and promotion.

How Much to Charge

Charge an hourly rate for your time. If the client lives some distance from your home, you can charge a reasonable mileage rate for your drive.

With permission, you can purchase and bill for the cost of games, books, CDs, and other things you feel are valuable for your client.

Some of these jobs are filled by agencies that specialize in services to the elderly. You may be able to work for the agency and be paid by that group instead of directly by the client.

Legal and Insurance Issues

① **Legal**

② **Legal**

③ **Legal**

④ **Accounting**

⑤ **Insurance**

Elder Care Consultant

Description of Job

- Consult with elderly clients and their immediate families about available options for health care, long-term care, and in-home services.
- Review client's eligibility for benefits under Medicaid, Medicare, private health insurance, and other sources of public and private assistance.
- Coordinate with attorneys, accountants, insurance agencies, medical providers, and others involved in the establishment of a plan for care and the means to pay for it.

The Need

Old age is relatively easy to bear for two economic classes of people: the very wealthy and the very poor.

The richest among us can afford to pay the huge cost of medical care, long-term care, and special services from their own resources; they don't need to ask for permission or meet government criteria for programs.

The poorest qualify for federal and state programs that provide a safety net. They have few if any investments and no property of any value that the government might take.

It is the vast group in the middle who must face the most difficult of choices, including the need to spend down their assets to pay for much of their own care and perhaps to reach near-poverty levels before they qualify for government programs.

The role of the elder care consultant is to offer expert advice on decisions, then to work with the client and other members of the family support team to implement the plan. Together with the family, you may work with elder care attorneys, accountants, and insurance agents to help implement a plan.

Among the areas you'll need to address:

- Assessing Social Security and Medicare benefits
- Coordinating private health insurance and long-term care insurance with Medicare

- Understanding the services available to veterans
- Reviewing Medigap insurance to fill in for areas not covered by existing policies
- Assisting with prescription drug strategies, including Medicare prescription cards, private programs, Veterans Administration pharmacies, and importation of drugs from Canada or Mexico, where legal
- Knowing the eligibility requirements for Medicaid
- Protecting investments and assets by transferring them to other family members well ahead of the point where government programs will consider them of interest

You'll also need to be aware of programs offered by local governments and offices for the aging and by area religious institutions, foundations, and charities.

Challenges

This job requires a tremendous amount of research and organization, and a commitment to keeping up-to-date on changes in laws, programs, and economics.

You'll often be dealing with people in times of personal stress because of illness, finances, or just the escalating concerns of old age. The elderly may have difficulty hearing or understanding complex concepts. Every client will have different needs.

Don't play lawyer, doctor, or insurance agent yourself. Your job is to be an impartial advisor to your client and an independent representative in dealings with professionals.

Know the Territory

The federal Medicare program is essentially the same across the country. Medicaid, which is funded jointly by state and federal governments, varies greatly from state to state. Private Medigap insurance fills in some of the gaps in government programs, and private health insurance and long-term-care policies can replace or supplement government plans.

Begin by learning everything you can about the local situation. Make contact with the county and state offices for the aging and learn about programs they offer; read web sites and brochures produced by state and federal agencies.

Meet with area insurance agents who sell Medigap, health insurance, and long-term-care policies to learn about available offerings. Any agent who is especially cooperative should be at the top of your list of recommended resources for your clients.

Check with the local bar association to find out about area lawyers who specialize in elder law. Contact some or all of them and ask about the services they provide; some may offer to meet with you to discuss their practice. Again, you can include their names among your recommendations.

Visit area nursing homes and long-term-care facilities. A helpful administrator may be able to help you learn more about the economics of long-term care. You should be able to offer an independent assessment of the atmosphere and conditions you find; state regulators are in charge of rating the quality of medical care and supervision.

How to Get Started

Post your services in senior centers, community centers, and religious institutions. Place ads in newspapers and shoppers.

Send notices of your services to area doctors and gerontologists, elder law attorneys, and senior centers.

Offer to give a talk at senior centers and make it known that you are available for hire for personal consultations.

Up-front Expenses

You'll need a collection of current research and reference materials. A computer with a connection to the Internet is also very important.

Other up-front expenses are principally for advertising and promotion.

How Much to Charge

Charge by the hour for your consultations and research. If you are asked to visit facilities, lawyers, accountants, or other specialists on behalf of your client, you can include a reasonable mileage charge.

Legal and Insurance Issues

① **Legal**

② **Legal**

③ **Legal**

④ **Accounting**

⑤ **Insurance**

Genealogical Research

Description of Job

- Research the ancestry and family history for a client.
- Present a report with information and analysis based on your research.

The Need

Who are we, and where did we come from? For most of us, what we know of our family history dates back only a generation or two. Our roots were lost when ancestors emigrated from foreign lands, moved around the country, or were buried with poorly maintained governmental, military, and religious records.

The urge to trace personal history often begins with the innocent interest of youngsters and progresses to the more urgent inquiry of adults who see the glimmers of mortality.

The professional genealogist uses traditional tools of library research, probate records, birth and death certificates, records of religious ceremonies, and marriage licenses. Some of the information exists in dusty paper records, but increasingly the bits and pieces of our lives are floating in cyberspace and accessible through the Internet. Even so, it requires some decent investigative skills and dogged determination to do the job properly.

Challenges

You'll need to understand the processes of genealogical research, have the determination and drive of a detective, and know how to work equally well with computer databases and old record books in musty vaults.

You'll also have to maintain a professional skepticism in pursuit of the truth. Your client may start out by telling you that he is descended from the royal family of Denmark, or that she is the great-great-granddaughter of a Civil War general. Your response, whether said aloud or kept to yourself, has to be: "We'll see about that."

Though nearly all current personal information is available in electronic form, many modern laws are intended to protect the privacy of individuals. You may need to obtain permission from your clients to examine records, or it may be necessary for them to directly request the records and pass them along to you.

Know the Territory

Some searches will go back several generations in the same town or area; many others skip around from town to town, state to state, and reach back across borders to family members who emigrated from Europe, Asia, Africa, and the Americas.

Begin by learning about available local and regional resources. Does your town or state offer online access to records? What sort of identification or permission is required?

Learn about the most common family histories for the people in your area. For example, some parts of the country have a large proportion of second- or third-generation immigrants from Ireland, Italy, or Scandinavia. Other places have more recent immigrants from the Caribbean, Latin America, Russia, and eastern Europe.

Become an expert on the sort of information you can expect to obtain from foreign sources. In some countries, most of the records are likely to come from church sources. In some former Communist states, records may be very detailed, although access over the Internet may be limited.

United States and Canadian officials kept reasonably good records of new arrivals during periods of major immigration, including the early part of the twentieth century, and much of that information is available through government and private web sites. Many of these sites have museums or visitor centers that can provide information on those who entered through the port. Most Europeans entered the United States through major ports in New York, Alexandria, Baltimore, Boston, Galveston, Miami, and Savannah; in Canada, major ports included those in Halifax and Quebec City.

The National Archives & Records Administration (NARA), a federal agency, publishes guidebooks and offers publications and leaflets that may help you get started in searching government records.

How to Get Started

Polish your skills by tracing your own ancestors before you start with paying customers.

Develop a checklist of questions to ask your clients in the initial interview, and a list of documents you would like to review. These include birth and death certificates, wedding licenses, divorce decrees, adoption papers, and anything else that might include details of your clients' lives and those of their ancestors.

Ask for the details of any unsubstantiated family stories; even if they are completely incorrect, there may be some kernels of information you could use in your research.

Post your availability on bulletin boards at community centers, senior centers, religious institutions, and elsewhere. Place ads in family- and community-oriented newspapers and shopping guides.

Up-front Expenses

Invest in some good guides to genealogical research. You should also have access to a computer with an Internet account, plus a good-quality printer.

Other expenses include advertising and promotion.

How Much to Charge

Charge an hourly rate for research; you may want to offer a basic search that is limited to no more than 8 or 10 hours, or promise to check in with your clients after each block of 10 hours to advise them of your progress and to get the okay to keep the clock running for further research.

Legal and Insurance Issues

① **Legal**

② **Legal**

③ **Legal**

④ **Accounting**

⑤ **Insurance**

Family Biographer

Description of Job

- Research, write, and publish a personal biography or family history for a client.
- Prepare a personal story on videotape, DVD, or CD for presentation at a family celebration or commemoration.

The Need

For eons, family history has been something handed down by word of mouth from one generation to the next. In more recent times, records of who we were have progressed from formal oil portraits of the rich and wealthy to studio photography to modern snapshots and videos.

Today, we have available incredibly powerful, easy-to-use, and easy-to-store media, including videotapes, CDs, and DVDs, as well as computer tools that allow anyone to create a near-professional-quality book with a press run of as few as one. The tools can be used to produce biographies for family reunions, weddings, anniversaries, birthdays, and memorial services.

The job of the family biographer is to facilitate the creation of a biography or history using modern tools and research methods. The result can be published using computer word processors and high-quality printers, or transferred from computer to videotape or DVD to be played on a television set.

Challenges

You will need to be an accomplished researcher and able to work with a wide variety of clients of varying ages and backgrounds. You will ask family members to give you photos, films, and precious documents to serve as the backbone for your work.

You'll need to be able to verify details, work with government agencies, religious institutions, and other record keepers. There is a great wealth of information available on the Internet, and you'll need to be able to search and retrieve data.

If you will be writing a biography, you will need to be able to express yourself in a clear voice. If you will be producing a DVD or videotape, you will need to master the technology of digital editing, videotape capture, and preparation of a PowerPoint (or similar) presentation.

The more advance time you have and the more the client is willing to pay for, the better the job you will be able to do. You may have to deal with situations where a client approaches you on Friday for a presentation to be made on Sunday.

In some situations, you may be asked to embellish stories or even report information you suspect or know to be wrong; you will have to come up with your own rules about how far you are willing to stray away from journalism and toward fiction.

Know the Territory

No two life stories are the same, and no two biographies or family histories will be alike, either.

You will begin by meeting with your client to discuss the process and to hear the oral history of the family, which will help you plan your research and writing. Collect as many photos, films, videos, and documents as possible. Bring a sturdy, dry case to transport material to your office; make copies as quickly as possible and return the originals to your client.

As a writer or producer for hire, you should make certain that you fully understand your clients' wants and needs. They may want to emphasize a particular accomplishment or event, and they may want you to ignore or downplay a skeleton in the closet.

It will be up to you to decide whether you are willing to report information you cannot verify.

The process for creating a book or an electronic presentation includes:

- Researching the story based on a verbal history given by the family
- Checking with independent sources to verify information
- Scanning documents, photos, films, and videos to convert them to digital form
- Using a digital editor, such as Adobe Photoshop, to repair and improve the quality of documents and images
- Using publishing software, such as Quark or Adobe InDesign, to produce printed versions
- Using digital publishing software, such as Adobe Acrobat, Microsoft PowerPoint, or other programs to produce a version on-screen, and then using a CD or DVD-burning program to create a CD or DVD, or outputting the version from a graphics adapter to a VCR to make a videotape

How to Get Started

Post flyers on bulletin boards at community centers, schools, churches, and other places. Place ads in newspapers and shopping guides.

You may be able to get bookstores, photo shops, and other retail outlets to allow you to post flyers and recommend you to their clients; offer a bonus or commission. Ask friends, acquaintances, and satisfied customers to tell others of your services; offer them a bonus or discount on future work.

Seek publicity about your work through the lifestyle editor of your newspaper, who may find it interesting enough to run a story.

Up-front Expenses

You will need a computer with access to the Internet and a professional-quality printer. The computer should include word processing software and a publishing program to produce printed output.

To convert photos and documents to digital images for printed materials and electronic presentations, you'll need a scanner. If you will be working to capture images from a videotape, you'll need a video-capture adapter.

To create a CD or DVD, you'll need presentation software and a CD or DVD burner and software. To create a videotape, you'll need a video adapter with a TV output and a video recorder.

Other costs include advertising and promotion.

How Much to Charge

Charge an hourly rate for research and production, plus the cost of materials such as CDs, DVDs, and videotape. You might want to offer a package price for a set number of hours.

Legal and Insurance Issues

①	**Legal**

②	**Legal**

③	**Legal**

④	**Accounting**

⑤	**Insurance**

CHAPTER 11

Educational Services

61 Tutoring

62 Language Instructor

63 Music Teacher

64 Computer Instructor

65 SAT or ACT College Test Preparation

66 College Selection Advisor

67 College Application Consultant

68 Instructor at Community School

Tutoring

Description of Job

- Help a student—of any age—achieve success in school.
- Provide training in a specialized subject to meet business or professional needs.

The Need

Sometimes we—or our children—need some extra help or one-on-one instruction to achieve success in school or in our jobs.

Your child may be a whiz when called on to produce written reports, but may struggle mightily in algebra and geometry. Your young student may be a math prodigy, but may be unable to master a foreign language.

As a parent, we all want our children to do well and succeed in school. However, any parent will quickly learn that it is somewhere between extremely difficult and impossible to teach your own child without a descent into screams and tears . . . and we're not just referring to the kids.

As an adult, you may want the assistance of a professional to help you learn how to operate a computer, master the art of knitting, or brush up on your 20-year-old French skills before taking a trip to Europe.

Challenges

It is not enough to know the subject; you also have to be capable of teaching. You have to be a good communicator, and you have to be patient.

You'll also have to work with school teachers where appropriate, and you'll have to get along with parents and guardians who may be a help or a hindrance in the process.

If you are offering tutoring to adults seeking to improve their skills in a professional area, you should work to coordinate your efforts with human resources and training departments where appropriate.

Know the Territory

Parents learn quickly that success in school, especially high school, is critical in getting into a good college and may play a role in obtaining financial aid and scholarships. It may not be sufficient to point to a child's extreme success in language skills and ask that poor results in math be ignored.

Another modern issue is the increased use of standardized testing in schools.

If you are working with a student in school, ask to see the textbooks the student is using and become familiar with the subject matter you will be covering. If you are coaching the student for a particular test, seek copies of past tests and work with them as a base.

How to Get Started

The best qualification for this sort of job is an advanced teaching degree or certificate and experience as a teacher. That doesn't mean you can't offer your services based on other experiences and background; for example, your own background as a computer user may be more than enough to qualify you to teach others how to navigate the Internet.

Whether you are currently a schoolteacher or are coming from industry, you should be up-to-date on current information, specialized language, and teaching methods.

In some school districts you may be able to work closely—though informally—with guidance counselors, teachers, and administrators. Make them aware of your resume and references and ask them to recommend you to parents who seek help for their children, as appropriate.

Place flyers and business cards on community bulletin boards, at schools, and in libraries. Place ads in the school newspaper, community shopping guides, and local newspapers.

Up-front Expenses

The principal up-front costs for this job are for advertising and promotional expenses. You could set up a web site, which would also involve costs.

You may need to purchase some textbooks and research materials to help you in your preparation and teaching.

How Much to Charge

Tutors usually charge by the hour. You might consider offering a discounted rate for a package of hours; for example, sell 10 hours of tutoring for the cost of 9. If the student lives a great distance from your home, you can ask for a reasonable reimbursement for the cost of travel.

Legal and Insurance Issues

① **Legal**

② **Legal**

③ **Legal**

④ **Accounting**

⑤ **Insurance**

Language Instructor

Description of Job

- Teach basic foreign language skills to students or business professionals.
- Offer brushup training to students with previous instruction in a foreign language.
- Provide advanced training in a foreign language beyond high school or college courses.

The Need

English may be the predominant language of business and tourism, but it is by no means the only way to communicate when you travel to, or deal with people in, foreign countries.

Understanding at least the basics of a foreign language will increase your chances for success in business. As a tourist, the ability to communicate in the local language and understand street signs and advertising will greatly enhance your experience. You are much more likely to enjoy your meals in Paris if you understand exactly what you are ordering and are able to communicate with your waiter.

Challenges

To be able to teach a foreign language, you need a strong command of the language, a good ear for pronunciation, and the ability to teach people who have a tin ear and a thick tongue.

You should also understand regional differences in accent and colloquialisms. For example, the French language of Quebec has some significant variations from the accent and idioms of Paris. The Spanish of the Caribbean and Latin America varies in some important ways from the Castilian dialect of Spain.

You may be called on to help business clients communicate about specialized topics such as finance and computer terms.

Know the Territory

One way to sharpen your language skill is to listen to foreign language broadcasts; many cable and satellite television providers offer news and entertainment channels from other countries. Many foreign language movies are available on videotape or DVD. You can also read daily newspapers and newsmagazines on the Internet.

How to Get Started

Advertise your availability through community bulletin boards and at schools. Place ads in area business newspapers and community shopping guides. Send letters about your services to training and human resources officers at area companies.

Teaching a course at a community school or college can get you some recognition and some clients who want private lessons. An advertisement in a student newspaper may win some clients who need extra tutoring.

Up-front Expenses

Purchase a library of reference books and dictionaries; subscribe to foreign language newspapers and magazines and view television shows and movies in the language.

Other expenses include advertising and promotion.

How Much to Charge

Charge by the hour for private instruction. Add the cost of any books or course material you require. (Take care not to violate copyright law by making unauthorized copies of published materials.)

Legal and Insurance Issues

① **Legal**

② **Legal**

③ **Legal**

④ **Accounting**

⑤ **Insurance**

Music Teacher

Description of Job

- Teach people—young and old—to play a musical instrument.
- Offer refresher courses and advanced instruction.

The Need

Learning to play an instrument is somewhat like learning to play a sport. A handful of people are born with an innate musical sense; the vast majority of us need instruction, at least at the start.

A music teacher begins with the fundamentals—how to handle an instrument, how to read music, and how to listen to your own playing.

Challenges

It's not enough to be able to play an instrument well; you have to be able to teach others to play. You have to be patient enough to withstand the screeches and wails of untalented—or at least untutored—students.

An important decision is whether you will go to students in their homes or teach them at a studio.

If you teach in the homes of students, you can save the expense and complication of setting up a studio. You will, though, have to spend the time to travel, and you will have to deal with whatever distractions exist in the home.

Setting up a studio allows you to control the environment. But you have to make provisions for students—and perhaps family members—to wait while other lessons are conducted. If you are teaching piano, organ, or drums you'll have to provide an instrument for students to play at the studio.

A third option is to work with an area piano or musical instrument store; many offer instruction and hire subcontractors to teach at studios in the store. This option saves you the expense of setting up a studio and gives you a professional setting.

Know the Territory

The heart of the market for musical instruction is likely to be elementary through high school students, although some people will want to pick up an instrument—or renew a decades-old acquaintance—in their adulthood. Spend the time to learn about musical programs offered at area schools, and don't forget that your services can complement school bands.

Make contact with area piano and musical instrument stores and offer your services for instruction in the home.

How to Get Started

Advertise on school bulletin boards, in shopping guides, and in music stores.
Seek referrals from friends and relatives.

Up-front Expenses

You'll need teacher's copies of musical instruction books. (Some publishers will offer free or discounted copies to teachers who agree to specify the books as required purchases for students.)

If you set up your own studio, you'll need to create a private space with sufficient room for you, a student, and the instruments you'll be teaching. If you're going to teach piano, organ, drums, harp, or other instruments not easily transported, you'll need to provide equipment in the studio.

How Much to Charge

Charge by the hour. Remember to factor in the cost of travel to distant clients. If you're going to be teaching in a studio, include a portion of the setup costs in your hourly rate.

If you will be teaching as a subcontractor in a music store, you will likely be paid by the store and not the student.

You may be able to make some additional money by selling instruction books and music to students. If you are running your own business, you may be able to receive a commission from the rental of musical instruments by an outside company or store.

Your contract with the student should be specific regarding hourly rate and any special conditions. The agreement should include a charge for any student who fails to cancel an appointment with sufficient notice.

Legal and Insurance Issues

Special notes: Investigate a business owner's policy for any studio you set up in your home or for any work you perform in the homes of students or at a music store. If you perform work in a studio operated by a music store or other third party, you may need to obtain a workers' compensation policy.

① **Legal**

② **Legal**

③ **Legal**

④ **Accounting**

⑤ **Insurance**

Computer Instructor

Description of Job

- Teach neophytes how to perform basic tasks on a personal computer.
- Give personal lessons on advanced software applications and operating systems.
- Provide telephone support for software tasks and problems.

The Need

Computers can be wondrous assistants in almost everything we do in our business and personal lives. Computers can also be maddeningly stubborn and difficult impediments that speak a language of their own.

Some people seem to be born with an instant connection to the ways of a computer, while others are baffled, bewildered, and sometimes terrified of the machine.

The job of the personal computer instructor is to help users learn the lan guage of computer operations and make use of software in their daily lives.

Challenges

By now, personal computers have become very close to commodities. Think in terms of cars: Though a Ferrari is quite different in features, speed, and price from a Ford Focus, the two vehicles nevertheless are quite similar; both have four wheels, an engine, a steering wheel, and a set of brakes.

Although one computer may have different hardware components than another (microprocessor, memory, disk drives, and the like) the operating system unifies them all. The vast majority of personal computers use a version of Microsoft's Windows to control the hardware and work with standardized software applications; a small but loyal cadre of users run Apple's Macintosh operating system.

The challenge for the personal computer instructor is to help nontechnical users understand how their PC is configured and to learn how to use the software that is appropriate for the work they want to perform: For the new user, the basic trio of applications is a word processor for writing and editing, a browser to gain access to the Internet, and an e-mail program to send and receive messages.

As with any tutoring job, you have to not only have a strong understanding of the subject, you have to be able to teach, as well.

It's also very important to have firm boundaries on the tasks you are taking on:

- Unless you are qualified to make repairs or install new hardware, you should insist that the student's computer be functioning properly before lessons begin.
- Don't offer to sell, give away, or install unauthorized copies of computer software.
- Insist that clients install and keep current an antivirus program to help protect their data from damage by infected e-mail and other programs.

Know the Territory

You should be fully comfortable with the use of common software applications and able to teach yourself about advanced facilities and techniques as needed.

The nearly ubiquitous Windows operating system exists in a number of versions, but at the user level all are quite similar, and mastery of the most current edition allows easy use of any of the earlier versions. A similar story applies to Apple's Macintosh operating system.

Some computer instructors and consultants are quite capable of moving back and forth between Windows and Apple clients, while others prefer to specialize. (Keep in mind that the Windows market is much larger.) Microsoft has the lion's share of software for both operating systems; Microsoft Office (which includes Microsoft Word and the Microsoft Excel spreadsheet) operates much the same in both systems.

Get to know the facilities of area school districts. Students working on a Macintosh during the day may want to use the same sort of system when they get home at night; adults taking a community school course on Windows equipment are likely to want to use the same operating system and software at home.

Sessions will generally be conducted in the homes or offices of your students, using their computer and software. You can also offer telephone support from your office or home; a developing trend involves use of special software installed on both the student's and the teacher's machine that allows the instructor to demonstrate tasks and make adjustments to settings by remote control over the Internet.

Some computer retail stores offer classes and tutoring for customers; contact area managers to see if there are openings for new instructors.

You should establish liaisons with computer consultants who perform repairs and upgrades so that you can make recommendations to your clients when necessary; in return, you should expect these consults to refer clients who are seeking instruction.

How to Get Started

Post flyers and ads in community schools, community centers, and senior centers. Computer stores that don't offer their own classes may allow you to advertise your availability on their bulletin boards.

Place ads in student newspapers, community newspapers, and shopping guides.

Up-front Expenses

You'll need a capable computer of your own, connected to the Internet for research and communication with manufacturers and students. You should also be running the latest version of operating systems and software applications.

Other expenses include advertising and promotion.

How Much to Charge

You should set an hourly rate for instruction; some teachers sell a block of hours or lessons at a discounted rate. Add a mileage charge for the cost of driving to clients.

Legal and Insurance Issues

① **Legal**
② **Legal**
③ **Legal**
④ **Accounting**
⑤ **Insurance**

SAT or ACT College Test Preparation

Description of Job

- Help a high school student prepare to take PSAT, SAT, or ACT college aptitude tests.
- Offer coaching on test strategies.
- Give tutoring in math and verbal skills.
- Administer practice tests.
- Grade tests and interpret results to aid in further practice.

The Need

For the majority of college-bound high school students, the first official step toward the doors of academia is taking one or more national assessment tests. The most common exam is the Scholastic Aptitude Test (SAT) and its practice test, the Preliminary Scholastic Aptitude Test (PSAT).

Some students choose to take the ACT Assessment, which is more closely linked to high school curriculum than to raw aptitude.

Colleges and universities use the student's score as a major component—along with class rank, GPA, teacher recommendations, and extracurricular activities—in their decisions to admit students and in doling out academic and merit scholarships.

Studies have shown that students who study skills and subject matter in advance of the test generally score 20 to 50 points higher (on a scale of 0 to 800) than those who do not prepare. For some students with particular strengths or weaknesses, preparation can add even more to their score and could make the difference in getting into the school of their choice or making it possible to afford going there.

In 2004, academic tutoring was a $4.5 billion business in the United States, according to Eduventures Inc., a Boston-based education market research and consultant.

Challenges

You have to know the subject matter and the tips and tricks to boost scores, and you have to be able to communicate that information to bored, terrified, needy, or uncooperative 16- and 17-year-olds. You may also have to deal with high and sometimes unrealistic expectations of parents. In other words, you'll need a great deal of patience and understanding.

Some of the work can be spread out across the entire year; students can begin preparation as much as a year before taking preliminary or actual tests and may take the exams several times (colleges generally look at the highest scores achieved in each section across all test sessions). However, the bulk of tutoring is likely to be done in the spring of the student's junior year and the summer before the senior year begins.

Don't make promises about specific test results, and don't raise unreasonable expectations for improvement. You can fairly say that almost every student receives higher scores as the result of coaching. Some tutors and commercial programs offer a money-back guarantee if the student does not receive a score at least 20 to 25 points higher than a previous reference test, which is not the same as a guarantee of improvement.

You will be competing against several major national college preparation companies that offer classroom lectures and testing; there are also a number of web sites that administer sample tests and analyze results. Your competitive pitch should emphasize personal attention and one-on-one tutoring.

Do not make unauthorized copies of copyrighted materials for your students.

Know the Territory

The SAT is a three-hour test that measures verbal and mathematical aptitude. In 2005, the test was expanded to include a written essay component; a perfect score on the now three-part exam is 2,400. The revised test eliminated analogies and quantitative comparisons and added a short essay and grammar questions to the writing section.

The ACT consists of tests in English, math reading problems, and science, and it also includes an optional essay section.

Some students get better results on one test or the other, and an advisor may assess a student's performance and make a recommendation.

Preparation usually begins with administration of a practice test that discloses strengths and weaknesses and provides a baseline to measure improvement. Most students and their tutors prepare by using actual tests administered in previous years.

Typical tutoring classes include a review of math and verbal skills and vocabulary, tips and strategies for reading and writing passages, and several actual SAT or ACT tests administered on a schedule and in an environment that closely matches the actual test setting.

This job may be most appropriate as a second job for a current or retired teacher or guidance counselor.

Begin with your own preparation; get to know the tests inside and out. Many books and web sites offer practice tests and strategies. You can track your own improvement over time as an indication of the effect of practice and planning.

How to Get Started

Place flyers and ads on bulletin boards in community centers and schools. Place ads in the high school newspaper, in local newspapers, and in shopping guides.

Meet with the high school guidance counselor. Present your references and resume and ask to be kept in mind if a student or parent requests a private tutor.

Up-front Expenses

Build up a library of SAT and ACT preparation books. A capable PC with Internet access allows use of many online resources for testing and research. Other costs include advertising and promotion.

How Much to Charge

Charge by the hour for tutoring and consultation. You can add the cost of any books or sample tests you provide to the student; you may be able to purchase materials at wholesale or discounted prices and resell them at retail prices.

The well-known SAT and ACT preparation companies typically charge from a few hundred dollars to as much as $1,000. A personal tutor is likely to bill somewhere between 20 and 100 hours.

Legal and Insurance Issues

① **Legal**

② **Legal**

③ **Legal**

④ **Accounting**

⑤ **Insurance**

College Selection Advisor

Description of Job

- Help high school students and parents make informed decisions about college.

- Keep current on college offerings, admission criteria, scholarships, and financial aid.

The Need

Each year nearly 4 million American students head off to one of more than 4,000 accredited colleges and universities. Of course, before they pack their bags they have to get past a significant headache: choosing the school that offers the best combination of academic excellence, college life, and affordability . . . and where the student stands a good chance of being accepted.

In theory, this is the job of a high school guidance counselor, and many do a fine job in advising students. However, in many systems, the guidance counselor is stretched way too thin, overseeing the academic decisions and job choices of hundreds or even thousands of students each year.

The College Selection Advisor works as a personal guidance counselor, augmenting or substituting for counselors within the school system.

If you think of college as an investment of as much as $125,000 for a four-year program at a private university, the idea of spending a few hundred dollars for some professional shopping advice makes a great deal of sense.

This is a good job for a retired guidance counselor, teacher, or college administrator. The process begins by meeting with the student and parents, gathering information about academic standing, extracurricular activities, and college aspirations. If the parents request it, you may also gather general information about family income and investments to help advise about financial aid.

Based on what you learn in the interview, you will make recommendations on colleges, taking into consideration location, city or rural setting, size of student body, and courses of study. The list will include an assessment of the student's chances of acceptance, based on academic record, SAT scores, and other criteria.

Challenges

The biggest challenge accepted by the college selection advisor is to help students and parents make realistic decisions. Almost any serious student might list Harvard as a preferred school, but only 1,500 or so freshmen are admitted each fall. And competition for many larger colleges is just as intense.

Another challenge involves the ability to make a dispassionate recommendation about the type or size of school based on your appraisal of the student. A shy, sheltered child who has spent her entire life in a small rural community might not fare well in a huge, big-city college; a brash city kid might be a fish out of water at a small school in the Midwest. Advisors need to help the parent and students examine this element of the college decision.

Though they may have been preparing to send their children to college for more than a decade, few parents have a real understanding of the exact costs of college: tuition, room, board, fees, books, and travel. The advisor can offer information on lesser-known schools that offer a good education at a relatively low price.

In many cases, it is also very important for students to apply to more than one college in case they are not accepted by their first choice. The advisor assists in categorizing schools as best choices, acceptable backups, and "safety" schools, where the student is all but certain to be accepted.

In general, the job of the college selection advisor ends once the list of appropriate schools has been drawn up; later in this chapter you can read about a related job, the *college application consultant,* who assists students and parents in filling out applications and other forms.

Know the Territory

Spend the time to keep current on colleges and universities. Nearly every school has a detailed web site with information about academic offerings and requirements. You can also visit public and high school libraries to examine brochures on file there.

Find out from area high schools which colleges have enrolled recent graduates and request application materials for your own collection. Several guidebooks to colleges are published annually, including offerings from *U.S. News & World Report, Princeton Review,* and Peterson's (e.g., *Four-Year Colleges*).

Learn how to categorize schools based on information about acceptance levels in recent years. What is the average range of scores on the SAT or ACT? Where did the typical student place in high school class standing?

To appraise the school itself, look for information about the size of the student body, the cost of tuition, room, and board, and the average size of financial aid grants.

How to Get Started

Meet with area high school guidance counselors and ask whether they would be willing to work with you and recommend your services. Some counselors may welcome your involvement; others may feel you are intruding on their turf. Be diplomatic in all of your dealings.

Place ads and flyers in community centers and stores. Advertise in local newspapers, shopping guides, and the high school newspaper. Ask friends and relatives to spread the word, and ask satisfied clients to refer friends to you.

Up-front Expenses

Minimal expenses include advertising and promotion and purchase of college guidebooks.

How Much to Charge

Charge by the hour, or charge a flat fee for a standard assessment covering five to six hours of work. A typical schedule might include an initial consultation of one to two hours, office research of two hours, and a presentation to the student and family of one hour.

If you are called back for additional advice, charge an hourly rate.

Legal and Insurance Issues

① **Legal**

② **Legal**

③ **Legal**

④ **Accounting**

⑤ **Insurance**

College Application Consultant

Description of Job

* Help students—and their parents—navigate through the confusing maze of college application forms.
* Assist in gathering required letters of recommendation and transcripts.
* Aid in preparation of financial aid forms.

The Need

Few processes are more stressful, less predictable, and more important than applying to colleges. A typical application packet for a private college includes dozens of pages of forms, several booklets of instructions, and requests for additional information.

If that were not enough, most college applicants today apply to more than one school—perhaps as many as six or eight—including "safety" schools, where they believe they have a near certainty of acceptance; schools where they believe they have a good chance; and schools that are worth reaching for even though the odds of acceptance are low.

Challenges

A college application consultant assists with the completion and filing of forms and other information, but does not offer advice on selection of colleges; that is a job for a high school guidance counselor or a specialized college selection advisor.

Similarly, an application consultant should not become involved in coaching a student on essays or in obtaining recommendations; again, a high school guidance counselor may be of assistance here. The application consultant should be concerned with making certain that the essay and recommendations are submitted properly as part of the process.

People taking on this sort of job need to be highly organized, detail-oriented, and capable of meeting deadlines.

Consultants also have to demonstrate confidentiality as they work with applicants and their families to fill out financial aid forms, including the Free Application for Federal Student Aid (FAFSA) which is used as the basic request for aid at most colleges. Some schools also ask for supplemental information on forms of their own and may ask applicants to mail in copies of current federal tax forms.

Consultants may also offer assistance in applying for scholarships from community organizations, national service groups, unions, and corporations.

Be sure you make no promises about acceptance to any school; your job is to present the student's information in an accurate and timely fashion. *Do not* become involved in falsification of credentials, scores, recommendations, or other elements of the application; it's not just the student's reputation that could be damaged.

Know the Territory

Applications for college are generally filed by high school students in the fall of their senior year. Early-admission deadlines are generally in November, and final deadlines are usually in January.

A well-prepared and motivated student may be ready to work on applications months ahead of the deadline. However, many students—perhaps a majority of those who seek assistance from a college application consultant—may delay until almost the last possible moment.

Your work may well be squeezed into the period between Labor Day and New Year's Day, which includes the Thanksgiving and Christmas holidays.

You'll need a steady supply of high school seniors. Your chances of getting assignments is also related to the percentage of students who apply to college and the proportion who seek admission to private colleges, which generally have more complex application processes than do state or community colleges.

Research the most common college choices made by students in your area. Many schools publish this information in year-end newsletters; you may also be able to obtain a list of schools from a cooperative guidance counselor.

Most important, spend the time to become an expert on college applications. Establish a collection of them, noting those with unusual or nonstandard requests or confusing questions.

How to Get Started

Most major colleges now post their applications and supporting information online. Visit the web sites and download copies of the forms, or request that application packets be sent to you.

At most web sites you can practice filling out the forms without actually submitting them.

Feel free to call college admissions offices and ask questions about the application process.

Up-front Expenses

You'll need to set up and maintain a computer system to help you research colleges and obtain applications; many schools also permit filing of applications online.

Advertise for clients in school newspapers, on bulletin boards in schools, libraries, and community centers, and in shopping guides and community newspapers.

How Much to Charge

Jobs can be priced on an hourly basis or as a flat fee for the first application and a slightly reduced charge for multiple colleges. It will be easier to gather information for subsequent colleges once the first application is completed, but it still takes time to go through each application line by line to enter data.

Note, too, that the amount of work you have to do is related to how organized the student and his or her parents are in gathering information. If you work on an application only to find that the essay has not been completed or that details of the student's resume have not been prepared, you will have to have your clients put in more of their own time and then revisit the paperwork.

Charging on an hourly basis allows you to make a reasonable profit even if the tasks multiply and you must make more than one visit to a student.

If the work is done at your students' homes, using their computer, printer, and telephone, there should be no extra charges involved. If you work on the forms partly or completely at your home or office, you may incur costs for Internet use, printing, and telephone; your agreement should allow you to add these charges to your bill.

Legal and Insurance Issues

① **Legal**
② **Legal**
③ **Legal**
④ **Accounting**
⑤ **Insurance**

Instructor at Community School

Description of Job

- Teach a specialty course at a community school.
- Facilitate a regular gathering of like-minded hobbyists.

The Need

Do you have a special skill or interest? Why not earn some money sharing what you know?

Community schools offer classes on subjects as diverse as literacy and foreign languages to knitting, cooking, baking, money management, retirement planning, creative writing, and dog obedience training. Popular classes include explanations of modern technologies such as computer training, digital photography, and auto repair and maintenance.

Informal groups also explore hobbies such as sports memorabilia, stamp and coin collecting, and directed reading groups.

Challenges

You need knowledge and skills in a specialized area, and you need the ability to teach. You also need the ability to establish and maintain a professional atmosphere for learning.

The good news is that in most cases the students who sign up for a community school course are doing so because of a strong interest in the subject or the need to master a skill; they are likely to be highly motivated to succeed.

Know the Territory

Many area educational institutions seek to extend themselves to all residents, including taxpaying adults who otherwise have no connection to the school district. Most of the classes are taught at night or on weekends.

Once you are established, you may be able to use your experience and skills as an instructor to provide personal tutelage to students outside of the community school. The class may also help you gauge whether there is sufficient interest in a subject or service to allow you to start your own business.

How to Get Started

Begin by studying the list of course offerings at local community schools and colleges. If you see courses similar to the one you want to teach, that is probably good news; you're on the right track. Instructors may come and go, opening up new opportunities, or you may be able to offer a complementary or advanced version of the same course.

Write up a description of the course you want to teach, emphasizing your credentials on the subject and your communication skills. Develop a basic curriculum that extends across the typical length of a term—it might be 10 or 12 weeks or longer. Include information about any required books or materials students would be asked to purchase.

Submit your letter of interest to the director of your local community school or the dean of a community college that offers a night program.

Up-front Expenses

You may need to purchase books and other reference materials to assist in drawing up a curriculum. Other research can be done over the Internet and in libraries.

Take care not to make unauthorized copies of copyrighted material or to plagiarize published material.

You may want to spend some of your own money to publicize your course.

How Much to Charge

Instructors may be paid a flat fee, an hourly rate, or a percentage of the fees collected from students.

If you do additional private instruction, you can charge an hourly fee directly to students.

Legal and Insurance Issues

① **Legal**

④ **Accounting**

⑤ **Insurance**

CHAPTER 12

Arts, Crafts, Jewelry, Clothing, and Musical Instruments

69 Alterations

70 Custom Tailoring

71 Custom Knitting, Sweater, and Afghan Design

72 Custom Quiltmaker

73 Jewelry Making

74 Portraiture from Photographs

75 Custom-Built Dollhouses

76 Musical Instrument Tuning and Repair

Alterations

Description of Job

- Adjust sizes and fit of new or old clothing.
- Add hems to dresses and pants.
- Make minor repairs to fix costume malfunctions.

The Need

One size does *not* fit all . . . and we all change size over time.

Those two facts of life support the need for clothing alterations. Although you may think of yourself as a perfect size 8 or a 40 regular, your new dress or sport coat may not be quite ready to wear. The gown or the pants that fit you so nicely a year ago may have mysteriously shrunk . . . or, more likely, you may have added a few pounds.

Sometimes a minor costume malfunction—a missing button, an open seam, a broken zipper—can be repaired to rescue a favorite or valuable piece of clothing.

Another fact of life is that relatively few people in modern society have the time, skills, or equipment to make clothing alterations or repairs.

Challenges

Don't experiment on jobs that are beyond your skills or experience.

As a business, you will be liable for any damage you cause; your agreement with customers should limit the liability to the cost of replacement, excluding claims for sentimental value or loss of use. Even so, you should be very careful about accepting a job to hem a $2,000 wedding dress for a $20 fee; the risk is much greater than the reward.

Know the Territory

Your principal advantages: You have skills that are no longer common and equipment that is not generally possessed.

Another advantage is the fact that almost all of us purchase clothing off the rack and are forced to deal with the fact that even though an item may be labeled a particular size, modeling forms of different manufacturers vary widely.

Spend the time to get to know as much as you can about fabrics, designs, and methods to let out or take in clothing.

How to Get Started

Contact area clothing stores—for both new and used apparel—and make them aware of your services. They may be willing to let you perform work as a subcontractor at the store, or they may refer customers to you for alterations.

Local bridal stores may be willing to contract with you to perform alterations; these jobs may involve an entire wedding party, including bridal gowns and bridesmaids' outfits.

Community theaters may need help adjusting costumes to fit their actors. Small restaurants that provide uniforms to their waitstaff may need alteration and repair services. (Larger restaurants, hotels, and factories generally use uniform rental companies that probably have their own tailoring services.)

To reach individuals, place ads on bulletin boards at malls, in retail clothing stores, and in fabric stores. You can place an ad in community newspapers.

Up-front Expenses

You'll need basic tailoring equipment, including a sewing machine with some professional features such as buttonhole serging. You should have an iron for touch-up; you can also send oversized or specialty clothing to a dry cleaner for pressing.

Necessary supplies including thread and buttons.

How Much to Charge

Charge a flat rate for simple mending. Add a charge for buttons, zippers, lining, and special threads you must purchase.

Your agreement should list additional charges for more difficult jobs, such as hemming a lined dress.

If the clothing must be cleaned or pressed, add a charge for services you perform or for services you subcontract to a dry cleaner. (As a professional, you should seek a discount or a commission from outside companies. You can mark up these costs when you bill your customer.)

Legal and Insurance Issues

Special notes: In dealing with your client's property, seek to limit your liability for damage or loss to the actual replacement value of items in your possession. You should protect yourself against claims for sentimental value or loss of use.

① **Legal**

② **Legal**

③ **Legal**

④ **Accounting**

⑤ **Insurance**

⑥ **Insurance**

Custom Tailoring

Description of Job

- Choose fabric and custom-fit clothing for special occasions.
- Adapt and custom-fit patterns to create clothing for plus-size clients.
- Custom fit and adapt clothing for children.
- Create doll clothing.

The Need

Not every woman is a perfect size 8 or 16. Not every woman fits properly into a plus-size garment. Women and their clothing come in an infinite number of variations.

Any woman who has searched for a mother-of-the-bride dress or has had her teenage daughter drag her along on the hunt for a once-in-a-lifetime senior-prom gown knows how frustrating and exhausting shopping can be.

At any age, custom clothing is an opportunity to choose fabric and notions and obtain a perfect fit in the process. In some situations—for example, brides-maids' outfits—it may be less expensive to choose fabric and commission a tailor than to purchase an article of clothing off the rack and have it altered.

While we're on the subject of custom clothing: Apparently, there are times when even a doll needs that extra-special, perfectly fitted outfit.

Challenges

You must be able to take precise measurements and know how to adapt patterns or take in garments to be a capable tailor. Even if you are working from a pattern, your client is paying for a custom fit.

If you are making clothing for a special occasion, you must be able to meet deadlines; don't accept the job of outfitting a bride and her three bridesmaids if you know the date of the wedding is too close at hand.

Know the Territory

The process begins with careful measurements. Then you will adapt a pattern to create a perfect fit for your client, taking into account the fabric and notions chosen. Finally, you will conduct a series of fittings to adjust the finished garment.

In addition to being an expert at the sewing machine, you must know about fabrics and how they work with various patterns, sizes, and styles. You need to understand how silk and satin wear, clean, and stretch differently than cotton or synthetic fabrics.

Clients may come to you soliciting your advice on fabric, style, trim, and what patterns work best with their measurement; or they may have done their homework and have a specific outfit and pattern number in mind.

How to Get Started

Place flyers and ads at community centers, in schools, and in stores. Place ads in newspapers, shopping guides, and school and church publications.

Ask friends and acquaintances to recommend your services; offer to give them a bonus or discount for business they steer your way.

Rent space at crafts shows, holiday fairs, and bridal shows. Teach a class in sewing at a local community school for publicity and perhaps to gain new clients.

Up-front Expenses

You'll need a professional-quality sewing machine and other clothes-making equipment. You may be able to farm out some specialized work such as embroidery and decorative stitching.

Other up-front costs include advertising and promotion.

How Much to Charge

Most jobs will be done at a flat rate based on your estimate of the number of hours involved plus the cost of material and notions. It could also be quoted as a cost-plus job, with the client paying the actual cost of all materials plus a set charge for your time as a tailor.

Adjust your flat rate, or change to an hourly rate, for jobs where the garment—or the client—will require a great deal of extra effort. Your price should take into account extra work for special features such as sequins, pearls, or lace, and the extra time required to work with certain fabrics.

Legal and Insurance Issues

Special notes: In dealing with your client's property, seek to limit your liability for damage or loss to the actual replacement value of the items in your possession. You should protect yourself against claims for sentimental value or loss of use.

① **Legal**

② **Legal**

③ **Legal**

④ **Accounting**

⑤ **Insurance**

⑥ **Insurance**

Custom Knitting, Sweater, and Afghan Design

Description of Job

- Custom-knit clothing to specifications.
- Personalize knitted clothing prepared from patterns.

The Need

Almost everyone can appreciate the beauty of a hand-knit sweater or afghan. But relatively few have the skills or time necessary to produce one.

A custom-knitted sweater or other article of clothing is a great gift for the hard-to-please or the hard-to-fit. It is a way to obtain clothing made of machine-washable or hypoallergenic yarns.

You can supply keepsakes to celebrate special occasions including holidays, reunions, and births.

Challenges

You'll need the skill to produce work of professional quality in a reasonable period of time. You may be called on to take measurements and create clothing to fit, or you may need to follow someone else's instructions.

Make sure you have a written agreement about the work to be done, including full specifications and sizes. Give details about the type of yarn and other components, and make reference to a specific design if one exists.

Know the Territory

Keep current on available yarns, materials, and designs. Visit fabric and knitting-supply stores for ideas, and consult web sites and magazines.

You may be able to purchase supplies locally, or you may have to order yarn, needles, and components by mail or over the Internet.

How to Get Started

Post flyers and business cards at knitting stores, community centers, and supermarkets. Place ads in shopping guides, newspapers, and church bulletins.

Consider setting up a web site to promote and sell your work, posting photos of completed work. Customers can call you by telephone or send specifications by e-mail.

Up-front Expenses

The primary expenses are for advertising and promotion. If you set up a web site, you will have to pay for design and hosting.

Consider setting up a merchant account to accept credit cards.

How Much to Charge

This sort of work is generally done on a flat-rate basis, although you will set your rate based on your estimation of the number of hours required to complete the job. You can include the cost of materials in your overall price, or break them out as a separate element.

Legal and Insurance Issues

① **Legal**

② **Legal**

③ **Legal**

④ **Accounting**

⑤ **Insurance**

Custom Quiltmaker

Description of Job

- Design and produce custom handmade quilts to the specifications of a client.
- Sell handmade quilts directly to customers or offer them over the Internet.

The Need

A handmade quilt is an instant family heirloom. It's a great way to commemorate special occasions such as the birth of a baby, a wedding, a graduation, an anniversary, and anytime it's important to give a quality, personalized gift.

Challenges

Making a quilt is a combination of skill and artistry. You should be very familiar with different methods, styles, and patterns.

If you are producing a custom design, make sure you understand the needs and wants of your customer. Show sketches, samples, and work in progress.

The quality of your product should be on a professional level, well above that of amateur work. You should be working with superior materials, sewing machines, and other supplies.

You have to be able to meet deadlines. If a quilt is intended to be presented at an anniversary or a christening, it has to be finished before the date.

Know the Territory

Become an expert on available fabrics and techniques. Establish a relationship with the proprietor of area fabric and craft stores for advice on products; you should be able to purchase products at wholesale or discounted prices.

Many books and patterns are available, and you'll find a wealth of information on web sites. You can order materials and accessories online as well.

How to Get Started

Post flyers and business cards in community centers, schools, and retail stores. Place ads in newspapers and shopping guides.

Make yourself known to managers of craft and hobby stores, interior decorators, and managers of home decorating stores. They may be willing to display some of your work or recommend your services to their customers; offer a commission or bonus for business they send your way. Ask friends, acquaintances, and satisfied customers to recommend your services; you can give them a bonus or discount on future business.

Rent a table at craft fairs or holiday shows to promote your products. Offer to teach a class at a community school—this will give you publicity and perhaps some clients. You can create and maintain a web site to showcase some of your creations and offer your services.

Up-front Expenses

Prepare some samples of your work to show would-be clients. Display photographs in a scrapbook or online.

You'll need a reliable, heavy-duty sewing machine and other sewing supplies and a collection of books and reference materials. Other costs include advertising and promotion.

How Much to Charge

Sell your quilts for a fixed price based on your well-learned estimate of the amount of time involved in creating the item plus the cost of materials.

Another option is to sell work on a cost-plus basis, charging one fee for your labor and a second fee for the cost of materials and supplies.

Legal and Insurance Issues

① **Legal**

② **Legal**

③ **Legal**

④ **Accounting**

⑤ **Insurance**

Jewelry Making

Description of Job

- Design and produce handcrafted necklaces, rings, bracelets, earrings, and beaded or jeweled purses.
- Customize off-the-shelf jewelry and purses to the specifications of customers.

The Need

All of us can appreciate a beautiful piece of jewelry. Even more impressive is a one-of-a-kind or customized piece.

The market for this sort of work is someone who wants something different from the standard offerings of retail stores.

Challenges

The difference between simple and ornate jewelry is a great deal of experience, time, and expense. Start out with simple, high-quality work and build your skills and business.

You must deliver what you promise. If you contract to provide a necklace of sterling silver or beads, Murano glass, or Swarovski crystal, you are legally bound to deliver that product.

Working with diamonds, platinum, gold, and other expensive materials requires a large investment and exposes you to liability for loss. Most jewelry makers start with simpler and less costly projects.

Know the Territory

Learn as much as you can about jewelry making from books, the Internet, and classes or workshops offered at craft and bead stores or community schools. Some suppliers offer training in the use of their tools or materials.

You may be able to gain experience by working as a helper or apprentice to an artisan.

Simple, handcrafted bead jewelry—using precious or semiprecious stones, crystal, gold, sterling silver, or clay—can be made from commercial and hand-made beads available from a variety of sources and strung on wire or beading thread. Some makers visit antique stores, flea markets, and craft shops in search of unusual components. Advanced work includes use of tiny seed beads.

Precious metal clay (PMC) jewelry is a clay substance that becomes a metal-like silver or gold material when fired in a kiln.

Working in gold, silver, copper, and other metals requires experience with jeweler's saws, solder, pliers, and other tools.

How to Get Started

Show off some of your handiwork at craft shows and flea markets. Find out whether some specialty stores will stock your products for resale to their customers; you can sell your items to the dealer or place them there on consignment until they are sold and then pay the dealer a commission.

Post ads and flyers at community centers, at schools, at senior centers, and in retail stores. Place ads in newspapers and shopping guides, especially around holidays, including Christmas, Valentine's Day, and Mother's Day. You can also create and maintain a web site to sell your products.

Ask satisfied customers to recommend your products; offer a bonus or discount for work they send your way.

Up-front Expenses

You will need a jeweler's tool kit that includes pliers, clamps, vises, hammers, cutters, saws, wire, clasps, soldering tools, torches, and thread. You may need a kiln to fire clay; you may be able to obtain access to a kiln at someone else's studio.

Other costs include advertising and promotion. If you choose to sell over the Internet, you will need to pay for a web site and the capability to accept credit card transactions.

How Much to Charge

Price your products based on the cost of the materials plus the amount of time involved in completing each project. Add extra charges for more customization and for shipping if necessary.

Legal and Insurance Issues

Special notes: If your client gives you something of value to be customized, seek to limit your liability for damage or loss to the actual replacement value of items in your possession. You should protect yourself against claims for sentimental value or loss of use.

① **Legal**

② **Legal**

③ **Legal**

④ **Accounting**

⑤ **Insurance**

⑥ **Insurance**

Portraiture from Photographs

Description of Job

- Paint custom oil or watercolor portraits of individuals, families, and pets.
- Create custom portraits of homes, boats, and cars.

The Need

A custom portrait is a want, not a need. For many people, a hand-painted oil or watercolor portrait is a step up in class from a framed snapshot or one of those all-too-familiar gauzy portrait studio photographs.

Capable artists can create painted versions of photographs of individuals, husband and wife, a family scene, or a favorite pet. Some people will pay handsomely for an art rendition of their yacht, sailboat, hot rod, sports car, or summer home.

One of the great advantages of a painted portrait is that the painter can take artistic liberties: peeling years off a face, adding a handsome or famous landscape, turning a young pistol into a cherub, or removing an out-of-favor friend or family member from a picture.

Challenges

You'll need strong artistic skills, including the ability to copy likenesses from photos.

Make sure you fully understand your clients' hopes and expectations. Do they want photo-realism, or do they want you to add some embellishments and improvements?

Know the Territory

Since the birth of photography nearly two centuries ago, artists have used photos as the basis for paintings and watercolors. Four common procedures are used, from old and basic to state-of-the-art and advanced:

1. Hanging the photo alongside the blank canvas or high-quality watercolor paper and re-creating it freehand

2. Projecting the photo onto the canvas or paper using an overhead projector or slide projector and painting it with watercolors or oils

3. Scanning the photo into a computer and using digital editing software to create a version of the photo that can be projected onto a blank canvas or paper and painted using watercolors or oils

4. Printing out a digitally edited version of the photo, mounting the print on a backboard, and applying oil paint to create a portrait

This job can easily be done from your home or studio without ever having to meet clients directly. You can post a portfolio of your work on a web site, and you can accept photos sent by regular mail or by by e-mail (as a digital file).

You can ship completed oil canvases or watercolors to the client either framed or unframed.

How to Get Started

Post flyers and business cards at community centers, at senior centers, and in schools. Place ads in newspapers and shopping guides.

Create a web site to show examples of your work. (Obtain permission from clients before posting their commissioned portraits online or in any other advertising medium.)

Ask satisfied customers to recommend your services to friends and acquaintances; offer a bonus or discount for any business they send you. Make contact with area photographers and ask them to suggest oil or watercolor versions to clients; offer a commission for referrals.

Up-front Expenses

You'll need an artist's kit: brushes, paints, palettes, and other supplies. If you will be promoting your work over the Internet or accepting submission of e-mailed photos, you'll need a capable computer with Web access.

How Much to Charge

Offer your clients a bottom-line price based on the size and complexity of the portrait. For example, a small 12- by 16-inch portrait of one person might be priced at $200 for a head-to-toe painting; it would be slightly less for an upper-body-only painting. Each additional person in the portrait might cost another $125.

A 48- by 60-inch portrait (15 times more space to cover) might be priced at $900 to $1,000 for one person.

Some artists quote a basic price for a portrait set against a plain background and charge a higher rate for more complex backdrops.

Oil paintings are generally priced about $50 to $100 higher than watercolors because of the higher cost of canvas and paints.

Add to the price the cost of framing and shipping the completed piece. A framed work requires a more robust container and higher shipping costs than a bare piece of work.

Legal and Insurance Issues

Special notes: In dealing with your client's property, seek to limit your liability for damage or loss to the actual replacement value of items in your possession. You should protect yourself against claims for sentimental value or loss of use.

① **Legal**

② **Legal**

③ **Legal**

④ **Accounting**

⑤ **Insurance**

⑥ **Insurance**

Custom-Built Dollhouses

Description of Job

- Build dollhouses to order, with custom colors and flourishes, based on plans and precut kits.
- Create one-of-a-kind dollhouses based on the dreams and wishes of clients.

The Need

Little dollhouses are big business for some youngsters (and their doting parents).

In many cultures, dollhouses are an important part of a young girl's childhood. Many adults look on them as a family heirloom or collector's item that can be passed on from one generation to the next.

For a child who is serious about finding a proper home for a family of dolls, a cheaply made, mass-produced plastic dollhouse from a toy store may be completely unacceptable.

Challenges

A custom-made or specially adapted dollhouse can cost hundreds of dollars. Although dollhouses don't quite follow the building code of a real home, some of the same construction skills and techniques are necessary. Because they are viewed close-up, the attention to finishing details must be meticulous.

Know the Territory

The simplest way to operate this sort of business is to assemble and custom-finish precut kits that are sold by a number of national and regional companies. Your customers can choose any home and specify colors, wall and floor coverings, and other elements.

More demanding of your skills is building dollhouses based on plans selected by your client. You will be responsible for obtaining wood and other materials, cutting them to size, and assembling them. You'll find many sources for plans, including books, catalogs, and web sites.

Experienced woodworkers can offer to draw plans, specify materials, and build a home from scratch. The ultimate in customization is also the most expensive process.

You can sell your products at craft fairs, through direct sales generated by ads and web sites, and in cooperation with high-end toy stores and home decor stores that want to offer custom products to their customers.

How to Get Started

Build some sample homes to show to clients; take extensive photographs of all jobs you complete to include in an album or to display online.

Post flyers and business cards in community centers, schools, and shopping centers. Place ads in newspapers, shopping guides, and specialized newsletters aimed at collectors.

Make contact with high-end toy stores, hobbyist shops, and home decor stores and seek places to display samples of your work. Offer to pay a commission or bonus to stores for business they refer to you.

Rent a table at craft shows and holiday fairs to display some of your work and to show catalogs of possible projects.

Offer to teach a course at a community school; you will receive some publicity and perhaps some clients. Offer to give demonstrations at community and senior centers—grandparents may commission your work for that special grandchild.

Up-front Expenses

You'll need a woodworking tool kit, plus supplies for painting, staining, and decorating. You should also plan on building a few samples of your work to show to customers and to display at craft fairs and in retail stores that agree to refer clients to you.

Materials for a relatively simple custom dollhouse can cost in the range of $150 to $300; more complex jobs use more expensive materials. Prefabricated kits can require just a few hours to assemble and a few more hours for painting and finishing. Working from plans requires additional hours for purchasing and cutting materials and for assembly. The most time-consuming projects involve custom design, specification, cutting, and assembly; these jobs may require 20 to 40 hours of work plus the cost of materials.

How Much to Charge

Most dollhouse builders quote a bottom-line price that includes the cost of materials and time spent in assembly and finishing. Add an extra fee for designing the house from scratch, taking into account that assembly will require considerably more time than working from a kit.

The cost of prefabricated kits—before labor, paint, and finish—ranges from as little as $50 for a simple plywood-faced shed to several hundred dollars or more.

Legal and Insurance Issues

① **Legal**

② **Legal**

③ **Legal**

④ **Accounting**

⑤ **Insurance**

Musical Instrument Tuning and Repair

Description of Job

- Inspect musical instruments to determine maintenance needs or assess damage.
- Repair or replace defective parts; work with a specialist to repair major damage.
- Restring instruments as required.
- Tune instruments to improve the sound.

The Need

Musical instruments need to be maintained and repaired, and most require a professional's touch and equipment to stay in tune.

The heart of the market is piano tuning. Other jobs include restringing and adjustment of stringed instruments and correction of problems with keys and other controls on woodwinds.

Challenges

The biggest challenge is to find a steady source of new and repeat customers.

You'll need a good ear for music as well as some basic mechanical skills.

Most people who perform this sort of work specialize in one area, such as pianos, stringed instruments, woodwinds, band instruments, or percussion instruments.

Modern electronic organs and amplifiers for electric guitars and other instruments require special training and background in electrical and computer circuits.

Work on large instruments such as pianos is usually performed on location in private homes, schools, and places of entertainment. Smaller instruments are often given over to the technician to be adjusted in a workshop.

Make sure you have limited your liability before working on an antique or especially valuable instrument.

Know the Territory

The traditional method of tuning an instrument was a well-trained ear and a set of tuning forks: The technician would strike or pluck a string, for example, and compare it to the reference pitch of the fork. That method still works, although many technicians today use electronic devices that give precise readouts on the frequency of an instrument's sound.

To adjust a piano, for example, a tuner strikes a key and compares the sound to the matching tuning fork; using a special lever or wrench, the tuner tightens or loosens the strings. A standard piano has 88 keys and 230 strings; a typical tuning session requires about 90 minutes.

Piano repair begins with checking the action of the mechanical linkages between the keys and the hammers. Minor repairs can be accomplished by cleaning or replacing worn parts; major repairs usually require removal of the piano to a workshop and a complete or partial disassembly.

Guitar technicians repair and replace tuning pegs, saddle, and bridge. They may also repair minor damage to the body and restring the instrument. The final step is to precisely tune the strings.

Repairs and tuning techniques for violins are similar to those for guitars; the technician may also fill in scratches and apply a fresh coat of appropriate varnish.

For brass and woodwind instruments, the technician checks the condition of keys, pistons, and other parts; if they cannot be repaired, they can usually be replaced.

Repairs to percussion instruments, including drum sets, require woodworking and metalworking skills in addition to musical training.

How to Get Started

You don't need to be able to play a piano or a guitar in order to tune or repair the instrument, although you may have to fend off requests for demonstrations by clients. The necessary skills are mechanical and auditory.

Some technical schools offer classes in tuning and repairing instruments. Check for classes offered at community schools or colleges. You may be able to train as an apprentice or assistant to a professional.

There are also many self-teaching books and some web sites that offer instruction on repair and maintenance of musical instruments. Read magazines aimed at musicians for leads.

Post flyers and ads in music stores, theaters, schools, and community centers. Place ads in newspapers and shopping guides.

Make yourself known to music teachers at local schools. If there are any orchestras or musical theaters in your area, meet the director.

Ask friends and acquaintances to recommend your services; offer a bonus or discount for business they direct to you. Ask satisfied customers to do the same, and offer them a discount on future services for new customers they refer.

Up-front Expenses

For ordinary tune-ups you'll need a small tool kit of wrenches, small pliers, and special-purpose tools. For piano tuning, as an example, you'll need tuning hammers, mutes, capstan tools, and tuning forks. Prepackaged tool kits range in price from about $50 to $200.

Most tuners use an electronic tuning meter as their primary or backup method for adjusting the pitch of strings; meters range in price from about $50 to $250.

Other costs include those for training, reference manuals, and an inventory of replacement parts. You'll also need to pay for advertising and promotion.

How Much to Charge

Basic tuning is usually charged at a flat rate. Repairs are charged at an hourly rate plus the cost of parts and materials; you should be able to purchase parts at wholesale or discount prices and resell them to your customers at retail prices.

Legal and Insurance Issues

Special notes: In dealing with your client's property, seek to limit your liability for damage or loss to the actual replacement value of items in your possession. You should protect yourself against claims for sentimental value or loss of use.

① Legal
② Legal
③ Legal
④ Accounting
⑤ Insurance
⑥ Insurance

CHAPTER 13

Transportation, Delivery, and Auto Services

77 Car Service

78 Independent Delivery Contractor

79 Auto Detailing

Car Service

Description of Job

- Provide scheduled pickup and transportation for clients.
- Meet clients at airports and cruise terminals.
- Provide scheduled service for nonemergency medical transportation, weddings, proms, and special events.
- Requires rental, lease, or purchase of appropriate vehicle.

The Need

Sometimes it makes a lot of sense to leave the driving to others.

If you're heading for the airport, you might prefer to leave your personal car home in the garage instead of at an airport lot; it might be less expensive, too. You can also save some time on early morning departures, and there is the comforting luxury of knowing someone is waiting to meet you at baggage claim when you arrive back home.

Older people without their own transportation can rely on a car service to deliver them and pick them up from doctor's appointments. Parents can relax (a bit) on prom night and other special occasions knowing that a professional driver and safe car is on call to transport their children.

Challenges

A car service is not a taxi service; in most jurisdictions, you need a special permit to pick up customers who flag you down on the street. You will need to limit your business to responding to reserved appointments and to telephoned requests for service.

In most states, you will need a chauffeur's license or endorsement to your personal driver's license. The vehicle may need to be registered as a limousine or commercial vehicle. Your insurance company will require full coverage of your vehicle for commercial use.

Depending on your clientele—and by extension the price range you plan to charge—you will need a clean, well-maintained, and spacious vehicle. You don't need a Cadillac limousine for ordinary car service jobs, but your 1994 Ford

Escort with fuzzy dice hanging from the windshield and dents in the passenger-side front door just won't do.

You will need to have a flexible schedule, especially if you will be accepting jobs picking up clients at airports; if a plane is several hours late, you will have to wait around for your incoming customer or arrange for another service to take your job. (For that reason, some car services do not accept airport pickups or limit the amount of time they will wait for a delayed flight.)

If you will be operating the car service on a part-time basis, you may be able to use the vehicle for other purposes. Be sure to consult your accountant about proper record keeping for mixed use of a business asset.

Know the Territory

Assess the market by working backward: Where do people need to travel? Is there much traffic from your area to an airport or a bus terminal? Is there steady business to area hospitals and doctors? Are there businesses in the area that might dispatch employees for air travel regularly?

Before you purchase a vehicle, research its cost of operation (gas mileage, maintenance, and depreciation) and determine its capital cost. Your business plan should be based on reasonable estimates of the number of jobs you can expect and cash flow you will receive.

How to Get Started

Place flyers and ads in community centers, schools, and retail stores. Advertise your service in newspapers and shopping guides.

Make contact with the travel planner for companies in your area. List your services with business associations and in newsletters.

Establish contacts at local senior citizen centers, hospitals, and doctors' offices who may recommend your services to clients.

Up-front Expenses

You will need a clean, reliable sedan or small van. Other expenses include a commercial or limousine driver's license, appropriate vehicle plates, and commercial insurance.

Some localities require car services to obtain a permit, and you may need to pay for the right to pick up or drop off passengers at airports, convention centers, and other government-owned or -licensed facilities.

You will also need a cell phone to accept bookings while you are on the road, to call airlines to check on schedules, and to keep in touch with clients who may call to advise you of delays.

How Much to Charge

Most car services charge an hourly rate for transportation around town, generally in the range of $35 to $50 per hour for a sedan or minivan; limousines may charge $80 to $100 per hour. Calculate your hourly rate on the basis of the operating cost for the vehicle plus fixed expenses such as licenses, insurance, and a profit for your time.

Services also commonly offer fixed rates from a particular region to an airport, bus terminal, or other popular destination.

Some services charge for time spent waiting for delayed flights, lengthy doctors' office appointments, and so on.

Customers must pay any tolls and entrance fees. It is also customary for customers to give a gratuity, usually about 15 percent.

Regular accounts are usually given a discount on hourly rates or a percentage off the monthly bill for service above a certain level.

Legal and Insurance Issues

Special notes: An insurance agent can counsel you about commercial vehicle insurance and liability coverage.

① **Legal**

② **Legal**

③ **Legal**

④ **Accounting**

⑤ **Insurance**

Independent Delivery Contractor

Description of Job

- Deliver packages, supplies, small appliances, and other items on demand for local retailers.

- Pick up and deliver packages and boxes as an independent representative of a national or regional carrier.
- Rent, lease, or purchase an appropriate vehicle.

The Need

It does not always make economic sense for retail outlets to buy or lease trucks and pay drivers for occasional deliveries.

Major national shipping companies, including FedEx, often hire independent delivery contractors for their on-demand pickup and ground delivery services.

When a company makes a deal with an independent contractor, it typically does not have to pay federal payroll taxes, Social Security taxes, federal unemployment insurance tax, state unemployment insurance premiums, and workers' compensation insurance premiums. It also is excused from most employee benefits, such as health insurance, vacation time, sick leave, retirement benefits, and life or disability insurance. In addition, the contractor has to provide the truck, the office, and a telephone.

Furthermore, the company can hire a contractor for a short period of time or for a special project without worrying about capital expenditures.

Challenges

You will bear the expense of purchasing or leasing a van or truck, plus the cost of licensing and insurance. This business will succeed only if you can bring in a steady stream of jobs at prices that cover your expenses and time.

Work may be seasonal, with spikes of business around holiday periods. In tourist or vacation areas, companies may need extra help in the summer or winter seasons.

By signing up as a contractor for a national shipping company, your job flow may be more regular, but such companies are very strict about driving records, court records, and insurance requirements.

Consult an attorney before setting up a trucking company with scheduled deliveries that cross state lines. Although the Interstate Commerce Commission no longer has a stranglehold on trucking, there are still many state and federal agencies, including the U.S. Department of Transportation, that will take an interest in your operations.

Know the Territory

Spend time with an accountant or consultant to go over your business plan to ensure that you can be economically successful as an independent contractor. The margin for error is slim.

Study the contracts offered by major carriers and make sure they will work for your situation. For example, FedEx's published rules for independent contractors dictate that drivers can have no more than three moving violations within the previous three years and no more than one in the previous 12 months. Drivers must have a commercial driver's license with a hazardous materials endorsement and must pass a U.S. Department of Transportation–defined physical exam and drug test.

How to Get Started

Contact area office supply stores, appliance stores, and other merchants and offer your services for on-demand deliveries.

Check with major national carriers about availability of independent contractor deals in your area.

Up-front Expenses

You'll need a van or truck large enough to meet the needs of your clients, but not so large that its purchase or lease and the cost of operation would eat up all of your profits.

You will also be required to have a commercial driver's license and tags, plus adequate collision and liability insurance coverage.

How Much to Charge

Contracts with major carriers usually pay by the mile, plus a stipend to cover some of the costs of the vehicle itself.

Deals with smaller local retailers may be priced by the hour or the mile, with extra payments for overweight items, night or weekend deliveries, and inside deliveries (versus those left outside the door).

Legal and Insurance Issues

Special notes: An insurance agent can offer counsel about commercial vehicle insurance and liability coverage.

① **Legal**

② **Legal**

③ **Legal**

④ **Accounting**

⑤ **Insurance**

Auto Detailing

Description of Job

- Clean cars inch by inch to return them to factory-new condition . . . or better than that.

- Perform some jobs on a regular basis, others on a one-time basis for resale to a new buyer.

- Work closely with your client to understand expectations; every job is unique.

The Need

Some people's cars are like a teenager's room, carpeted with six months of newspapers and fast-food wrappers and possessed of an exotic but nonspecific odor. Other people like to maintain their cars in better-than-factory-fresh condition.

The auto detailer uses hoses, sponges, vacuum cleaners, toothbrushes, toothpicks, and magnifying glasses to pick up every crumb, polish every surface, and renew every cosmetic feature of a car.

Challenges

Your job is to run a beauty salon, not a plastic surgeon's operating room. An auto detailer's job description does not include removing dents or significant interior or exterior work; clients should be referred to an auto body shop or an automotive paint shop for that sort of preparatory work before the vehicle is brought in for detailing.

Do you go to the car, or does it come to you? You'll need the same equipment either way, but if you travel to the job, you'll need a vehicle—perhaps a truck or van—to carry supplies. (Your vehicle should become an example of your work; it should sparkle like a showroom demonstrator.)

If the cars come to you, your setup and cleanup will be easier, but you may bear some liability for the vehicle while it is on your property.

Record existing damage to the car and the odometer reading on the contract, and have the client initial that section to protect you against certain claims.

Know the Territory

Detailing is, for most car owners, a luxury. Take a look around a neighborhood and appraise the value—and condition—of the cars you see.

Before you accept a vehicle for detailing, make a close inspection in the presence of the owner and note any damage or special conditions. Look for tears in the upholstery, scratches or dents in the sheet metal, and missing parts.

Think twice before accepting antique or collectible vehicles. You don't want to be responsible for replacing African burl wood in a Rolls-Royce if you scratch it.

How to Get Started

Post flyers in auto supply stores. Place ads in auto club and collector newsletters.

Ask friends and relatives for referrals.

Up-front Expenses

You'll need a few hundred dollars worth of detergents, vinyl and leather renewers, tire and wheel cleaners, polishes, and waxes.

Necessary equipment includes clean, soft towels—many detailers use cloth diapers—for polishing and cleaning. Sponges and washing mitts are useful to clean the exterior. To apply wax and polish, many detailers use real or synthetic chamois cloths; final buffing can be done with a power orbital buffer, although purists prefer hand finishing.

You'll need stiff-bristled brushes to clean tires and wheels; you'll need small, soft brushes, including toothbrushes, to clean inside small enclosures.

Spray bottles and cans are needed for glass cleaners, vinyl and leather renewers, and other chemicals.

Interior cleaning begins with a powerful vacuum. Carpets can be cleaned with a steam cleaner or shampoo machine.

Cleaning the engine compartment is usually a job for a power washer, carefully applied to avoid damage to sensitive components of modern motors. Detailers use a degreasing solution and a brush to remove oil and grease, taking care to avoid getting the chemical on the paint surface. Rubber belts, hoses, and door gaskets can be renewed with a silicone dressing.

How Much to Charge

Proper detailing of a car that is already in reasonably good shape will take from several hours to a full day; a car that has major cleanliness issues may demand as much as two days.

You can charge on an hourly basis or set a flat rate based on an underlying hourly rate. Plan on additional charges for difficult cases; conversely, offer discounts for repeat customers who bring cars to you regularly.

Add extra charges for special polishes, cleaners, or paints.

Estimated charges: $50 to $100 for ordinary jobs, $100 to $200 for difficult cases.

Legal and Insurance Issues

Special notes: In dealing with your client's property, seek to limit your liability for damage or loss to the actual replacement value of items in your possession. You should protect yourself against claims for sentimental value or loss of use.

An insurance agent can offer counsel about commercial vehicle insurance and liability coverage.

① **Legal**

② **Legal**

③ **Legal**

④ **Accounting**

⑤ **Insurance**

⑥ **Insurance**

Computers, Graphics, and Photography

80 Computer Buying Consultant

81 Computer Repair and Upgrade

82 Web Design and Maintenance

83 Graphic Designer

84 Freelance Photographer

85 Film to Digital Scanning

86 Photo and Document Restorer

87 Videographer

Computer Buying Consultant

Description of Job

- Advise individuals and small companies in making computer purchases.
- Assist with setup of hardware and installation of software.
- Help install telephone, DSL, or cable modem connection to the Internet.

The Need

For some people, buying and installing a computer is a terrifying prospect. They fear buying the wrong equipment, paying way too much for it, and then being totally unable to figure out where to plug in which end of the cable.

Other people may throw up their hands at the prospect of figuring out how to connect to the Internet or how to set up a small wireless network in a home or office to share printers, modems, and other devices.

The computer buying consultant is like a contractor for the construction of a house: someone who arranges for delivery of all of the pieces and services and makes sure everything is working properly. Then he or she fades away (heading for the bank), leaving the operation and maintenance of the house to others.

The job of the computer buying consultant ends once the computer system is up and running properly. If a client runs into problems with software or if a piece of hardware fails six months or a year later, the client should be referred to a computer repair or software consultant.

We recommend separating the jobs of a computer buying consultant and a repair service because the level of complexity is vastly different. Once the computer is up and running, you will have no control over what the user does to it.

Challenges

Make sure you understand the needs, wants, and technical abilities of your clients. You don't want to specify a machine that is beyond the needs (and budget) of your client, yet you don't want to recommend a cheap and underpowered or poorly assembled machine just because the price tag is low.

The vast majority of computers in homes and business are based on the PC design and are intended to work with the Microsoft Windows operating system. A small portion of the computer industry is devoted to the Apple Macintosh design and its operating system. The two universes are relatively similar to each other, but you will need to be well educated about the differences.

Learn the various Internet connection options available in your area. Telephone dial-up service is the most mature and usually the easiest to set up, but it is the slowest system available. Cable modem service, where available, is usually the fastest for residential and small-business use. In between is DSL service via telephone cable; setup can sometimes be very complex and problematic, and connection speeds are faster than dial-up but generally slower than cable.

Be sure the client understands the brick wall you will erect between consulting on the purchase of a system and its later operation. Establish relationships with computer repair services and software consultants who will be available to your client if needed.

Know the Territory

You need to be the sort of person who can quote prices and specifications from memory, someone who reads computer ads and web sites for enjoyment. You should be familiar with the offerings of the major online vendors of computers (including Dell, Hewlett-Packard, and IBM) and the web sites and catalogs of direct sellers of other machines.

Make regular visits to area computer retail stores to see the range of offerings and understand their sales and support procedures.

How to Get Started

Place flyers and ads in community centers, schools, and retail stores. Advertise in community newspapers, shopping guides, and school newspapers.

Ask satisfied customers to recommend your services to friends and acquaintances; offer a bonus or discount for business they refer.

Up-front Expenses

Build up a library of technical manuals and computer magazines to keep current on the latest technologies and products. Consult web sites of manufacturers of hardware and software and be a regular visitor to Internet homes for companies that sell computers, peripherals, and services.

You'll also need a basic tool kit containing screwdrivers and nut drivers for installation of systems.

Other expenses include advertising and promotion.

How Much to Charge

Charge by the hour for your services, or offer a package rate for a set number of hours for buying consultation and installation of equipment. To offer the most independent and unbiased service to your client, you should not ask for or accept commissions or other payments from the sellers of hardware.

Legal and Insurance Issues

① **Legal**

② **Legal**

③ **Legal**

④ **Accounting**

⑤ **Insurance**

Computer Repair and Upgrade

Description of Job

- Fix or replace failed components of personal computers.
- Perform upgrades of memory, microprocessor, and drives.
- Salvage data from functioning hard drives in failed computers.
- Work with data recovery companies to salvage data from failed hard drives.

The Need

There are very few of us whose lives and businesses are not inextricably bound up with computers. We balance our checkbooks, research our homework, send e-mail, play games, and work on our Great American Novel on our PCs at home.

In businesses, sometimes the entire enterprise exists within the memory banks of the computer; companies also depend on their machines for communication, accounting, human resources, inventory, sales, and research.

Here's something that every computer owner should know: Hard drives, CD-ROMs, fans, memory, and just about every other part of a computer will eventually fail. It's not a question of *if*, just *when.*

The bottom line: When something breaks, it needs to be fixed. Sometimes, when the computer itself fails, a capable technician needs to perform a transplant of vital data from one machine to another.

The other element here is the need to keep up-to-date with improvements in hardware: faster and larger hard drives, faster and larger memory, and new and improved CD and DVD drives. In most cases, it is not necessary to throw away an otherwise functioning PC. Instead, it can be upgraded piece by piece.

Challenges

We recommend that you avoid mixing hardware apples and software oranges. Your clients should have support agreements with the providers of their software or with a consultant.

When you are called in to make a repair, your first diagnosis should be to determine whether you are dealing with a corruption of the software, an improper setting for the application, a problem with the operating system, or a failure of the hardware. You should be able to make basic adjustments to the operating system, but be very careful about offering to make fixes to application software unless you are fully capable of doing so.

Know the Territory

The good news about modern computers is that they are highly modular. Think of them as a series of independent components linked together by an electronic superhighway called a *bus.* Within various classes of machines, sealed boxes holding hard drives, CD-ROMs, DVD players, and memory can be plugged in or taken out to replace failed units or upgrade them.

You can move a functioning hard drive from one machine to another to keep the data, or arrange for a transfer of the data over a network or by direct connection by a cable that links the new and old machine.

If a hard drive fails, though, there is the issue of finding a way to retrieve the information that has been stored on it. You can remove the drive and send it to a company that specializes in emergency recovery of data; sometimes the experts have to physically disassemble the drive in an operating room–like sterile environment, remove the magnetic platters, and install them in special readers.

The vast majority of personal computers are based on the PC design pioneered by IBM; a small percentage use the Apple Macintosh design. The two systems have more in common than they have differences, but you should make certain you understand their peculiarities if you plan to offer repairs on both designs.

How to Get Started

Post flyers and ads in community centers, business supply stores, and schools. Place ads in newspapers and shopping guides.

Ask satisfied customers to recommend your services, and offer them a bonus or a discount for business they refer to you.

Up-front Expenses

You should build up a library of technical reference books about PCs and their components. There is a great deal of information available on the Internet from support groups and from manufacturers.

You'll need a basic tool kit, including screwdrivers of various sizes. Other valuable tools include a simple voltage tester and an antistatic strap.

How Much to Charge

Charge by the hour for your time, plus the cost of any parts you install. As a professional, you should be able to buy components at discounted or wholesale prices and resell them to your clients at a marked-up retail rate.

For regular customers you might offer to sell a block of hours at a discounted rate. You can add a premium to your rates for after-hours and weekend work.

Legal and Insurance Issues

① **Legal**
② **Legal**
③ **Legal**
④ **Accounting**
⑤ **Insurance**

Web Design and Maintenance

Description of Job

- Create a business or personal web site to meet the needs of your client.
- Add commerce features such as a shopping cart, catalog, and forms.
- Add communication features such as chat rooms, e-mail, and blogs.
- Create photo albums, online samples and demonstrations, and FTP transfer facilities.
- Arrange for registration and hosting of a domain.
- Maintain the site as contracted.

The Need

For most modern businesses, a web site has become at least as important as a storefront, a listing in the Yellow Pages, or a full-page ad in the Sunday newspaper. Customers expect the stores they deal with to have information about hours, sales, and products readily available online.

Today, many companies make a large portion of their sales directly over the Internet; some enterprises exist only as virtual businesses, with no brick-and-mortar stores for people to visit.

The job of the web site designer is to work with a company's marketing department to extend the firm's offerings onto the Internet.

Major companies are likely to work with large advertising agencies or major web site design companies; don't expect to design the next Amazon.com or eBay.com as your first customer. Much more likely are assignments to create the first web presence for a local store or professional service (lawyer, accountant, consultant, and the like).

You may also be asked to assist individuals in creating a web site to share their thoughts, pictures, and presence with the world.

Challenges

If you don't recognize the details of the job description, you've got a whole lot of preparation ahead of you before you can consider performing this sort of work.

Creating and maintaining a web site is not rocket science, but it does demand a great deal of attention to detail . . . and there are hundreds of details.

Web sites can begin as very simple home pages that list hours of operation, telephone numbers, driving directions, and basic products or services offered. At the other end are web sites based on huge databases of products and information, including animation, video, music, shopping carts, shipping information, and direct chats with technical support or customer service agents.

Even a simple web site may be beyond the skills and interest of a small company or an individual, and a complex site is an extremely labor-intensive undertaking.

When you meet with clients, make sure you understand exactly their needs and desires. Don't spend hours of billable time on something they don't like and won't want to pay for.

Take great care to avoid copyright infringement and plagiarism. If the clients provide photos or other types of art, determine whether they own those items or have purchased the right to reproduce them on the Internet. Don't "borrow" images from other sites or sources; don't think for a moment that the lawyers for Mickey Mouse won't be legal tigers if you use his picture without permission.

Know the Territory

Study the Internet and watch for new trends and tricks. Read computer and marketing magazines and consult the web sites of software makers for information about their products. Some software companies offer demo versions of their tools that allow you to learn how to use them and to create (but not save and use) some sample pages.

Your clients should supply the text to support the pages, and they may supply images as well, or you might be called on to work with an outside artist or service bureau to create images to the specifications of the client.

You may also be able to purchase collections of royalty-free images and music that have been cleared for use on web sites.

Use the filmmaker's tools of storyboarding to plan a web site and show it to your client before major work is under way.

Spend the time to learn the offerings of various web-hosting companies. The market is extremely competitive; look for a reasonable price for your client, but keep in mind that the most important thing these companies have to offer may be their reliability (uptime) and the availability of technical assistance.

Selling products online requires a shopping cart that manages inventory and the ordering process and interfaces with a merchant account sponsored by one or more credit card companies or with an electronic check-acceptance service.

Some web-host companies offer packages that include hosting, e-mail, and shopping cart services.

How to Get Started

Start by becoming an expert on web site creation and maintenance. There are many books on the subject, and you can take courses online or through colleges and training companies.

Create a portfolio that you can demonstrate online or on a laptop computer you bring with you to presentations.

Promote your availability through flyers and business cards placed in office supply stores, computer stores, community centers, and schools. Ask satisfied clients to spread the word about your services, and offer a discount or bonus to them for new business they refer to you.

Up-front Expenses

You'll need a capable computer with a high-speed Internet connection, plus software for web site creation, illustration, and photo editing. Expect to pay about $1,500 to $2,000 for the computer, plus $300 to $1,500 for software.

Additional expenses include the cost of advertising and promotion.

How Much to Charge

You can charge by the hour (with an estimate of total cost) or offer a flat rate based on the size of the job. Add to the bill charges for any images or music you must purchase and any specialized service bureaus you must use. Be sure to advise clients before you make any significant commissions on their behalf.

Web hosting is usually billed on a monthly or annual basis. In most cases, you will want to set up an account for your clients, but have them provide credit card or bank information so that they pay the hosting company directly.

Legal and Insurance Issues

① **Legal**

② **Legal**

③ **Legal**

④ **Accounting**

⑤ **Insurance**

Graphic Designer

Description of Job

- Design logos, letterheads, business cards, and other graphics for businesses.
- Produce electronic files for brochures, catalogs, and forms.
- Specify and coordinate printing.

The Need

The "paperless" office is a myth. We still live in a clutter of forms, business cards, and written correspondence. Even though the Internet has taken over a significant slice of wholesale and retail sales, electronic commerce, too, uses logos and graphics.

The job of the graphic designer is to translate the corporate identity of a business into a readily recognizable logo and to help create order and logic in printed materials, including brochures, catalogs, and forms.

Once the design has been made, the graphic designer works with a professional printer to specify colors, paper, and process.

Challenges

Graphic beauty is in the eyes of the beholder; make sure you work closely with your client and obtain approval for work in progress before it is committed to print.

Your agreement with the client should be very specific regarding the ownership of any designs you make. In most cases you will be selling all rights to your work, but anything is open to negotiation; consider the case of Harvey Ball, who designed the original bright yellow happy face button as a promotion for State Mutual Life Assurance Company in 1964. He was paid $45 for the design, and neither he nor the insurance company trademarked the image, which has gone on to uncounted millions of uses and has made millions of dollars for others.

In some cases, the graphic designer may be called on to produce newspaper advertisements or flyers; unless you choose to accept the additional assignment of writing and editing advertising copy, you should ask the client to involve a professional copywriter.

Know the Territory

Although many artists and designers begin with a blank piece of paper and a pencil (with eraser), nearly all production work is completed on a computer using a drawing program such as Adobe Illustrator or a digital editor like Adobe Photoshop. Page production for books, magazines, brochures, and catalogs as well as smaller jobs like business cards are typically produced using software like Quark XPress.

The digital files can be reviewed on-screen or as printouts, then edited before being transmitted to a printer.

How to Get Started

Post flyers and ads showcasing your work in community centers, retail stores, and schools. Place ads in newspapers, shopping guides, and newsletters to the business community.

Send samples of your work to area businesses. Ask friends and relatives to recommend your services; offer a bonus or discount on future work for business they send your way. Do the same with satisfied customers.

Create a portfolio of your work to show potential clients; the work can also be made available over the Internet or on a CD you can produce by yourself.

Contact area advertising agencies and printing companies; they may recommend you to their clients if you use their services for the project.

Up-front Expenses

You'll need an artist's tools for sketches. For production you'll need a capable computer, plus digital drawing and editing software and a high-speed Internet connection to communicate with clients and printing companies. Artists can work with either PC or Apple Macintosh computers, although over the years the art community has been one of Apple's mainstays.

Other expenses include advertising and promotion.

How Much to Charge

Basic work is charged on an hourly basis plus the cost of any materials and supplies. Some artists charge a flat fee for designing a logo, with the understanding that the client can then use that logo for any future purpose. (Remember the happy face.)

Legal and Insurance Issues

① **Legal**

② **Legal**

③ **Legal**

④ **Accounting**

⑤ **Insurance**

Freelance Photographer

Description of Job

- Take photos of social events and celebrations, as commissioned by a client.
- Produce photos of products and projects for business catalogs and advertising.
- Take passport and ID photos.
- Document real estate and automobiles for insurance companies.

The Need

Anyone can click a shutter on an automatic camera, but there is often a wide gap between an amateur snapshot and the work of a professional.

The freelance photographer has the skills, artistic eye, and advanced equipment needed to produce work of professional quality for individuals, companies, and official documents.

Among the clients for a freelance photographer are:

- Families seeking high-quality photos of social events and milestones, including parties, prom night, graduations, new babies, and the like
- Individuals in need of passport photos or other simple ID photos
- Home contractors or their customers seeking to document the progress of a renovation or new construction

- Insurance agencies or companies, real estate agencies, or appraisers needing documentation of automobiles, homes, and businesses
- Businesses in need of basic product or project photos for reports, catalogs, and simple advertising

Challenges

Unless you have years of experience and training, don't expect to compete against professional studio photographers for fashionable, high-end advertising and formal portraiture jobs. Although the pay for these sorts of assignments can be quite high, so, too, is the investment in equipment and the time needed to establish relationships with clients.

As you start your business, you should be careful about accepting major assignments such as wedding photography. These jobs are often in chaotic settings, with uncertain lighting and sometimes unreasonable expectations. Build your experience with simpler, less stressful jobs.

Passport photos are easy to produce, but most follow some very specific guidelines regarding size, background, and printing method, as published by the U.S. Department of State's passport services agency.

You will need to become completely proficient in the use of your equipment. Many if not all of your photos will be of events or moments that cannot be duplicated.

You will need to continually demonstrate your ability to produce work of professional quality every time you are engaged. Each time you take a job you will be competing against amateurs who believe they are perfectly capable of taking snapshots.

Know the Territory

Since the development of photography nearly two centuries ago, we have used the camera to document important personal milestones, public events, and art. In business, we have grown into a highly visual society that uses photographic images to sell products, services, and political messages.

Traditional photography uses light-sensitive film to produce negatives or slides that can be used to make prints. Increasingly, professional and commercial photographers are switching to digital cameras. These devices allow for near-instant availability of high-resolution images in electronic form for use on web sites and in printed advertisements and catalogs. An image file can be transmitted over the Internet to a client just moments after it has been taken.

As a digital photographer you'll need to become proficient in the use of photographic editing software and Internet transmittal of files to clients or to service bureaus for printing.

How to Get Started

Post flyers and ads in community centers, schools, and retail stores. Place ads in local newspapers, school publications, and organizational newsletters.

Make your services known to party planners, caterers, entertainers, and others who might recommend you to their clients; offer a commission or bonus for any business they refer to you. Ask satisfied customers to recommend you to friends and acquaintances; pay a bonus or offer a discount to customers who help you expand your business.

Contact other professional photographers and offer to take on jobs that are too small for them or where they have a time conflict; offer to share your fees for work you receive through them.

Contact insurance and real estate agencies to let them know you are available to take photos to document insurance applications, insurance claims, real estate ads, and other business uses of photography.

Up-front Expenses

You'll need a capable camera with interchangeable lenses or a high-quality zoom lens. For conventional photography you'll need to work with a professional photo lab to produce negatives, slides, and prints.

For digital photography you'll need a high-resolution digital camera, sufficient memory cards for storage, and access to a computer that has photo editing software such as Adobe Photoshop. If you will be supplying prints, you'll need access to a high-quality printer, or you'll need to work with a service bureau that can convert electronic files to prints.

How Much to Charge

You can charge an hourly rate plus the cost of film, prints, and other expenses; you should be able to purchase supplies and photo darkroom or printing services at wholesale or discounted prices and resell them at retail rates.

Another business plan is to offer a package price for a set number of hours and services, and then charge for each print or for use of your electronic files.

Legal and Insurance Issues

① **Legal**

② **Legal**

③ **Legal**

④ **Accounting**

⑤ **Insurance**

Film to Digital Scanning

📖 👤 🎨 💻 🏢 ⚛ 🔧 📜 🖧 ♿

💰 💰–💰 💰 💰

Description of Job

- Convert old photos, negatives, and slides to digital files that can be displayed on computers and televisions and reprinted using modern digital printers.
- Enhance the quality of and remove flaws from old negatives or videotapes.
- Transfer videotape to CD or DVD for display on computers and televisions.

The Need

For many of us, our photos and videotapes are our most precious possessions, but time and technology march on . . . and closets fill with old photos and outdated media. Remember Betamax tapes, Super 8 movies, and Instamatic slides?

Photographic prints have a limited life; they deteriorate over time. Slides fade. Negatives become brittle and are subject to scratching.

Videotapes have a shelf life, and they are dependent on the availability of a working playback device. A closetful of old Betamax tapes is useless if all you have is a modern VHS player.

Super 8 and other film-based movie systems require the appropriate projector and a screen.

Today, the headlong rush is into digital media. Digital cameras outsell film cameras, and nearly all of us have become used to looking at images on computers (from our own collection or downloaded from the Internet) or on television using CDs or DVDs as the source.

A single DVD can hold hundreds of high-resolution photos or several hours of video. DVDs are easier to store and handle and offer a much longer life expectancy. In addition, images stored in digital format have another very important advantage over older analog media (including photos, slides, film, and negatives): Pictures can be copied and moved an endless number of times without degrading the quality.

The job of the film-to-digital-scanning professional is to gather the technology and the expertise to convert media from analog to digital.

Challenges

The principal complexity of this job is managing all of the various combinations of before-and-after media. You'll need to purchase scanner equipment and a powerful and capacious PC and become expert at using them.

Another challenge is the fact that you will be entrusted with irreplaceable family treasures. You'll have to take special care to avoid loss or damage to media you are working with.

Know the Territory

Among the most popular types of conversion:

- Film slides in 35mm, 110, 126, and 127 formats to CD or DVD. Older cameras might use larger 120 or 220 film.

- Negatives in any of the same formats, reversed to positive images and recorded to CD or DVD.

- Color or black-and-white prints scanned to digital files and recorded to CD or DVD.

- Movies in 8mm, Super 8, and 16mm formats, converted to CD or DVD.

- Videotapes in Beta, VHS, S-VHS, 8mm, Hi8, MiniDV, and Digital 8 formats, converted to CD or DVD.

All of these conversions use a PC for processing, storing, and creating CDs or DVDs.

Offer a selection of output options. Let clients choose between CDs that play on computers or DVDs that have more capacity and can be used on either computers or television sets. Each scan can be done at a range of resolutions (degree of fine detail). The higher the resolution, the sharper the image in display and the better the print that can be made from the file; on the downside, it takes considerably longer to scan at higher resolutions and the files take up more space on the CD or DVD.

How to Get Started

Begin by becoming an expert on the technology. Read computer and photography magazines, visit trade shows, consult web sites, and tap the expertise of knowledgeable equipment salespeople.

Draw up a detailed business plan with reasonable assumptions to determine how much of an investment makes sense. You might want to start out offering just slide, negative, and print conversions; the technology is more mature and the investment a bit less.

Advertise your availability through flyers at community centers, senior centers, and schools. Place ads in newspapers and shopping guides.

You might be able to establish a relationship with area photo, art supply, or framing stores to allow you to advertise there in return for referring customers to them for services you don't provide.

Up-front Expenses

You'll need a current PC with a large amount of memory and storage; plan on spending at least $1,500 for the computer. The PC will need to have a recordable CD or DVD burner.

A high-resolution 35mm slide scanner ranges in price from about $500 to $2,000, and most include holders for negatives and software that can reverse images from negative to positive. The more expensive scanners generally include advanced features that can automatically remove scratches and improve the quality of the image being scanned.

Flatbed scanners, for use with color or black-and-white prints, range in price from as little as $100 to as much as $1,000.

Prices for high-end drum scanners for large slides and prints begin at several thousand dollars and go up from there.

Digital capture boards and external capture devices range in price from about $200 to $1,000; these are used to scan incoming video from a VCR or camera and convert it to digital.

You'll also need capable software on your PC to edit digital files and to transfer them to a recordable CD or DVD.

How Much to Charge

You can get a sense of prices by consulting web sites of companies offering these sort of services.

We found prices for slide scanning ranging from about 45 cents to $1 each for basic work and from about $1 to $2.50 per slide for high-resolution scanning.

Prices for scanning negatives were higher because of additional time required on most systems; we saw prices of about 80 cents to $1.60 for basic work.

For transfer from film to VHS tape, prices were about 10 cents per foot at basic levels of resolution and without digital restoration. Prices for transforming film images to DVD were priced from 12 to 25 cents per foot, depending on level of resolution and amount of restoration.

Scanning a print to digital form and restoring it can range in price from $5 to $50, depending on the amount of touch-up required.

In addition to per-image or per-foot charges, companies add charges for CDs and DVDs provided to the client, plus shipping costs.

Legal and Insurance Issues

Special notes: In dealing with your client's property, seek to limit your liability for damage or loss to the actual replacement value of items in your possession. You should protect yourself against claims for sentimental value or loss of use.

① **Legal**

② **Legal**

③ **Legal**

④ **Accounting**

⑤ **Insurance**

⑥ **Insurance**

Photo and Document Restorer

Description of Job

- Scan and digitize old black-and-white or color photographs.
- Scan and digitize old documents such as birth certificates, marriage licenses, and diplomas.
- Apply advanced computer software effects to restore color, improve contrast, remove scratches, and fill in holes.
- Edit or crop images as requested.
- Print new digital images and store edited files on disk for archival purposes.

The Need

In case of fire or natural disaster, almost all of us would (1) see to the safety of family members, (2) rescue cats and dogs, and (3) grab the photo albums. In many ways, the photos we accumulate are the most important remembrances of our lives.

That said, we almost all have a closetful of family treasures, at best gathering dust, at worst moldering away.

Photos have a life span of as little as 10 years—less if they are exposed to sun or extreme humidity. They'll last longer if stored in sealed boxes at controlled levels of heat and humidity.

Older color prints fade away more rapidly than those produced in more recent years using improved papers and finishes.

Many people retain only the prints, having long ago lost or misplaced the negatives. Negatives themselves, if stored in high humidity or heat, can become damaged and unusable in ordinary photo processing.

The job of the photo and document restorer is to use modern digital tools to scan images and documents and restore them to their original—or better than original—condition. The images can be reprinted using modern methods, and the edited digital files can be stored on CD or DVD for future use.

Challenges

The most critical task is to catch the images before they fade away to nothingness. The process of photo repair and restoration is nondestructive—it does not damage the original; you should use reasonable precautions in handling them, though, such as lintless cotton gloves and archival storage boxes.

You'll need to learn to use your computer hardware and software tools to their full extent and in an efficient manner.

You will have custody of irreplaceable family treasures and must use all reasonable efforts to safeguard them from loss or damage.

Know the Territory

Almost everyone has precious photos, but relatively few have the skill and time to convert them to digital form and store them for the ages.

You'll be in competition with national companies that sell their services over the Internet or resell through major photo store chains. Your sales pitch should emphasize your local availability and custom services.

You'll scan images and store them on disks. A color scan of an 8- by 10-inch photo at high resolution can require as much as 400 megabytes of storage space; reducing resolution slightly, to 600 dots per inch (dpi), yields a file of about 103 megabytes. Black-and-white images are smaller, about one-third the size of color images.

Once an image is scanned and stored on disk, you'll first use advanced software to adjust the color and contrast, sharpen details, remove scratches, and fill holes. Then you may be called on to do some editing to crop the image, to digitally remove background trees and signs that seem to be growing out of people's heads, or to delete strangers (or old boyfriends or girlfriends) from otherwise acceptable pictures.

Completed images stored on a hard disk can then be transmitted over the Internet to a professional processor who will produce high-quality photographic prints. The images can also be printed locally using high-quality inkjet printers; such images can be done quickly and are of high quality, although they may not last as long as a photographic copy. The client also receives a CD or DVD containing a copy of the edited file; the disk may also contain an electronic photo album that displays the edited files on a television or computer.

How to Get Started

Begin by becoming an expert on photo scanning and restoration. The investment is not huge if you already have a capable personal computer.

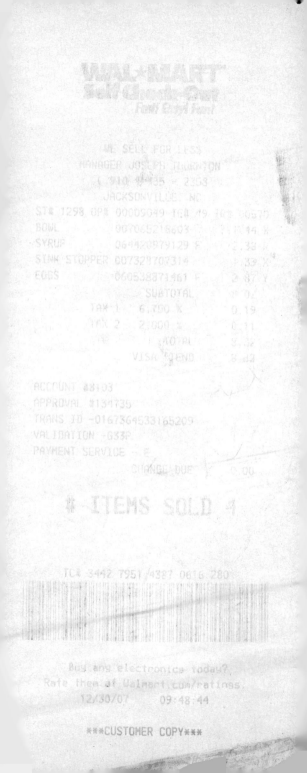

WAL★MART
Self Check-Out

WE SELL FOR LESS
MANAGER JOSEPH BURNTON
(910) 455 - 2253
JACKSONVILLE, NC
ST# 1298 OP# 00009049 TE# 49 TR# 00575
BOWL   007065218603   1.44 X
SYRUP   064420979129 F   2.38 R
SINK STOPPER 007329707314   1.39 X
EGGS   060538871461 F   2.87 T
              SUBTOTAL   8.07
    TAX 1   6.750 %   0.19
    TAX 2   2.000 %   0.11
              TOTAL   9.32
           VISA TEND   9.32

ACCOUNT #8103
APPROVAL #134735
TRANS ID -0167364533165209
VALIDATION -G33P
PAYMENT SERVICE - E
              CHANGE DUE   0.00

ITEMS SOLD 4

TC# 3442 7951 4387 0616 280

Buy any electronics today?
Rate them at Walmart.com/ratings.
12/30/07   09:48:44

CUSTOMER COPY

There are many books about photo restoration using software such as Adobe Photoshop. You can take courses over the Internet or at community schools. Adobe also conducts its own series of traveling classes.

Promote your availability with ads and flyers at community centers, in senior centers, and through religious organizations. Seek cooperative arrangements with area photo labs and picture framers.

Up-front Expenses

You'll need a PC with an abundance of memory and storage; we recommend at least 512 megabytes of RAM and at least 40 gigabytes of hard disk storage space. Purchase a high-resolution flatbed scanner for photos; even better is a drum scanner, although prices for these devices can run into the thousands of dollars.

Your PC should also include a CD-R or DVD-R burner and high-speed broadband access to the Internet for uploading files to service bureaus for photograph printing. You should also have a photo-quality printer to produce prints using ink-jet technology.

In addition, you'll need professional-quality photo editing software; the industry leader is Adobe Photoshop, which has some special-purpose add-in modules that help perform tasks such as isolating a single person or a small detail from a crowded image.

If you need to purchase all of the equipment, plan on spending $2,500 to $3,500. (Adobe software alone costs about $750 to $1,000.)

Additional costs include advertising and promotion.

How Much to Charge

Billing is done on an hourly basis, plus the cost of the disks and the prints you produce. You can add a reasonable markup to the cost of photos produced by service bureaus based on the files you have created. You should offer clients an estimate of the amount of time that will be required for restoration. Add charges for pickup and delivery. Working with a professional picture framer, you can offer to deliver finished photos mounted in frames; seek a discount from the framer and charge your client standard retail rates, or add a reasonable markup.

Legal and Insurance

Special notes: In dealing with your client's property, seek to limit your liability for damage or loss to the actual replacement value of items in your possession. You should protect yourself against claims for sentimental value or loss of use.

① **Legal**

② **Legal**

③ **Legal**

④ **Accounting**

⑤ **Insurance**

⑥ **Insurance**

Videographer

Description of Job

- Videotape weddings, amateur sports events and competitions, parties, and celebrations.
- Record meetings, public events, and speeches for business clients.
- Edit tapes into a professional presentation.
- Produce copies on videotape, CD, or DVD.

The Need

We live in a visual age; we are used to having photos, movies, and television to record nearly every moment. Modern families and businesses have VCRs, DVDs, video cameras, digital cameras, cell phones with built-in cameras, and increasingly antiquated film-based cameras.

However, it is obvious to most of us that a great gap exists between an amateur point-and-shoot effort and a polished, edited production by a trained expert using professional-quality equipment. It may be acceptable to shoot your own video of your son's debut in the school play or your daughter's game-winning goal in a lacrosse game. However, when it comes to what we expect to be once-in-a-lifetime events—a wedding, an award presentation, or a keynote address—it makes a lot of sense to hire a professional freelance videographer.

Challenges

You have to know what you're doing, and you have to have reliable, professional-quality video, audio, and lighting equipment. You'll be shooting live events, with no second chance in case of a technical problem.

It may be possible to take on some jobs by yourself, but most productions will require assistants to help with setup and to stand by to help during the work itself; some events will need multiple cameras and audio pickups.

Know the Territory

Make sure you fully understand your client's needs and wants, and be very careful about what you promise. In most cases you should not take on a job without visiting the location to make sure you will be able to function properly there.

Not every location permits installation of bright video lights and microphones, and some may have limited electrical outlets. Modern equipment can usually be run from battery-powered sources.

Some churches and other religious institutions may not permit any intrusion on their ceremonies, and you should carefully look into any request for taping of a theatrical performance to make sure you are not violating the rights of the copyright holder.

At some hotels and convention centers, you may be required to work with unionized employees. Any extra costs should be passed along to your client.

If permitted, videotape a dress rehearsal of the event. This will allow you to confirm that all your equipment is functioning properly, help you determine the proper placement of cameras and microphones, and acquaint clients and guests with your style of operation.

Some of the dress rehearsal tape may be of use in the final video you prepare for the client.

How to Get Started

Contact area party and wedding planners, banquet halls, community centers, and schools to make them aware of your availability. Post flyers and ads on area bulletin boards and advertise in newspapers and shopping guides.

Obtain permission from your clients to use portions of their events in creating a sample tape or DVD to show prospective customers. Offer a bonus or discount to satisfied customers who refer new clients to you.

Up-front Expenses

You'll need at least one professional-grade video camera, plus external wired and wireless microphones, an audio mixing board, and a set of video lights. A basic setup could cost from $1,500 to $5,000.

Some equipment, including additional cameras, lighting, and audio devices can be rented from professional supply houses. (Be sure to carefully test any rented equipment before using it on a job.)

Once the video has been shot, you'll need editing equipment. These can be special-purpose video editing controllers and rerecorders, or you can use video capture and editing systems for use with high-end personal computers. Plan on spending between $3,000 and $5,000 for editing equipment and computers.

You'll need video libraries of images, fades, dissolves, and special effects to liven up the edited tape. Other helpful software includes audio editors and a library of copyright-free music.

Finally, you'll need a way to produce multiple copies of the final video. This can be done on a professional-grade video recorder or with a CD or DVD burner that is part of your PC.

You'll need a van or large vehicle to transport your equipment to jobs; make sure it can be made secure to protect valuable gear.

How Much to Charge

For most jobs you can charge a set price for videotaping, editing, and producing the final version of the video. Include in your price the time required to visit the location, tape a dress rehearsal, return for the actual event, and edit video. Add the expense of any special requests by the client and for multiple copies of the finished video.

Legal and Insurance

① **Legal**
② **Legal**
③ **Legal**
④ **Accounting**
⑤ **Insurance**

Office and Professional Services

88 Temporary Secretary

89 Transcription Services

90 Temporary Worker at Conventions and Business Meetings

91 Bookkeeping

92 Billing Service

93 Resume Design

94 Letter Writing

Temporary Secretary

Description of Job

- Perform short-term, temporary secretarial or clerical assignments.
- Assist with special projects using computer or secretarial skills.

The Need

You're tapping into the fact that it is almost always considerably less expensive for a company to hire short-term or temporary workers for special projects and seasonal work. Hiring temporary workers generally relieves companies from the expenses for medical insurance, paid leave, and other benefits.

Small firms such as medical offices, accountants, and construction companies may need coverage to fill in when their only clerical person is on vacation or called away for an emergency.

Challenges

You must have up-to-date office and computer skills and be flexible enough to adapt to various assignments. It is also critical for you to be able to work professionally with a changing cast of supervisors and coworkers.

You must be a quick learner, and you must be able to follow instructions exactly. Most of the time you will be hired to help out during times of stress; you have to be part of the solution, not part of the problem.

Although your work will be short term and temporary, you have to demonstrate that you are dependable, that you will be at the job on time, as required, and that you will not walk away for a vacation or a better offer during the term of your commitment.

As a temporary worker, you will be expected to act and dress as professionally as full-time staff.

Know the Territory

Learn as much as you can about businesses and stores in your area. Check web sites to learn about each company's operations.

How to Get Started

Advertise your availability in newspapers. Send letters, with a resume and summary of your qualifications, to the human resources departments of companies in your area.

Notify the companies you already deal with about your availability. Tell your personal doctor or dentist that you are available, and submit your qualifications.

A number of small companies rent space in large professional buildings. Visit them and leave your business card, resume, and references.

Up-front Expenses

The primary expenses are for advertising, promotion, and business cards. You'll also need an appropriate wardrobe for professional settings.

How Much to Charge

Temporary work is paid on an hourly basis; state laws usually dictate higher rates of pay for nights or weekends and set a multiplier for overtime.

Legal and Insurance Issues

① **Legal**

② **Legal**

③ **Legal**

④ **Accounting**

⑤ **Insurance**

Transcription Services

Description of Job

- Transcribe taped or digitally recorded memos, notes, and manuscripts to a computer file or printout.
- Perform basic spell-checking and editing on files.

The Need

Many professionals, including lawyers, doctors, researchers, corporate executives, and authors, prefer to dictate notes, letters, and drafts of articles, speeches, and books. Corporate and government committees often seek transcripts of meetings. Academic institutions may want a transcript of a speech.

It often makes economic sense to hire a professional transcription service for temporary or project-based work.

Challenges

You need a good set of ears, a fast pair of hands, and the ability to work with clients in technical, academic, governmental, and other specialties. For instance, transcription for a doctor would include medical words and phrases; lawyers use legal and court terms and special forms of citation for cases and law.

The good news is that a number of tools are available to help you perform work in specialty fields. You can purchase medical, legal, or technical dictionaries, and electronic add-ons can expand spell-checkers in word processors to cover specialized terms.

You will need to have equipment capable of working with different types of media, including microcassettes, full-size cassettes, and digital memory. Most word processing software, including industry leader Microsoft Word, is able to accept or output files to or from most other programs.

Most businesses use PC equipment; a relatively small number of companies use Apple Macintosh hardware. In most cases, both types of machines are capable of reading data files from each other. One way to transfer your files without having to worry about converting from one type of media to another is to send them electronically over the Internet.

Know the Territory

Begin by becoming an expert on the use of a computer word processor, electronic fact-checking and spell-checking software, and the Internet. You'll also need to become completely comfortable with the use of a *transcriber,* a specialized machine that allows you to control the playback of a tape or memory with a foot pedal; a good machine includes settings that allow you to speed up or slow down playback, adjust the amount of backspacing, and change the tone of the audio to make it clearer.

Some professionals add speech-recognition software to their bag of tricks. This sort of program is capable of recognizing speech and converting it to text on a computer; the conversion is not perfect and requires a human to edit the files.

Your next assignment is to get to know the market. You'll have the greatest success in an area that includes businesses, colleges, and professionals.

How to Get Started

Make yourself and your availability known to the business and professional community in your area. Contact local chambers of commerce and associations and ask for leads; consider placing ads in their publications. Do the same at area colleges; post notices in student centers, faculty lounges, and place ads in college newspapers offering your services to professors and students.

Speak with the town or city manager and ask about needs for transcription of governmental meetings.

Send letters to corporations, legal firms, and physicians in your area.

Ask friends and relatives whether they know of area authors or researchers who might need transcription services.

Up-front Expenses

You will need a professional-quality transcription machine; the most common format uses microcassettes, but you may need to buy several machines to handle tapes or digital memory that use other types of media. Machines range in price from about $200 to $400.

You will also need a current personal computer that runs a major word processor such as Microsoft Word, plus a professional-quality printer. If you plan to accept digital files over the Internet or send your completed transcripts that way, you will need access to the Internet.

Other expenses include advertising and promotion.

How Much to Charge

Charge by the hour for services at the prevailing professional rate in your area, which might range from about $15 to $40 per hour. Add a surcharge for rush jobs or work that must be performed over the weekend.

You can also add charges for floppy disks or CD-ROMs you provide to the client, plus a reasonable charge for each printed page of the final product.

If you are required to travel to an office, add a mileage charge. Add the cost of postage or courier service if used to deliver the work.

Legal and Insurance Issues

Special notes: In dealing with your client's property, seek to limit your liability for damage or loss to the actual replacement value of items in your possession.

You should protect yourself against damage claims for sentimental value or loss of use.

① **Legal**

② **Legal**

③ **Legal**

④ **Accounting**

⑤ **Insurance**

⑥ **Insurance**

Temporary Worker at Conventions and Business Meetings

Description of Job

- Provide reception, registration, clerical, or other professional services at conventions.
- Assist salaried staff at business gatherings, shareholder meetings, and other special events.

The Need

Most businesses are not equipped to fully staff conventions and large business meetings. They usually contract with temporary personnel agencies or hire individual workers as needed. The work includes registering guests, assisting in setup of events, secretarial services, and support staff.

Workers may spend time in the meetings, or they may be dispatched to area hotels and conference centers to assist visitors.

Challenges

Temporary helpers need to be professional in their actions and dress and very flexible in accepting assignments. Working hours may include weekends and early-morning or late-evening assignments.

You'll need to commit to being available through the entire period of an event.

Some convention centers may require that all employees be members of a union; find out the details and determine whether it makes sense to join for a temporary job such as this.

Know the Territory

Contact area convention and visitors bureaus to find out about upcoming events; most are scheduled months or years ahead of time. Ask whether the bureau hires temporary workers for its clients, or ask for referrals to companies that do the hiring themselves.

Maximize your appeal: Do you have any special skills, such as speaking a foreign language or interpreting for the deaf? Are you capable of working at a computer or helping at the registration desk?

Do you know area restaurants and entertainment well? Many events could use the services of guides or concierges for their guests.

How to Get Started

Market yourself through the area convention and visitors bureau and local chamber of commerce. If you obtain the names of upcoming conventions and large meetings, contact the meeting planners at the sponsoring companies or groups directly.

Contact area hotels that have convention space or those used to house guests for large meetings elsewhere; inform business centers that host large meetings of your availability.

Up-front Expenses

The principal expenses are for promotion and advertising.

How Much to Charge

Expect to be paid on an hourly basis, with overtime for lengthy days or weekend and holiday work. If you are asked to transport materials or move from one location to another, you should be reimbursed for mileage.

Legal and Insurance Issues

① **Legal**

② **Legal**

③ **Legal**

④ **Accounting**

⑤ **Insurance**

Bookkeeping

Description of Job

- Handle bookkeeping, accounting, and record-keeping services for a small business.
- File monthly, quarterly, and annual tax forms, or coordinate with client's tax accountant or attorney to provide necessary information for tax purposes.

The Need

Every business has to maintain records of receipts, expenditures, sales taxes collected, income tax withheld, and many other details of interest to local, state, and federal governments as well as to banks and other lenders. Other records relate to expense accounts, depreciation, inventory, accounts receivable, accounts payable, and various benefits.

Yet few small businesses can justify putting a full-time bookkeeper or accountant on the payroll, and some larger companies may prefer outsourcing the job to save money or to establish a presumably independent arm's-length relationship.

Challenges

In addition to strong bookkeeping or accounting skills and experience, you'll need to be able to work with many different types of businesses and clients.

The lexicon, accounts receivable, and accounts payable will be much different at a restaurant than at a pet shop; the types of tax forms and information required by a DBA or partnership may be not the same as those required for a corporation.

You may be called on to fill in for vacation absences or for special projects; in such cases, you will have to follow someone else's plans and methods exactly.

Outside or part-time bookkeepers and accountants must demonstrate professionalism and discretion, keeping private the proprietary information of their clients.

Make sure your bookkeeping and accounting skills are up-to-date. If your skills and knowledge are limited in a particular area, you should probably decline a related job rather than do damage to your clients and to your reputation.

Know the Territory

You'll need to keep current on accounting practices and on the local business environment. Make contact with local chambers of commerce to learn about new and expanding companies.

Make sure you are capable of working with state-of-the-art accounting software.

How to Get Started

Identify possible clients by contacting your local chamber of commerce and other business associations; place ads in newsletters to their members. Send letters to new and expanding companies.

You may be able to post your business card or a flyer at area business supply stores, including some of the major chains.

Up-front Expenses

The primary expense will be advertising and promotion. You may also want to have a listing or ad in the Yellow Pages under "Accountants," "Bookkeeping services," or "Temporary services."

How Much to Charge

You should charge by the hour. Investigate companies in your area that perform similar services.

Legal and Insurance Issues

Special notes: In dealing with your clients' property, seek to limit your liability for damage or loss to the actual replacement value of items in your possession. You should protect yourself against claims for sentimental value or loss of use.

① **Legal**

② **Legal**

③ **Legal**

④ **Accounting**

⑤ **Insurance**

⑥ **Insurance**

Billing Service

Description of Job

- Aggregate accounts and take over billing for products and services.
- Collect payments and post them to proper accounts.
- Monitor accounts receivable and report to client about any problematic customers.
- Work with collection agencies when appropriate.

The Need

Many businesses and professionals are fully dedicated to the services they provide or the products they sell. At some smaller companies, there is much less interest in, and sometimes inadequate attention paid to, billing customers and collecting the money—tasks that keep the whole enterprise afloat.

Even when a company is fully prepared to send bills and collect revenues with well-trained staff and state-of-the-art systems, it might not make economic sense to do so.

The job of the independent billing service is to devote full attention to accounts receivable as needed, which eliminates the need for a company to hire and pay salary and benefits for a full-time employee. Your basic pitch is this: Your services as an outside billing agency will cost less than doing the work in-house, and/or your agency will do a better job of managing receivables (and working with a collection agency when necessary). If you can't make that claim, you have no appeal to the client.

You can also appeal to small businesses that have suffered from turnover in their billing departments; you should be able to promise that services will be standardized and available every business day of the week.

Challenges

You'll need to mesh your experience and practices with the systems and methods of your client. Among special challenges: not ruffling the feathers of valued customers who are used to preferential treatment. There may also be times when you'll have to play the heavy in dealing with certain customers.

Some billing scenarios are much more complex than others. Medical practices, for example, have to deal with a dizzying collection of federal and state government agencies, major insurance companies, union and association medical plans, and private payers. If you have previous experience in the medical field, you may be able to pick up doctors as clients; if not, medical billing is probably not the place to start.

Know the Territory

You must be current on computer communications, billing software, and accounts receivable programs. Most accounting or billing programs can be customized with modules that adapt them to the specific needs of particular types of businesses.

The best qualification for this sort of job is your previous experience working in an accounting or billing department.

You must promise and demonstrate discretion in managing the private affairs of your clients, and you will be subject to audit by your client's accountant or other representative.

Your client must be capable of transmitting the raw data for billing in an efficient manner. The state-of-the-art way is to send files to your office via the Internet. Less modern, but still relatively common, is to physically ship boxes of paper invoices that you will have to enter into your computer system and process.

How to Get Started

Contact area businesses to let them know of your credentials and availability. Place ads in business publications and general newspapers.

Ask satisfied clients to recommend your services to other businesses; give them a bonus or a discount for any new business they bring to you.

Up-front Expenses

You'll need a current PC with access to the Internet, standard accounting or accounts receivable software, and a printer capable of producing invoices, labels, and envelopes for mailing. If your client requires you to use a specific software program, you may have to purchase and learn to use that package.

Other expenses include advertising and promotion.

How Much to Charge

The most common billing scheme for small businesses is to charge by the hour or to offer a flat rate based on the number of bills processed per week or per month. Add to the bill the cost of paper and envelopes, postage, phone calls, and any special services requested by the client; alternatively, those expenses could be built into the hourly or flat rate.

Legal and Insurance Issues

Special notes: In dealing with your client's property, seek to limit your liability for damage or loss to the actual replacement value of items in your possession. You should protect yourself against claims for sentimental value or loss of use.

① **Legal**

② **Legal**

③ **Legal**

④ **Accounting**

⑤ **Insurance**

⑥ **Insurance**

Resume Design

Description of Job

- Interview clients for details about academic, professional, and relevant personal details.
- As appropriate, fact-check and verify information.

- Design a resume suited for the type of position sought.
- Print resumes and create an electronic version suitable for e-mailing and posting online.

The Need

A well-crafted resume is one of the primary ways for a job applicant to get a foot in the door. Human resources officers, executives, and recruiters appreciate a well-written cover letter, but they zero in on employment history, appropriate experience, and specialized education. (Some companies use computerized software to screen e-mailed and online resume submissions for keywords that relate to the job they are looking to fill.)

A resume must be easy to read and understand, accurate, and accessible in any form requested. The resume designer combines reporting and designing skills.

Challenges

You must be honest in dealing with your client and scrupulous of your reputation; any mistakes or willful misrepresentation will reflect poorly on both you and your client. Do not agree to falsify information or unreasonably inflate the importance of a particular job or experience.

You must also be discreet about the information you gather; not all of your client's history may be positive, and the client may want to keep confidential some of the information, including salary history.

You will be expected to keep your involvement in a client's job search to yourself. Not all job seekers want their present employer to know they are in the market to leave.

You must know how to use a word processor to create a resume, and you will need to have design skills to make it attractive and easy to read.

Many companies now ask applicants to send resumes by e-mail or by posting to a web site. For these purposes, you need to learn how to create a text-only version of the resume, without formatting, or to create an HTML-coded version. (HTML is the underlying code used to apply formatting to web sites.)

Know the Territory

Gather information from previous resumes, employment and academic records, and interviews with your client that yield relevant details about job responsibilities and accomplishments. With your client's permission, research and verify any details that are not supported by documents.

Working with your client, develop a list of references who are willing to respond to inquiries about the client's work history and character. Verify names, addresses, titles, and phone numbers, or assist the client in doing so.

How to Get Started

Advertise at colleges, in community centers, and in newspapers and shopping guides. Be prepared to show prospective clients generic versions of resumes you have produced, with names and other personal details removed or replaced with fictional names or randomly generated addresses and phone numbers.

Up-front Expenses

You'll need a capable computer with Internet access and a professional-quality printer. You may produce resumes on your own machine, or upload them to a service bureau for professional printing. In the case of electronic submission of resumes, you will need the ability to send the file over the Internet.

Other expenses include advertising and promotion.

How Much to Charge

Bill for your time on an hourly basis. You might want to offer a basic package that includes a set number of hours plus production of a resume, with additional charges if research or fact-checking goes beyond ordinary efforts.

You can add a charge for printing resumes on your own equipment or for arranging for printing by an outside service bureau.

Legal and Insurance Issues

① **Legal**

② **Legal**

③ **Legal**

④ **Accounting**

⑤ **Insurance**

Letter Writing

Description of Job

- Prepare letters from individuals to businesses, government agencies, and others.

- Provide guidance and assistance in filling out forms and responding to inquiries.

The Need

We live in a highly verbal and visual world; much of what we do in life is accomplished with a conversation or a point-and-click computer function. However, sometimes you need to *put it in writing,* and that is not something that everyone feels comfortable doing.

How do you notify a credit card company that you want to dispute a charge? What is the most gracious way to thank someone for a favor? How should you acknowledge condolences? What is the best way to outline your concerns or requests to a politician or a government agency?

A carefully composed letter to a neighbor or a business may help fend off the possibility of an expensive legal action. A properly written letter of return or complaint may result in a full refund for a faulty product or an unsuccessful service call.

The advantages of written communication include the ability to carefully hone your message to make it as clear and unambiguous as possible and the advantage of retaining a written record of your correspondence.

Challenges

You need to be able to communicate clearly and concisely in writing. Equally important is the ability to communicate clearly with your clients; you'll need to understand their needs and get the exact details necessary for the letters you write.

Know the Territory

Your clientele may come from any walk of life—from the young and inexperienced to the overly busy professional to senior citizens who need an outside advocate.

Become familiar with forms of address and the proper style for written communication. There are a number of books that would be of help. One easy-to-use letter-writing book is *1001 Letters for All Occasions* (Adams Media), by Corey Sandler and Janice Keefe, the authors of the book now in your hands.

You should be an accomplished user of a computer and word processor, and make full use of the spelling-and-grammar function. You should also be comfortable using the Internet to research information and to submit electronic mail and forms on behalf of your client.

How to Get Started

Place flyers and ads in community centers, schools, and senior centers. Place ads in newspapers and shopping guides.

Consider offering classes on letter writing at senior centers or community centers as a way of earning money and generating new clients.

Up-front Expenses

Invest in books on letter writing as well as reference books. You should have access to a capable computer with a word processor and access to the Internet.

Additional expenses include the costs of advertising and promotion.

How Much to Charge

Charge an hourly rate for your services, plus the cost of any special services you provide, including mailing.

Much of your work can be conducted over the telephone. If you must travel to a client's home to perform work, you can charge a mileage rate.

Legal and Insurance Issues

① **Legal**

② **Legal**

③ **Legal**

④ **Accounting**

⑤ **Insurance**

CHAPTER **16**

Sales

95 Yard Sale Organizer

96 Consignment Resale

97 Antique and Collectible Wholesaler

98 Used Book Reseller

99 Tool and Equipment Rentals

100 Newspaper Delivery Route

101 Online Auctions: EBay and Beyond

Yard Sale Organizer

Description of Job

- Help homeowners and renters conduct a successful yard sale, tag sale, or garage sale.
- Manage the organization, promotion, and sales of such events.

The Need

We're not sure which is more satisfying: clearing out your attic, basement, and closets or recouping some of the money you spent on dust magnets and clothing you can't believe you ever thought looked good on you.

You know the stuff we're talking about: that exercise bicycle in your bedroom that hasn't been used in two years . . . plus half the clothing hanging on its handlebars and all the shoes stacked behind the rear wheels. As your children grow older, you'll have a nice collection of clothing, toys, books, and sporting equipment ready for a new home.

Not everyone knows how to set up a sale and how to make it successful. As a yard sale organizer, your emphasis is on the *organization*. Among the skills you'll bring are:

- Understanding local ordinances about signs, hours of sale, and other matters
- Knowing the sort of items that sell well in your neighborhood
- Knowing the value of stuff around the house
- Cataloging the items for sale
- Knowing how to set up a display of items
- Knowing how to manage the cash box

Challenges

Some towns and community organizations place regulations on yard sales that limit hours of operation, posting of signs, and parking. In some states and municipalities, the law may require collection of sales tax.

It would be polite to notify neighbors in advance of the sale date; if the sale attracts a large number of cars, it might interfere with their ability to get in and out of their own driveways. Devote as much attention to taking down your signs after the sale as you do to putting them up beforehand.

Expect early birds to attempt to grab bargains before the official starting time for the sale; in fairness to all, most yard sale pros will ask them to wait until the posted time. Consider what you will do if it rains on the day of sale; you might want to list a rain date in ads and on signs.

You have to organize the wares for sale. Use tables (which could be old doors propped on sawhorses) or blankets and painter's tarps on the grass to display items. Place similar items together. Clean all clothing before sale, and neatly fold items so they can easily be seen and not wrinkled or damaged.

Place your most expensive items in a location where you or your client can keep a close eye on them. If you have antiques, works of art, or collectibles, do some research or hire an appraiser. You—or your client—should pay heed to the stories of yard sale buyers who have found paintings worth small fortunes or original documents of treasures such as the Declaration of Independence that sold cheaply and then earned a fortune for the "finder."

Mark items with labels that indicate the asking price or with a color code that corresponds to a price chart.

Although many buyers will give you the asking price, others consider it part of the game to haggle a bit. Using color codes allows the seller to play the game, too: Price an item at the high end of its price range if you are willing to accept less; adjust prices downward if sales are slow or to clear out items you don't want to lug back inside at the end of the day.

Another advantage to hiring an organizer is that some people are not comfortable dealing with friends and neighbors on a cash basis. In addition, the organizer will be less emotionally attached to items; his or her goal is to help clear out the merchandise, even if it requires cutting the price. (As an organizer, be sure you understand your client's bottom-line price for expensive items.)

Finally, an experienced yard sale organizer knows how to keep the books, manage the cash box, and keep an eye on the merchandise—all while handling a wave of customers.

Know the Territory

Attend garage sales or tag sales in your area to see what sorts of items they are selling and at what prices. Make note of the kinds of signs posted and ads placed.

Most yard sales are held on the weekends, and certain times of the year are better than others. In a vacation area, the best time may be in the late spring or early summer, when people are furnishing their summer residences. In a college town, students may want to buy furniture and furnishings in September and sell them off in May.

How to Get Started

Advertise your availability as a yard sale organizer in shopping guides and newspapers; post flyers in supermarkets, home supply centers, and community centers. Make contact with professional housecleaning companies and ask them to recommend you to their clients in return for a referral fee.

Up-front Expenses

You'll need to make your services known through ads in newspapers and shopping guides and by distributing flyers and business cards. Any expenses related to actual yard sales will be billable to your client.

How Much to Charge

Yard sale organizers can charge an hourly fee or ask for a percentage of the proceeds. Plan on several hours of organization, advertising, and setup, plus three or four hours for the sale itself and two hours for cleanup afterward. A typical job, then, might require 8 to 10 hours of your time.

If you charge a percentage of sales—perhaps 15 to 20 percent of the take—do so only if you have a reasonable expectation that sales will total more than a few hundred dollars.

Any out-of-pocket expenses to advertise the sale or for supplies should be reimbursed by your client.

Legal and Insurance Issues

Special notes: In dealing with your client's property, seek to limit your liability for damage or loss to the actual replacement value of items in your possession. You should protect yourself against claims for sentimental value or loss of use.

Consult your town clerk for information about local ordinances. Ask an accountant or your tax office for advice about sales tax collection; although it may be common for homeowners to ignore tax laws for yard sales, we are *not* going to endorse that practice in this book. First of all, sales tax is not an expense to you; however, if you or your client are fined for ignoring the law, the expense is quite real.

① **Legal**

② **Legal**

③ **Legal**

④ **Accounting**

⑤ **Insurance**

⑥ **Insurance**

Consignment Resale

Description of Job

- Accept items owned by others and offer them for resale at tag sales, at yard sales, and over the Internet.
- Receive a portion of the proceeds from the sale.

The Need

Not everyone is comfortable holding a yard sale outside or a tag sale inside their home, and not everyone has enough items to sustain a sale by themselves.

The consignment reseller gathers items from multiple sources, consults with the owner about pricing, and sets up a table at a flea market or yard sale to offer them for sale.

Another way to sell items is to offer them through Internet auctions and sales sites.

Challenges

Don't accept an item if you don't feel you have a reasonable chance of selling because of lack of demand or because the seller wants to put an unrealistic price on it. Maximize your profits by cherry-picking items that will sell quickly at a good price.

Do not accept items that might subject you to unreasonable liability: very expensive things, fragile items, guns and other weapons, tools that are obviously broken, and the like.

Take care to maintain a close inventory of items you have accepted for sale; each should be marked with a code that identifies the owner and refers to a listing of the minimum price. You will be responsible for paying the owner if an item is lost or stolen while in your possession.

Include in your agreement with the seller provisions for return of the item if it does not sell within a specified period of time. Many contracts specify that if the owner does not pick up an unsold item at the end of the for-sale period, the reseller can dispose of it at any price and pay the owner only the reduced yield.

Know the Territory

Search for opportunities to participate in flea market sales or to mount your own yard sale.

Consider placing valuable items on Internet marketplaces like eBay and Amazon; in doing so you will be relieved of the cost of advertising, promotion, billing, and accepting credit cards and other forms of payment. You will have to pay the Internet web site owner a commission or fee for products you list and sell; this cost should be deducted from the proceeds before you assess a fee to your client.

How to Get Started

Place flyers and ads in community centers and retail outlets offering to sell items. Place ads in newspapers and shopping guides.

Promote your flea market or tag sale in the same way, or participate with others in a general advertisement.

Learn how to use Internet auction and sales sites, and study the sorts of items they offer to find the best match for the products you will be selling.

Up-front Expenses

The principal up-front costs for a consignment business are advertising and promotion, plus any fees for participation at a flea market or a tag sale run by an organization.

If you choose to advertise some of your items on a web site, there may be expenses associated with setting up the site, hosting, and accepting credit cards. If you use an Internet marketplace such as eBay, there are no up-front costs other than computer access to the Internet.

How Much to Charge

Most consignment resellers charge a fee based on a percentage of the selling price of the item; a typical fee is 20 to 30 percent. Depending on your cost of doing business, you might ask owners to pay you an up-front fee when you accept their items for resale, and then deduct that amount from your commission when an item is sold.

Legal and Insurance Issues

Special notes: In dealing with your client's property, seek to limit your liability for damage or loss to the actual replacement value of items in your possession. You should protect yourself against claims for sentimental value or loss of use.

- ① **Legal**
- ② **Legal**
- ③ **Legal**
- ④ **Accounting**
- ⑤ **Insurance**
- ⑥ **Insurance**

Antiques and Collectibles Wholesaler

Description of Job

- Take your sharp eye on the road in search of hidden and underpriced gems at garage sales, tag sales, and flea markets.
- Research the market value of your finds and resell them to collectors or auction houses.

The Need

Any careful shopper at a tag sale stands a good chance of picking up bargains, like a never-used Crock-Pot for $5 or an extra set of plates that more or less match the ones in your kitchen cupboard.

The more observant eye shops in search of the treasure within the trash: real jewels among the faux, a valuable antique chair mixed in with cheap reproductions, a work of art or rare print hidden among the neon paintings on black velvet.

People have garage sales because they want to get rid of their extraneous stuff; some of it should go directly to the dump, but sometimes you can uncover great finds.

Don't count on emulating the story of the Philadelphia tag sale shopper who bought a painting for $4 because he liked the frame and, when he removed the canvas, found an original of the Declaration of Independence that later sold at auction for $2.42 million. That sort of lucky accident is nearly impossible to replicate.

Much more likely are the stories you'll see on television, like those on *Antiques Roadshow.* For example, a set of dusty old handwritten ledgers picked up at a tag sale were identified by a trained appraiser as former properties of Ben Franklin; the books were valued at $12,000 to $18,000.

The job of the antiques and collectibles wholesaler is that of the hunter-gatherer; your goal should be to turn around and resell the items to private clients or to a wholesaler.

Challenges

The biggest challenge facing people who shop tag sales and flea markets as a business is to avoid paying too much for items. You should develop and enhance your expertise in a reasonable number of areas: jewelry, wooden furniture, historical documents, Depression-era glassware, antique cameras, old radios, and the like.

Spend the time to learn how to separate real items from reproductions. Learn how to discover dates of manufacture, serial numbers, artists' names, and other identifying information. Find out the secrets of counterfeiters—artisans who make modern versions of valuable Chippendale chairs or reprints of old documents on artificially aged paper.

Know the Territory

Contact antique dealers and collectors to determine the sorts of items they are most interested in buying and selling. Ask friends and acquaintances to put you in contact with collectors who may have wish lists of items they are looking to add to their shelves.

Learn the seasons and the locations for tag sales, garage sales, and flea markets. Check prices for items at online web sites, including eBay.

Look for courses on antiques and collectibles at local community schools or colleges.

How to Get Started

Make yourself known to owners of antiques stores and establish relationships; you may be able to call them from the road and negotiate a price for resale before you buy something you find. Look for clubs and organizations that attract collectors and let them know you are available to help them fill their collections.

Up-front Expenses

You should build up a collection of books and research materials and have access to the Internet. You'll need to bear the expense of traveling in search of items.

You will have to lay out the money for your purchases and may have to pay for shipping and storing items until they are resold.

Other expenses include advertising and promotion.

How Much to Charge

You will make your profit by reselling items at a price higher than you paid for them, plus the cost of travel and shipping.

Legal and Insurance Issues

① **Legal**

② **Legal**

③ **Legal**

④ **Accounting**

⑤ **Insurance**

Used Book Reseller

Description of Job

- Resell used books from your own library to collectors and readers via web sites and online marketplaces.

- Resell textbooks and technical books to students and researchers.
- Purchase used books at tag sales and yard sales for resale.
- Act as a purchasing agent for collectors seeking specific books.

The Need

You love books. That's why you're holding one in your hands right now.

Sometimes, though, the cost of new books—especially textbooks and technical titles—can be quite high. Perhaps you want a book that is no longer in print and not available at a retail store.

Sellers of used books keep old books alive and deliver current but second-hand titles to willing readers.

Challenges

The margin of profit between the purchase price of a used book and its resale value is not very large. Therefore, any books you buy and cannot resell will eat away at overall profits.

Know the Territory

Reselling used books is a time-honored business that dates back to the time when the first new book was sold. Much of the business was once a low-paying enterprise with high costs: inventory, storage, advertising, and a retail location.

However, this business model was turned on its head by the arrival of the Internet, which allows virtual businesses to thrive because of the quick and inexpensive exchange of information without regard to location.

Study the used book marketplaces at Amazon.com, at BarnesandNoble.com, and at other web sites to learn about programs that allow registered users to sell used books. These sites essentially give you free advertising for your wares, as they are directly linked to searches performed by visitors to their well-promoted cyberstores. They handle the billing and collection of funds from purchasers and remit the amount—minus a reasonable commission—to you.

Amazon and Barnes & Noble allow resellers to post a price for their books and adjust it up or down based on their success. At various forms of eBay auctions, products are sold to the highest bidder; sellers are allowed to set a reserve price, which is the minimum price for a product.

You can also market your services as a book sleuth for collectors. Armed with a list of books they need or want, you can search the Internet, used book stores, estate sales, and other sources. When you find a wanted book, you purchase it on behalf of your client.

How to Get Started

Study the online web sites to learn about the used book market and resale programs. Register as a reseller. The web sites do all of the work of promoting their offerings and making visitors aware of the used book marketplace.

If you will be selling direct, place flyers and ads in high schools, at colleges, and on community bulletin boards.

To find books to sell, be on the lookout for tag sales, estate sales, and private offerings.

To find private collectors seeking titles for their libraries, place ads in newspapers and in newsletters of special-interest organizations.

Up-front Expenses

The principal up-front expense of a used book business is the cost of inventory. You'll want to avoid overpaying for any books you purchase.

If you are listing products on another company's web site, your only expense will be the minimal cost of computer access to the Internet. There may be some costs related to the storage of books.

How Much to Charge

If you resell books through an online web site operated by Amazon, Barnes & Noble, or similar operations you will receive the selling price of the book (minus a prearranged commission and shipping costs).

If you list books on a web site of your own, you will receive the full purchase price of the book plus shipping costs, but you will also bear the additional costs of advertising, promotion, web site creation and hosting, and credit card services.

Acting as an agent on behalf of a collector, you can charge a significant premium above purchase price to pay for your time and other expenses.

Legal and Insurance Issues

Special notes: In dealing with your client's property, seek to limit your liability for damage or loss to the actual replacement value of items in your possession. You should protect yourself against claims for sentimental value or loss of use.

① **Legal**

② **Legal**

③ **Legal**

④ **Accounting**

⑤ **Insurance**

⑥ **Insurance**

Tool and Equipment Rentals

Description of Job

- Rent specialized tools to hobbyists and professionals.
- Rent testing, measurement, and configuration equipment.

The Need

Do you need to own a high-powered brush cutter for a one-time clearing of a patch of ground on your property? Does it make sense to purchase an electronic testing device for a one-time installation or modification of a new feature for an automobile you are working on in your driveway? Can you justify purchasing an extra computer and monitor for a weeklong special project?

The answer in each case, and many others, is that it often does not make sense to make a capital expenditure for a one-time or occasional use of an expensive piece of equipment.

That's the rationale behind equipment rental companies; they spread the cost of a unit over many users. If the rental unit is managed and maintained properly, the owner may write off the depreciation over time and then sell the used equipment to recover some of its original cost.

Challenges

Don't try to compete against the major national franchise tool rental companies, at least at the start. These operations require a major up-front investment in equipment, training, retail operations, franchise fee, and mass-market advertising.

Instead, concentrate on renting out expensive and hard-to-find tools and equipment. Your business plan should be built on a high per-device fee for a low volume of daily or weekly rentals.

Research the cost and life expectancy for specialized equipment before you make any purchases. Some tools have an almost unlimited life; other pieces of equipment are so specialized or unusual that they may become outmoded or unusable after a very short period of time. Your business plan should be based on a realistic estimate of the number of times a device can be rented while in your possession; the total yield plus any resale value has to produce a profit.

In most agreements, you are responsible for the maintenance of equipment and must bear the cost of any equipment that breaks in normal use. However, your rental agreement should spell out situations where the customer must pay for repair or replacement of the equipment because of negligence or misuse. The customer is also responsible for replacement if the equipment is lost or stolen.

Know the Territory

If you have a special interest or hobby, you may already possess some unusual tools or equipment that others may want to "borrow"—for a fee—from time to time.

Learn as much as you can about the demographics, hobbies, and activities in your region. Look for clubs for hobbyists and special-interest groups; become familiar with shows and demonstrations aimed at hobbyists and do-it-yourselfers.

Attend meetings and ask about the sorts of tools and equipment members would like to use from time to time.

Look into selling insurance policies to customers to cover them against loss or theft of rented items and other unexpected costs; some rental companies self-insure, applying extra payments made by customers to a pool of funds earmarked for replacement of equipment.

How to Get Started

Post flyers and ads on community bulletin boards, in retail stores, and at community centers. Place ads in newspapers, shopping guides, and special-interest newsletters. Attend meetings of clubs and make members aware of your interest in acquiring and renting equipment they may need.

Up-front Expenses

Your principal up-front cost will be for the purchase of equipment. You may be able to buy some used or reconditioned equipment; be sure the items come with a warranty and a ready supply of parts for repairs.

Other costs include advertising and promotion.

How Much to Charge

Your business plan should include a realistic estimate of the demand for each item and its life expectancy. Calculate a price based on the expected revenues an item will generate over a reasonable period of time, taking into account the cost of the equipment, its possible resale value, and the cost to you for the money you have invested in inventory.

As an example, consider a $500 tool that you think will be rented once a month and that should have a value of $200 at the end of two years of use. Your real cost for the item is perhaps $350; rented 24 times in two years, your break-even price for the equipment alone is about $15. You'll also want to add in a portion of the cost of operating your business and paying for repair or replacement of items that break, and you should make a profit for your time and effort. In this example, you could justify charging about $50 for short-term rental of the tool.

Legal and Insurance Issues

Special notes: You'll want insurance on your equipment; don't expect to collect if a single power sander is stolen or if a wrench breaks, but you should be covered in case of a major loss of expensive equipment at your site or while rental items are in the possession of clients.

① **Legal**
② **Legal**
③ **Legal**
④ **Accounting**
⑤ **Insurance**

Newspaper Delivery Route

Description of Job

- Deliver the newspaper to residential and business locations, usually in the predawn hours.

- Perform other services, including stuffing Sunday newspapers with advertising inserts, magazines, and other special sections.
- You may need to rent, lease, or purchase an appropriate vehicle.

The Need

The days of a kid on a bicycle prowling the streets with a canvas sack of newspapers are mostly gone. In most communities today, newspapers are delivered by adult subcontractors who use a car or truck to cover large geographic areas and hundreds of subscribers.

In most areas, this is a five- or seven-day-a-week commitment that can be accomplished in the predawn hours. For that reason, it is often a second job.

Newspaper companies generally employ their own drivers or a trucking company to deliver large bundles of papers to newsstands and stores. Delivery to homes is usually subcontracted to individual carriers.

Challenges

First you need to get past the idea of taking on a job that may begin at 5 A.M. every day—despite wind, rain, or snow.

You'll need a vehicle that is large and sturdy enough to carry a heavy load of newspapers. The vehicle will sustain a great deal of wear and tear because of the start-and-stop nature of the route. In snowy climes, you may be out on the roads before the plows have arrived.

There's also the chance of some wear and tear on yourself: sore back and shoulders from loading the papers and getting in and out of the car at each stop on the route.

Drivers may be responsible for makeup deliveries for subscribers who do not receive their paper as promised, or who find their paper in the swimming pool instead of on the front porch.

As a subcontractor, you may be required to find, hire, and provide a substitute carrier to fulfill your deliveries if you are unable to do so because of illness or vacation.

Know the Territory

In most communities, the newspaper handles the sale of subscriptions and the collection of payments. Deliverers receive a listing of their route; the list of subscribers may change slightly from day to day because of new customers, cancellations, and vacation suspensions.

Some newspaper companies have sophisticated software programs that can provide carriers with a logically organized route (or local experts who perform the same function). If not, you'll need to know the area well enough to set up a logical plan by yourself.

Bundles of newspapers may be available for pickup at the printing plant, or they may be delivered to several regional locations to be picked up by carriers.

Depending on your state's regulations, you may need a commercial license and plate for your vehicle, and your insurance company may require coverage for use of the car or truck for commercial purposes. Consult a capable insurance agent for advice.

How to Get Started

Contact the circulation department of area newspapers and ask about delivery jobs. Most newspapers also advertise for carriers in their own classified sections.

Up-front Expenses

In most situations you will be responsible for providing your own vehicle, and you may be required to supply to your employer evidence of proper licensure and insurance.

You will have to pay for gasoline and maintenance of your vehicle; you should be able to recoup some or all of these expenses from the mileage reimbursement paid by the newspaper company.

How Much to Charge

The newspaper company will generally offer a fixed fee for each delivery. Many companies also pay a mileage reimbursement for use of your car.

In some communities, carriers are directly employed by the newspaper company, earning a salary plus benefits and mileage reimbursement for the use of their own vehicle.

Because most companies do the billing and collection by mail or by automatically charging credit card accounts, newspaper carriers can no longer count on weekly or monthly gratuities from customers. However, in some communities it remains common practice for regular carriers to receive a tip at Christmastime; some carriers encourage the practice by inserting a holiday card with their name and address in deliveries near the holiday.

Legal and Insurance Issues

Special notes: An insurance agent can offer counsel about commercial vehicle insurance and liability coverage.

① **Legal**

② **Legal**

③ **Legal**

④ **Accounting**

⑤ **Insurance**

Online Auctions: EBay and Beyond

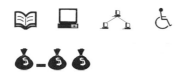

Description of Job

- Sell nearly anything to almost anyone over the Internet.
- Choose your method of sale: auction to the highest bidder, fixed price, or Dutch auction of multiple items to multiple bidders.
- Use automated processes to bill buyers, collect payment, and prepare shipping labels and computer-generated postage.

The Need

From the dawn of time, humans have bought and sold nearly every imaginable product and service. Commerce started as one-on-one sales from growers or artisans to individual buyers. It moved on to retail stores and later catalog companies that brought together inventories of goods to sell to many individuals. Built into the price of everything sold were the costs of showcasing goods in a store, printing and mailing catalogs, and paying the salaries of salespeople and telemarketers.

With the advent of the Internet, though, came an incredibly efficient, low-cost marketplace that blew down nearly all of the costly walls that stood between seller and buyer. The champion—and one of the few great successes of the Internet age—is eBay. Launched in 1995, the value of goods traded through its web site was expected to exceed $24 billion in 2004. More than 105 million users around the world buy and sell items in more than 50,000 categories.

As sellers, eBay and similar sites, including Amazon Marketplace and Yahoo! auctions, allow you to clear out your attic, empty your closets, and conduct a virtual yard sale, offering items to anyone with a connection to the Internet and a mailing address. Don't limit yourself to the idea of a yard sale; tens of thousands of businesses exist entirely as storefronts on eBay or other services. They buy new items at wholesale, used goods at other people's tag sales, whole collections from hobbyists, and antiques from estates, dealers, and individuals.

Challenges

As with any business, you have to find a way to buy low and sell high. The proceeds for items sold at auction should include your cost for the item, the cost of listing it with the service, computer costs, shipping costs, and a reasonable profit for your time and effort.

Before you go out and buy a truckload of bobble-head dolls to resell on eBay, make sure there's enough of a market for that item at a profitable price. Here's an example of how these online services can help you run a very efficient business: You can easily check the success of other sellers offering similar items. You can watch the progress of an auction, from its opening bid to its final selling price, and even determine the number of bidders.

Depending on the type of item and the auction site you use, you may have to deal with a certain percentage of returned merchandise and an occasional bad check. (Many sellers use the services of the auction site to collect payment by credit card, or insist on money orders or bank checks as payment.)

Know the Territory

The biggest and most successful online auction company is eBay. You can learn about its services and fees and browse through tens of thousands of items by going to its web site at www.ebay.com.

As eBay has expanded beyond its original auction-only business, it now offers several choices of selling methods:

- *Auction.* You set an opening price and promise to sell your item to the highest bidder above that floor.

- *Reserve price auction.* You set an opening price, which is published on the site, and a reserve price, which is not disclosed to bidders. If the highest bid does not meet or exceed the reserve price, you are not obligated to sell the item.

- *Dutch auction.* If you have multiple identical items, you can sell them in a single Dutch auction. Bidders offer a particular amount for one or more items, and all items sell for the lowest successful bid. For example, if you have three clocks for sale, all three will sell for no more than the third highest bid.

- *Fixed price.* You can offer items for sale at a fixed price, without an auction.

- *Buy it now.* You can set a buy-it-now price that will halt the auction if a buyer agrees to that price.

You can select the time limit for each type of offering. The standard run for an item on eBay is usually seven days.

Yahoo! auctions are listed at http://auctions.shopping.yahoo.com.

Amazon offers a service allowing sellers to list new and used books and many other items for sale at a fixed price. Listings for these products appear on the same pages as prices charged by Amazon and major retailers. Currently (as of 2004), there is no charge to list an item in the Amazon Marketplace; fees are levied only on actual sales.

Amazon also offers Amazon Auctions, which functions similar to eBay's offering. For information, consult www.amazon.com.

How to Get Started

Spend time trolling the sites of all of the online auction sites. There is no charge for electronic window-shopping.

Look at the sorts of products that are offered for sale. Most sites, including eBay, allow you to see the opening price and the progress of bids over the course of an auction.

If you see lots of people selling the same sort of product you hope to sell, that's not necessarily bad news; it probably means there is a healthy market for that item. Only you can decide whether you can make a satisfactory profit at the going prices.

If you cannot find similar products for sale, proceed cautiously. It may mean that there is no market for the item you want to sell, or it may mean that you have something that is extremely rare.

Up-front Expenses

You will need access to the Internet. There are no advertising and promotion costs associated with most auction sites.

Depending on the type of product you are selling, you may want to post a digital picture with your ad; you can purchase or borrow a digital camera or a scanner to create a file.

How Much to Charge

There are five elements to consider here: (1) the price you receive for the sale of the item, (2) the listing fee from the auction site, (3) the final fee based on the actual selling price for the item, (4) the cost of shipping the item to the customer, and (5) charges for accepting payment from your customer by credit card or debit card.

The beauty of an auction—if you are reaching the right audience for your product—is that you are participating in a relatively pure form of capitalism. The price you receive is the highest any of the bidders is willing to pay.

Of course, in most cases you don't want to sell items at prices that are lower than your costs or significantly below what you think the item is worth. There's bad news and good news here. In a standard auction, you are bound to sell the product to the highest bidder, which could be at too low a price.

The good news is that most online auction services allow you to set a *reserve price,* a floor below which you are not willing to go. For example, you could offer a used camera for sale and allow opening bids of $10 to get the process going. As part of your listing, though, you may set a reserve price of $100. Bidders are not informed of the reserve price, but the site will notify them if their bid is below the reserve.

Online auction sites generally charge a listing fee and then an additional charge based on the actual selling price of the item. You can also choose extra-cost services, including featured positions, boldface or color listings, and multiple photos.

We'll use as an example some of the elements of eBay's plan; others are similar. Currently (as of 2004), the insertion fee for items with an opening-bid price of less than $25 is about 60 cents; the fee for items with a starting price of $50 to $199 is about $2.40; and items with a price starting at $500 or more have an insertion fee of about $4.80.

If you register a reserve price with eBay, the company adds a fee of as much as 1 percent of the reserve price. If the item sells (which means it is purchased at a level above the reserve price), the additional fee is refunded.

Then there is a final value fee. As of late 2004, eBay charged 5.25 percent of the closing value for items that sell for $25 or less. For items selling for as much as $1,000, the final value fee is 5.25 percent of the initial $25 plus 2.75 percent of the remainder. Items selling for more than $1,000 are assessed a slightly lower overall percentage of the selling price.

For most online auction sales, you should add a set fee to your product to cover shipping. Spend the time to research actual costs, and list a realistic price for shipping. If you set the fee too high, you will scare off knowledgeable buyers; if you set the fee too low, you will reduce your actual profit. Most of the auction companies, including eBay, offer guidance on shipping costs and may even have links directly to the U.S. Postal Service, United Parcel Service, and FedEx to help you calculate costs and arrange for shipment.

Finally, you may have an expense associated with accepting credit cards or direct debit from checking accounts. In 2004, eBay's affiliated company Paypal charged about 3 percent of the total amount (including selling price and shipping costs) for its services.

You do not have to use a company like Paypal, although there is great value in receiving immediate payment for orders. If you deal directly with buyers, you may want to ask for bank checks, postal money orders, or other forms of guaranteed payment, or delay shipment until personal checks have cleared.

Legal and Insurance Issues

Special notes: The online auction site will require you to agree to its seller's agreement; there is little if anything you can do to modify it. You will likely have to give the company an active credit card account number or a debit account for direct payment, and the company may reserve the right to assess charges or penalties for actions that violate the agreement.

If you plan to make this an ongoing enterprise, consult an accountant to determine the proper form of business for your operations. An insurance agent may recommend a business owner's policy.

① **Legal**
② **Legal**
③ **Legal**
④ **Accounting**
⑤ **Insurance**

Government and Private Resources for Small Businesses

Small Business Administration (SBA)

This is a U.S. government agency offering training, publications, advisory services, financial offerings, and special programs for women, minorities, veterans, and other priority groups. The SBA has offices in most states.

For your nearest office, consult the telephone directory under U.S. Government or call 800-827-5722.

Web site: www.sba.gov

Service Corps of Retired Executives (SCORE)

Sponsored by the Small Business Administration, SCORE is a national organization of thousands of business executives who volunteer to provide free counseling, workshops, and seminars to prospective and existing businesspeople.

SCORE Association
409 3rd Street, SW, 6th floor
Washington, DC 20024
800-634-0245
Web site: www.score.org

Small Business Development Centers (SBDC)

These are state, local, educational, and private groups and individuals who provide assistance, counseling, and training on small business development.
   Web site: www.sba.gov/sbdc

Government Printing Office Publications

The government publishes pamphlets, online guides, and other information.
   Government Printing Office
   Superintendent of Documents
   Washington, DC 20402-9328
   Web site: www.gpoaccess.gov

U.S. Department of Agriculture (USDA)

The USDA offers information about food safety and preparation.
   U.S. Department of Agriculture
   12th Street and Independence Avenue, SW
   Washington, DC 20250
   Web site: www.usda.gov

U.S. Department of Commerce (DOC)

This agency offers information, advice, and grant programs, including business opportunities supplying goods and services to the federal government.
   U.S. Department of Commerce
   Office of Business Liaison
   14th Street and Constitution Avenue, NW
   Room 5898C
   Washington, DC 20230
   Web site: www.commerce.gov

U.S. Department of Labor (DOL)

The DOL provides information and publications about compliance with federal labor laws.

U.S. Department of Labor
Employment Standards Administration
200 Constitution Avenue, NW
Washington, DC 20210
Web site: www.dol.gov

U.S. Food and Drug Administration (FDA)

Contact the FDA for information about packaging and labeling requirements for food products.

U.S. Food and Drug Administration
5600 Fishers Lane
Rockville, MD 20857-0001
Washington, DC 20402
888-463-6332
Web site: www.fda.gov

Index

Entries in italics designate major categories.

Accidents, errors, and omissions, xiii
Accounting, xiv
Actual value of items, xiv
Airport transportation, 238–240
Alterations, 218–220
Antiques wholesaler, 293–295
Artistic skills, xv
Arts, crafts, jewelry, clothing, and musical instruments, 218–220
Attractive nuisances, 4
Auctions, Internet, 304–305
Auto detailing, 243–245
Automobile insurance, commercial, xiv, 9

Babysitting, 166–168
Babysitting agency, 168–171
Baker, specialty cake, 134–137
Bank accounts, legal requirements, xiv
Bartender, freelance, 140–142
Billing service, 280–282
Bookcase builder, 81–83
Bookkeeping, 278–280
Break-even point, 20, 21

Brick worker, 55–57
Brochure and catalog design, 256–258
Building permit, 47, 49
Business automobile insurance, 9
Business form, xiv
Business insurance and risk management, 1–9
Business interruption insurance, 7
Business licenses, xiv, 14
Business meeting temporary worker, 276–278
Business owner's policy (BOP), xiv, 3–4, 8

Capital expenditures icons, xvi
Car service, 238–240
Caretaker, 94–97
Categories icons, xv
Catering, 129–131
Certified Development Company (CDC) 504 loans, SBA, 28
Challenges icons, xv
Chemicals, 31, 42, 61, 64, 74–77, 101, 102–105, 106–107

Children, family, and pet services,
165–194
Children's event organizer, 123–126
Children's night out, 171–174
Children's outdoor playset installer, 51–52
Chimney cleaning, 102–105
Christmas tree service, 113–114
Client responsibilities, xiii
Client's home, entering, xiii
Closet organizer, 79–81
Collateral for loans, 27
Collectibles wholesaler, 293–295
College application consultant, 211–214
College selection advisor, 208–211
Comaker, loan, 27
Commercial general liability insurance, 8
Commercial licensing, xiv
Compensation, xiii, 17–23
Complexity icons, xv
Computer buying consultant, 248–250
Computer instructor, 202–205
Computer repair, 250–252
Computer skills, xv
Computer upgrades, 250–252
Computers, graphics, and photography,
248–270
Consignment resale, 291–293
Contracts, xiii
Convention worker, temporary , 276–278
Corporations, 13–14
Cost of goods and services, 17
Costs:
   fixed, 18–20, 22
   incremental, 20
   variable, 18–20, 22
Creative skills, xv
Criminal activity insurance risk, 6
Custom dollhouses, 231–233
Custom knitting, 222–224
Custom meal service, 137–140
Custom quiltmaker, 224–226
Custom tailoring, 220–222

Debt, 26
Deck cleaning, 41–43

Deck construction, 46–48
Digital scanning, 261–264
Disability insurance, 7
Document restorer, 264–268
Doggie day care, 182–184
Doghouses, 48–50
Dog walking, 178–182
Doll clothing, 220–222
Dollhouses, custom, 231–233
Dried flowers, 85–87

EBay, 303–307
Educational services, 196–216
Elder care consultant, 186–188
Elder companion, 184–185
Endorser, loan, 27
Entertainer, 143–145
Equipment rental, 298–300
Equity, 26
Errand runner, 92–94
Errors and omissions insurance, 9
Excess liability insurance, 9
Exposure reduction, 5

Family biographer, 191–194
Fertilizing, lawn, 30–33
Film to digital scanning, 261–264
Financing small business, 25–28
Firewood delivery, 108–110
Fitness trainer, 160–162
Fixed costs, 18–20, 22
Flower arrangements, 85–87
Food, xv
Form of business, xiv, 11–14
Freelance photographer, 258–261
Furniture repair, 77–79
Furniture stripping, 74–77

Garden tilling, 37–39
Genealogical researcher, 189–191
General partnership, 12–13
Gift basket maker, 152–155
*Government and private resources for small
business,* 309–318
Government Printing Office, 310

Graphic designer, 256–258

Guaranteed replacement value of items, xiv

Guarantor, loan, 27

Handicapped or homebound, xv

Handyperson, 90–92

Hazardous work, xv, 74–77, 102–105, 107

Health codes, xiv, 130, 132, 135, 138

Historical tour guide, 157–160

Holiday decoration service, 145–147

Home services:
    exterior, 29–57
    interior, 59–87
    specialty, 90–117

Housecleaning, 60–62

House painting, 100–102

House watcher, 97–99

How to use this book, xiii–xvi

Icons, xv–xvi

Incremental costs, 20

Independent delivery contractor, 240–243

Indoor painting, 72–74

Informational icons, xv–xvi

Installment loan, 27

Instructor, community school, 214–216

Insurable risks, 6–7

Insurance, xiv, 1–9

Insurance issues, heights, 40, 46

Interior decorator, 64–66

Internet services, 253–255

Invitees, insurance definition of, 4

Jewelry maker, 226–228

Key person insurance, 7

Knitting, 220–224

Ladders, 39, 104, 146

Landscape designer, 44–46

Language instructor, 198–200

Lawn care/mowing, 30–33

Legal concerns, xiii–xiv

Legalities and taxes, 11–15

Letterhead design, 256–258

Letter writing, 285–286

Liability, xiii

Liability exposure, xv

Liability insurance, xiv, 6–7

Licensees, insurance definition of, 4

Licenses or permits, xv, 36, 47, 104, 110, 111–112, 130, 132, 135, 138, 141

Light pollution ordinances, 54, 146

Limited liability corporation, 14

Limited partnership, 13

Line of credit, 26–27

Loans, type, 26–27

Logo design, 256–258

Long-term loan, 27

Loss or damage to items, xiv

Low-voltage outdoor electrical wiring, 53–55

Markups, 20–23

Medical training, 160–162, 162–164, 168–171, 174–178, 184–185

Mowing, lawn, 30–33

Musical instrument tuning and repair, 233–236

Music teacher, 200–202

Newspaper delivery, 300–303

Noise ordinances, xiv, 31, 146

Occupational safety regulations, xiv

Office and professional services, 272–286

Online auctions, 303–307

Outdoor lighting, 53–55

Parties, entertainment, and special events, 119–147

Partnerships, 12–13

Party and special event rentals, 126–129

Party planner, 120–123

Personal services, 149–164

Personal shopper, 150–152

Personal trainer, 160–162

Pets, xv

Pet sitter, 182–184

Photographer, freelance, 258–261

Photo restorer, 264–268
Physical damage insurance risk, 6
Plant care, 83–85
Playhouses, 48–50
Playset installer, 51–52
Pool service, 105–108
Portraiture from photographs, 228–230
Price of goods and services, 17
Price setting, 17–23
Professional liability insurance, 9
Property coverage insurance, 8

Quiltmaker, 224–226

Rentals, party and special event, 126–129
Resume design, 282–284
Risk management, 1–9
Risk retention, 5
Risk transfer, 6
Rototilling, 37–39
Rug cleaner, 62–64

Sales, 287–308
Sales tax on services and products, 14–15
SAT or ACT test preparation, 205–208
SBA. *See* Small Business Administration
Seasonal jobs, xv, 30, 33, 37, 42
Secretary, temporary, 272–273
Secured loan, 27
Self-insurance, 5
Service Corps of Retired Executives
    (SCORE), 309
Setting your price, 17–23
7(a) loan guarantee, SBA, 28
7(m) microloans, SBA, 28
Shelf builder, 81–83
Shopper, personal, 150–152
Short-term loan, 27
Silk flowers, 85–87
Skills icons, xv
Slipcover maker, 67–69
Small Business Administration (SBA), 28,
    309
Small Business Development Centers
    (SBDC), 310

Small engine repair, 115–117
Snow removal, 33–36
Social events, 127
Sole proprietorship, 12
Specialty cake baker, 134–137
Specialty painting, 72–74
Sponging, painting, 73
Stenciling, 73
Stonemason, 55–57
Storage sheds, 48–50
Subchapter S corporation, 14
Surety bond guarantee, SBA, 28

Tailoring, 220–222
Temporary secretary, 272–273
Tool rental, 298–300
Tour guide, historical, 157–160
Training or certification, xv
Transcription services, 273–276
Transfer of risk, 6
Transportation service, 238–240
Transportation, delivery, and auto services,
    237–245
Trash removal, 111–112
Travel planner, 155–157
Trespassers, insurance definition of, 4
Tutor, 196–198
Types of loans, 26–27

U.S. Department of Agriculture (USDA),
    310
U.S. Department of Commerce (DOC), 310
U.S. Department of Labor (DOL), 311
U.S. Food and Drug Administration (FDA),
    311
Umbrella insurance, 9
Unsecured loan, 27
Upholsterer, 67–69
Used book reseller, 295–298

Vacation-related jobs:
    child care, 174–178
    home caretaker, 94–97
    house watcher, 97–99
    pet visits, 178–182

Variable costs, 18–20, 22
Videographer, 268–270
Visiting chef, 131–132

Wallpaper hanger, 69–72
Web and phone sales, xv
Web design and maintenance, 253–255

Window cleaning, 39–41
Workers' compensation coverage, xiv

Yard sale organizer, 288–291

Zoning codes, xiv, 15

ABOUT THE AUTHORS

Corey Sandler is the author of more than 150 books on business, travel, and technology. He has worked as an executive for three national publishing companies and as an executive officer of an agency of New York State government. Current titles include *Performance Appraisal Phrase Book, 1001 Letters for All Occasions, Fix Your Own PC,* and the Econoguide Travel Book Series. *Watching Baseball: Discovering the Game Within the Game,* coauthored with Boston Red Sox broadcaster and former major leaguer Jerry Remy, was a *Boston Globe* number one best seller in 2004.

Sandler, a former Gannett Newspapers reporter and columnist, also worked as an Associated Press correspondent covering business and political beats. He became the first Executive Editor of *PC Magazine* in 1982 at the start of that magazine's meteoric rise. He also was the founding editor of IDG's *Digital News.* He has degrees in psychology and journalism.

Sandler has appeared on NBC's *Today* show, CNN, ABC, National Public Radio's *Fresh Air,* and dozens of local radio and television shows. He has been the subject of many newspaper and magazine articles.

Janice Keefe is coauthor of *Performance Appraisal Phrase Book* (Adams Media) and *1001 Letters for All Occasions* (Adams Media). She is a former manager for an agency of New York State government.

You can send e-mail to the authors at info@econoguide.com.